THE INDIVISIBLE ISLAND

THE INDIVISIBLE ISLAND

THE HISTORY OF
THE PARTITION OF IRELAND

by

FRANK GALLAGHER

THE CITADEL PRESS
NEW YORK

PRINTED IN THE NETHERLANDS BY JAN DE LANGE, DEVENTER

CONTENTS

LIST OF ILLUSTRATIONS

LIST OF MAPS

ACKNOWLEDGMENTS

This book would have been impossible to write were it not for the collaboration of others. I am indebted especially to Thomas P. O'Neill, M. A., Deputy Keeper of Printed Books at the National Library of Ireland, and Labhrás O'Nualláin, D. Econ. Sc., Lecturer in Economics at University College, Galway. Both put the benefit of their wide knowledge at my disposal. Mr. O'Neill who has made a speciality of history assisted in making the historical section of the book authoritative. Dr. O'Nuallain, who has made a particular study of the economic aspects of partition, enabled the chapters dealing with these questions to be as complete as is his own book *Ireland: Finances of Partition* in relation to financial matters. The advice and criticism of both Dr. O'Nualláin and Mr. O'Neill on the other sections of the book were indispensable. Most of the work of seeing it through the press fell on Mr. O'Neill.

I would also like to record the patience and accuracy of Miss Ita Durkin in dealing with the many revisions of the whole manuscript.

CHAPTER I

A NATION THROUGH THE CENTURIES

THE ORIGIN OF the early populations of Ireland is lost in the myths which surround pre-history. The earliest record, *Lebor Gabala Erenn* (the Book of the Conquest of Ireland), dates from the eighth century, though only a twelfth-century text survives. It traces Irish history back to many centuries before Christ, but like other records of its kind it mixes mythological and historical kings and rulers inextricably. Archaeology is regarded as a better guide on the question of early settlements in Ireland. Excavations have shown those settlements to date back beyond 2000 B.C. These and the later cultural remains—megaliths, dolmens and horned cairns—are found in every part of the island.

Out of the mists of antiquity it is possible to identify four main Celtic invasions: the first the Cruthin or Pretani; then, between the sixth and fourth centuries B.C., the Belgae or, as they became known in Ireland, the Fir Bolg. The Laginian invasion came mainly to Leinster and Connacht later, and finally the Goidels or Gaels reached Ireland direct from Gaul some time before 50 B.C. To these early inhabitants Ireland was a unit, and to the Fir Bolg the hill of Uisneach marked the centre of the country and was a holy place.

The division of the country into four provinces which met at Uisneach dates from before this last invasion; and soon after the Gaels had settled, their leader, Tuathal Techtmar, carved out a fifth province in the midlands, and these ancient divisions of Ireland became known as "fifths" or *Cóiced*. The Midland Gaels established themselves at Tara in Meath, while others of that invasion spread south and west and so brought Munster and Connacht, as well as Leinster, under their sway.

In the fourth century A.D. the Gaels of Meath had become so powerful that their kinsmen of Munster and Connacht accepted their King as Árd Rí or High King. Niall of the Nine Hostages is the first historical Árd Rí, and it was in his reign that the North, like the other provinces, was brought to acknowledge his High Kingship. He established his three sons, Eogan,

Conall and Enda, as the local monarchs in the fifth of Ireland known as Ulad (Ulster). That was before the end of the fourth century of our era.

The Roman Empire was breaking up in Europe but there was as yet no general emergence of nations. The Angles and Saxons came and teutonised England as the Romans withdrew, but more than five centuries were to elapse before the foundation of an English or a French monarchy. In Ireland, however, there was a national kingship and there was unbroken succession to it from among the descendants of Niall from A.D. 400 to 1022, with but two exceptions. A large number of these High Kings of Ireland came from Ulster, particularly in the sixth and seventh centuries.

Christianity was brought to Ireland during the time of Laeghaire, son of Niall of the Nine Hostages, in the fifth century. One of the earliest missionaries, and certainly the most famous, was St. Patrick. He knew the land well. He had been brought to it as a slave-boy by Irish raiders who at that time preyed on the disintegrating Roman provinces. They were daring and powerful, those Irish raids on neighbouring lands, and one of them made a footing for the conquest of Scotland by which that Kingdom was given a Gaelic stamp it has never lost.

At Slemish in Antrim the slave-boy Patrick tended sheep for six years. Then he escaped and at Auxerre in France he studied for the priesthood. It was in the fifth century that he returned to Ireland on the mission which filled the rest of his life. He landed at Saul on the coast of Down and it was there that he established his first church in Ireland.

But he was not long in the island before he realised that he must go to the centre, and so we find him coming to Tara to the High King of Ireland, Laeghaire. He did not convert the High King, but he did succeed in getting from him permission to preach, and that he did with success. He travelled through all parts of Ireland, and, organising the church on a basis at once monastic and episcopal, he founded his episcopal See at Armagh. When he died he left a flourishing Christian community in Ireland.

The monastic organisation of the early Irish church had a profound effect on Irish culture, for the monasteries became centres of learning and of the arts. St. Finnian of Clonard, Co. Westmeath, was the founder of this scholarly tradition and among his disciples were many who themselves established monasteries, like St. Comgall of Bangor, Co. Down; St. Ciaran of Clonmacnoise, Co. Westmeath; St. Brendan of Clonfert, Co. Roscommon; St. Ruadan of Lorrha, Co. Tipperary.

The crowning glory of these monastic universities was their gift for exalted craftsmanship such as illuminating manuscripts. The beautiful work which has survived the ravages of centuries shows to what an art this illumination was brought. Of the early manuscripts which are now available the *Book of Kells* is the most perfect. This book, which is an illuminated copy of the Gospels in Latin, is ascribed to the eighth century and has many pages decorated with superb ornament.

These monasteries, which were to be found in every province, gave their Irish and their foreign students the highest learning of their day. But if many from the noble houses of Europe sent their sons to Ireland to be taught, Ireland sent good measure in return. The Irish missionary effort, which was to become a tradition lasting even to this day, was begun in the earliest years of her Christianity.

St. Columcille, the first Irish missionary, left Derry in 563 and established a monastery at Iona off the coast of Scotland. That monastery was to be mother-house of the mission to Scotland, for from it came St. Adamnan, St. Columcille's successor. From Bangor, in Co. Down, another great Irish saint, Columbanus, set out on a mission to the Continent during which monasteries were established at Luxeuil, St. Gall and Bobbio by him and his disciples. This was the beginning of a period of Irish evangelical work in Europe which was extraordinarily fruitful. It went on through the sixth, seventh and eighth centuries. With never-ceasing zeal monks from Ireland travelled through the countries which had not yet recovered from the barbarian invasions that followed the fall of the Roman Empire. Their help was vital in the revival and restoration of Christian traditions.

Professor Toynbee, in his monumental work *The Study of History* [1] says:

> The period of Irish cultural superiority over the continent and over Britain may be conveniently dated from the foundation of the monastic university of Clonmacnois in Ireland in A.D. 548 to the foundation of the Irish Monastery of St. James at Ratisbon, *circa* A.D. 1090. Throughout those five and a half centuries, it was the Irish who imparted culture and the English and continentals who received it.

[1] vol. ii, p. 329.

This gift to the Western World was possible because of the settled nature of Irish civilisation and polity. Ireland's national unity was expressed not only politically through the recognition given by the component parts of the nation to her High-King, but also in a national law and a national language. The Brehon laws, the poetry, the ancient sagas, can be traced back to this period. Professor Edmund Curtis, who held the chair of Irish History in Trinity College, Dublin, writes of Ireland in A.D. 800 that "she was the first nation north of the Alps to produce a whole body of literature in her own speech"; and he continues:

> The structural unity of Ireland had now remained intact for four centuries in language, law, religion and culture. Scholars and poets could freely pass, be understood and entertain all listeners throughout the whole island. The national unity was visible in the High King, in occasional 'Rig Dáil' or national gatherings, and in the general assemblies held by the High King at Tailten and such centres. [1]

It was at this period—known to historians as the Golden Age of Irish civilisation—that a new series of attacks began on Western Europe which threatened to extinguish again the light so brightly re-kindled with Ireland's aid. The newcomers were the Norse, a sea-faring race from Scandinavia, who for two centuries raided and took booty wherever their broad and shallow boats could reach.

The Irish monasteries with their cultural treasures were attractive prey, and year after year of the first half of the ninth century the national records are filled with accounts of the forays of the Norsemen. The scope of these piracies was wide and the Irish foundations abroad suffered the same fate. Iona was pillaged even as were Bangor, Armagh, Clonmacnoise and Clonfert. The missionary endeavour in Europe, the cultural development at home, were undermined by the insecurity created by the raids. The Norsemen grew bolder as the years went on. From A.D. 830 onwards they made landings and established themselves on various parts of the Irish coasts.

One Norse leader, Turgesius, brought a powerful fleet into Lough Neagh, and, using that as a base, ravaged Ulster from Armagh to Derry. It was the King of Meath, Malachy, who, after fourteen years, ended that wild reign, defeating and drowning Turgesius in Lough Owel. Shortly afterwards Malachy became High King and continued to lead the attack on the foreigners.

[1] Lecky, *History of Ireland* (1950), p. 21.

In 866 his successor to the national throne, Aedh Finnliath, captured all the Norse settlements in the northern half of Ireland and inflicted such a blow that for forty years the raids on Ireland ceased, though the Norsemen held their settlements south of Dublin. They turned their faces to other lands, pillaging Britain and sailing up the Seine, the Loire and the Garonne on their predatory excursions. In this period they laid siege even to Constantinople and withdrew only on payment of a heavy ransom.

In the early years of the tenth century the great Norse attempt was made to subdue Ireland as they had subdued half of England. In a battle near Dublin in 919 they defeated and killed the High King, Niall Glundubh, and set up a kingdom covering the present two counties of Dublin and Wicklow. Their grip on Limerick, Cork and Waterford gave them control of Munster. But national recovery was on the way.

By their attack the ruling house in Munster was greatly weakened and gradually a new royal clann, that of the Dal Cais, took strength. It was led by two brothers, Mahon and Brian, and it was they who in the second half of the tenth century led the Irish revival which in the end broke the power of the Norsemen. They slowly asserted their superiority throughout Munster and at the battle of Sulcoit in 968 they overthrew the Norsemen in the Southern Province. Mahon became King of Munster and was succeeded by Brian eight years later.

The effort to wrest the nation free was continuing elsewhere. One Malachy had defeated Turgesius, another more than a century later, in 980, overthrew a great Norse army at the seat of his High Kingship, Tara. He and Brian agreed in 998 to divide the exercise of authority in the whole Kingdom between them, but in a few years Malachy transferred his High Kingship to Brian.

The new High King followed the traditional custom of marching around Ireland—"making the circuit"—and receiving from all the lesser rulers their tribute to his authority. Thence came his name Brian Boru, Brian of the Tributes. In the course of the circuit the High King visited the ecclesiastical capital. Here under date of the year 1004 his scribe entered in the *Book of Armagh* Brian's famous decree of the primacy of Armagh. The scribe in that entry gives his master the title of "Emperor of the Irish".

Ten years later Brian, as the national ruler, faced the final hosting of the invaders on the flat lands of Clontarf, close to Dublin. In a desperate battle the Norsemen were utterly defeated and fled, never to return. But the Irish had suffered grievous losses, most of all in that Brian was slain, and his son and his grandson. The direct line to the High Kingship had been broken. It was an unfortunate moment for Ireland to be without the unifying force of a central monarch, for beside her there was growing up a Power bent on new conquests.

Just as Wessex, Northumbria and Mercia had come into armed conflict in England as to which should provide the ruling house; and as Normandy, Anjou, Aquitaine and Burgundy contested in France; so in Ireland, Ulster, Leinster, Connacht and Munster sought the leadership. For a century and a half after the death of Brian and his heirs there was continual strife in the effort to decide the issue. It was not a difference as to the oneness of Ireland that caused this struggle but a question of who should be the monarch of the unit. It was not till 1166 that this political issue was decided. In that year Rory O'Connor was universally accepted as High King and Ireland, one for centuries in language, law and culture, was again under one supreme ruler.

The period of the monarchical conflicts had seen a contrary movement in the ecclesiastical sphere. The struggle with the Norsemen had disrupted the organisation of the Irish Church, and now came a period of reconstruction and reform. From the Continent came the Cluniac revival, and the great Irish reformer St. Malachy introduced some of the newly-founded orders. In 1152 a full national synod was convened at Kells and a diocesan organisation took the place of the earlier monastic system. The relics of this period imply a return of tranquillity, for the arts flourished, particularly works in metals. The Cross of Cong, the Tara Brooch and the Lismore Crozier are among the most beautiful examples of this revival. But just as the illumination of manuscripts received a blow from the constant Norse raids and plunderings, a new invasion was to kill this rebirth of Irish art.

The Normans in the neighbouring isle had as Irish ally Diarmuid MacMurragh, a deposed King of Leinster. He, to further intrigues of his own, invited them to Ireland, and they came in 1169. They had established a powerful monarchy in England and had expanded it into Wales. Their arrival in Ireland led to a struggle which has not ceased even after 800 years. A feudal race, they had created a great military organisation and had no superiors in the arts of fortification. They captured Dublin and defeated the High King and when Henry II of England came to Ireland in 1171 they had paved the way for the imposition of his sovereignty on Ireland not only with arms but with the psychological weapon of a Papal grant from Adrian IV. [1]

Henry promised, on the submissions of Irish chiefs, that Ireland would be treated as a feudal vassal. Instead it was treated as a conquered country to be parcelled out under nominees of the English crown. Hugh de Lacey was appointed Henry's Deputy and was granted land in Meath which he set out to conquer. Norman adventurers, despite a treaty made by Henry with the High King, were granted South Munster. John de Courcy and others were permitted to carve out principalities where they could, without even the pretence of a legal grant. Eight years after the Norman invasion the newcomers were masters of two-thirds of Ireland. McCarthy and O'Brien in the South, O'Neill and O'Donnell in the North, O'Connor in the West, were among the few Irish chiefs who still held their lands.

The need for a common defence impressed itself on the Irishmen, and in 1258 was formed the first Irish national Confederacy against the Normans. It did not long survive. Aedh O'Connor, King of Connacht, Tadhg O'Brian, King of Thomond (Limerick) and Brian O'Neill of Ulster, met at Caol Uisge on the River Erne and there chose O'Neill as King of Ireland to lead their resistance. They attacked the Normans in the battle of Downpatrick and were routed. O'Neill himself was slain. The Normans pressed forward with the conquest, and by 1311 the Ulster coastal territories of Down, Antrim and Derry were incorporated into the lordship of Richard de Burgo, Earl of Ulster.

Bannockburn in 1314 and the defeat of the Anglo-Normans by the Scots under Robert Bruce raised new hopes in Ireland. Edward Bruce landed in Antrim in 1315 and the Ulster Irish rallied to him. Domhnall O'Neill, son of Brian, who had been elected King in 1258, renounced his claim to the throne of Ireland and Edward Bruce was crowned High King, on May Day 1316. Again the nation rallied. There were insurrections in Munster, Leinster and Connacht in the effort to break the Norman power. They failed in part. Bruce was killed in battle

[1] Much had been written on this grant, most of it questioning its authenticity. See *Pope Adrian IV: A friend of Ireland* by Rev. Louis Chaillot, translated by Rev. W. McLoughlin.

in 1318, but outside Leinster, where the Normans held their ground, their position was greatly shaken.

The Irish Chiefs in the Bruce Confederacy publicly repudiated the Norman claim to the Sovereignty of Ireland. The close association with Scotland which had persisted through the centuries now manifested itself. From those Gaels across the narrow sea came help in arms, leading to a new element in Irish warfare: heavily armed Scottish mercenaries called Galloglaigh, or Gallowglasses, who made a much better showing against the mailed professional Norman soldiers than the lightly armed Irish kerns.

There was another element that favoured the Irish. The Norman lords soon achieved something of an independence of their own. The English Kings, though they held the title "Lord of Ireland", had little contact with Irish affairs. They were occupied with their French possessions and with struggles with the English barons. This weakness in control led to the Normans in Ireland first forming a detached community and then being absorbed by the civilisation of the nation in which they had settled. Their families gradually adopted Irish customs and in many ways transformed themselves into Irish men and women. They intermarried with the Gaelic chieftain families and made for themselves powerful alliances.

So widely had this happened that the "Statutes of Kilkenny" were passed against it. The son of Edward III of England, Lionel, called a Parliament at Kilkenny in 1366 which prohibited the "English of Ireland" from adopting Irish customs, culture or language and from marrying into Irish families. But the transformation had gone too far.

The political consequences soon manifested themselves. The "Pale", that area in Leinster in which the Norman power was strong, gradually receded. In the middle of the fourteenth century it had embraced at least ten counties: a century and a half later it had dwindled to a strip of territory fifty miles long and thirty miles wide, stretching from Dublin to Dundalk, little more than a bridgehead.

In the fifteenth century the long-drawn-out Wars of the Roses in which rival English dynasties struggled for the Crown still further weakened the English power in Ireland. The Fitzgerald family—Earls of Kildare—had obtained an ascendancy over the Irish Norman families and, while continuing to profess allegiance to the English King, in fact had become practically independent.

The Battle of Bosworth, with the death of Richard III, ended the Wars of the Roses, and Henry Tudor became Henry VII of England. The new monarch turned to extend his power in Ireland.

The Earl of Kildare, Garrett Mór Fitzgerald, was then the most powerful man in Ireland. In 1494 Henry sent Sir Edward Poynings as the King's Lord Deputy with instructions to undermine the Earl's prestige and bring Ireland to "whole and proper obedience". Poynings carried out his mission in a manner often repeated in history. He convened a Parliament and got them to pass statutes the effect of which was to make the British Privy Council supreme over the Parliaments of Ireland.

Henry VIII continued his father's policy of strengthening the English hold on Ireland. In 1534 he had the then Earl of Kildare imprisoned in the Tower of London. An insurrection was led by the Earl's son, "Silken Thomas", and it became part of the long chain of Risings, whether by the native Irish or the Norman families turned Irish, which was to go on down the centuries. The insurrection was crushed without mercy. The followers of Silken Thomas who surrendered to the King's Deputy were executed in cold blood and an attempt was made by Henry to wipe out the whole Geraldine clan when he had Silken Thomas himself and five of his uncles hanged at Tyburn.

This ruthlessness had an effect opposite to what was intended, for the treatment of this old Norman family tended only to make other Norman descendants embrace Ireland's cause more fervently. They found greater reason to do so when Henry changed his religion. The former Palesman, whether Old Irish or Anglo-Irish, stood by the Old Faith.

The change in religion merely intensified what was the permanent English aim. When the Catholic Mary succeeded the Protestant Henry, she set on foot (in 1556) a scheme for the establishment of a strong English colony in Ireland. Large areas in what are now the Counties of Laois and Offaly were declared forfeit and were granted to English settlers. The O'Mores and O'Connors, Irish possessors of those lands, rose in arms against this confiscation and for fifty years waged war upon the settlers, in the end causing the whole expropriation to fail.

Queen Elizabeth, if she reversed Mary's ecclesiastical policy, continued the plans of confiscation and plantation by which it was hoped to subdue Ireland at last. In Ulster Shane O'Neill was the strongest defender of the still vibrant Gaelic system, and he set out to re-establish the leadership of the O'Neills of Tyrone in that province. Elizabeth's Lord Deputy, the Earl of Sussex, used every intrigue to rouse other Irish chiefs against Shane O'Neill and succeeded in turning the O'Donnells, the O'Reillys and the Scots of Antrim into Shane's enemies. In the end Shane was defeated and slain. His death did not bring the expected reward of the submission of Ulster or even of Tyrone, and the English forces turned south to subdue Munster.

There the Old Norman Earls of Desmond had become leaders, and they fought back as gallantly as Shane O'Neill had done. It was not for thirteen years that the Earl of Desmond was defeated and killed, and by then the war had extended into Leinster. In Ulster, Munster and Leinster the old Irish and the new Irish fought the invader together.

The English campaigned with the cruelty and guile characteristic of sixteenth-century warfare. It was the age of Machiavellian strategy, and any of the Irish who were considered dangerous to the spread of English power were murdered. In 1574 Sir Brian O'Neill was host at a banquet at Belfast to his friend and Lord Deputy. The Lord Deputy arrived but had the Banqueting Hall surrounded, and two hundred of Ireland's noblest men and women, including the host and hostess, were massacred! [1] The same Lord Deputy had the old, the wounded, the women and the children, who had been placed for safety in Rathlin Island by MacDonnell of Antrim, hurled into the sea. In all parts of the land the same methods to establish Elizabeth's sovereignty were practised.

The defeat of the Earl of Desmond was followed by the plantation of the province of Munster which had been laid waste by the long war. This establishment of English settlers was no more successful than had been that of Laois and Offaly. As in so many later cases, also, those who were given the land brought over no English tenants and thus gave their holdings no permanence. In any case, the whole nation was soon involved in one of the greatest struggles for survival.

It centred around a new national leader who had arisen in Ulster. He was to weld the Irish chiefs into an unsurpassed unity for the liberation of their land. Hugh O'Neill had been educated in England and had been set up by the English in Ulster as Earl of Tyrone. The English purpose was to weaken his kinsman,

---

[1] Richard Bagwell, *Ireland under the Tudors,* vol. ii, pp. 288-9.

Turloch O'Neill, who was generally accepted as head of the clan, as "The O'Neill". Turloch retired in 1593 and Hugh was elected The O'Neill. By combining the Irish title with his earldom he created unity where the English had aimed at creating disunity. The head of the O'Donnells, "Red Hugh", acknowledged O'Neill's leadership and then was begun the last great war for the Gaelic system of government. The first blow was the defeat of the English at the "Ford of the Biscuits" near Enniskillen in 1594.

The war lasted intermittently for seven years. It had the character of a national Rising, for the McCarthys and O'Sullivans of Munster, the O'Mores and O'Byrnes of Leinster and all Connacht except the Earl of Clanrickarde sided with the Ulster leaders. The first years glowed with success. The Irish armies won battles at Clontibret, the Yellow Ford, close to Armagh, and Tyrell's Pass near Mullingar.

Queen Elizabeth, deeply disturbed at the prospect of her hold over Ireland being broken, changed her Lord Deputy several times and gave to each strong reinforcements, but the strength of Hugh O'Neill was unshaken. In 1600 he made a circuit of Munster and Leinster in which he was received by the Irish as virtual High King. Then came a new Lord Deputy from England, Lord Mountjoy. Under him a campaign of ruthless ferocity was carried out, and it gradually weakened O'Neill until he appealed to Spain for help.

To Kinsale, in the September of 1601, came a small Spanish force. Mountjoy and his Lieutenant in Munster, Sir George Carew, laid siege to the town but shortly afterwards found themselves besieged by O'Neill and O'Donnell, who had come from the North to relieve the Spaniards. In a pitched battle which changed the course of history the Irish were defeated, and they retreated in a march which is one of the epics of human endurance. But the turning-point had come for the Gaelic chieftains; the Gaelic system of law and organisation began at last to break up. On 30 March 1603 Hugh O'Neill submitted at Mellifont.

Elizabeth had just died and the new King, James I, was thought to be sympathetic to the Irish chiefs. O'Neill and O'Donnell were indeed confirmed in the ownership of their lands, which were to be held under English law, and they were guaranteed freedom of religion. But their enemies were in power in Ireland and soon showed that they were determined to destroy them. The promises of religious toleration were ignored. The end of that phase of Ireland's national resistance had come. In September 1607 ninety-nine of the leading men of Ulster, among them Hugh O'Neill, sailed from Lough Swilly into voluntary exile. O'Neill found asylum in Rome and there he died nine years later. The Gaelic polity which had existed for a thousand years had at last been broken, but the language and literature was to live on; and there lived on also among those who were left the determination somehow to break the subjugation of their nation. The next great attempt was led by a descendant of the leaders who had fled.

CHAPTER II

THE PLANTATIONS

THE FLIGHT OF the Earls gave the English monarch an opportunity he had long sought. He and his advisers had come to regard colonisation as the only way by which Ireland could really be subjugated. The lands of the chiefs who had fled were looked upon by the King's Deputy, Sir Arthur Chichester, as admirably suited to a new plantation. Thus there could be introduced into Ireland settlers who would act as a garrison against any future Irish struggle for independence.

Sir John Davies, the Attorney General in Ireland, wrote in 1609 to the Earl of Salisbury, English Secretary of State:

> They that expect and long for the settling of the peace of this Kingdom, assure themselves that, if the empty veins of Ulster were once filled with good British blood the whole body of this commonwealth would quickly recover perfection of health. [1]

King James in an instruction to his Lord Deputy set out plainly that the purpose of the plantation was to keep Ireland subdued:

> You will spare (he said) no flesh, English nor Scottish; for no man's private worth is able to counterbalance the safety of a kingdom, which this plantation, being well accomplished, with procure. [2]

Six counties were planted, for to the lands in Donegal, Derry (then Coleraine), Armagh and Tyrone which the Gaelic chiefs were considered to have forfeited by their flight, were added Cavan and Fermanagh.

The forfeited estates were principally divided into parcels of 2,000 and 1,500 acres, with bogland and woodland in addition. The larger areas were granted to English and Scottish undertakers who were to bring from England or Scotland at least forty-eight able-bodied tenants for each 2,000 acres. They were by law allowed to keep no Irish tenants and all the Irish residing on the lands were to be removed. The estates of 1,500 acres were given to English soldiers who had served in Ireland: "servitors" they were called. They were permitted to take Irish tenants, though concessions were granted to them if they too excluded

1 *Calendar of State Papers, Ireland,* 1608-10, p. 214.
2 *Concise View of the Irish Society* (1832), Appendix, pp. 183-4.

all but English and Scottish. Some small areas were granted to "deserving Irishmen" to whom were given about one-sixth of the confiscated lands.

The intention was clear. The Irish were to be removed from the large tracts of country given to the undertakers. The native population was to be concentrated on the lands given to the servitors and to the small group called the "deserving Irish" and on Church lands which had not been forfeited. This elaborate scheme failed as previous schemes had failed in Leix-Offaly and in Munster. The Irish occupants and tenants of the land would not surrender it easily. In July 1610 the Lord Deputy wrote to the Earl of Salisbury:

> the work of removing and transplanting being to the natives as welcome as the sentence of death. [1]

There was another reason why the basic population remained Irish. The undertakers were unwilling to part with the Irish inhabitants because of the dearth of labour and the fact that they could not import sufficient settlers in a short space of time to replace them. Also the Irish could pay higher rents and not acquire any legal interest in the lands they held, an important economic consideration.

This inability to remove the old residents in the planted lands was eventually recognised by the Government, which in 1628 permitted the undertakers to let one-quarter of their estates to the Irish. These were to live together in villages, to wear English clothes and to learn the English language. The other three quarters of the undertakers' estates were to be completely cleared of the Irish by May Day 1629.

But this last regulation could no more be enforced than those which preceded it, and the Irish remained for the most part on their former lands, though reduced from the status of proprietors to that of tenants-at-will. The only section of the people which a concerted attempt was made to remove were the Irish "swordsmen" or armed followers of Irish lords. They were ordered to be sent into Connacht and Munster or transplanted for service in Continental armies. Several hundreds were indeed rounded up and despatched to Sweden but a far larger number eluded capture and maintained themselves as outlaws in the hills and woods of their native territory.

The county of Derry was a special case. It was taken over by

1 *Calendar of State Papers, Ireland*, 1608-10, p. 479.

the city of London, which set up an Irish Society to do the work
of planting it. The London trades companies contributed to the
expenses and the lands of Derry were apportioned among them.
But their introduction of settlers went as slowly as that of the
other five counties. The kind of individuals who took the land
was described by the Lord Deputy to Lord Salisbury in
November 1610:

> Those from England are, for the most part, plain country gentlemen,
> who may promise much, but give small assurance or hope of per-
> forming what appertains to a work of such moment. If they have
> money they keep it close for hitherto they have disbursed but
> little.... The Scottishmen come with greater port (show) and
> better accompanied and attended, but it may be with less money
> in their purses. [1]

It was scarcely to be expected that such undertakers would
carry through the scheme of plantation with much energy. In fact
there is proof in plenty that they did not. A Captain Nicholas
Pynnar made a survey of the planted counties in 1618 and 1619.
He showed the number of British families and able-bodied men
in each estate. There were in all 1,974 families in the whole of
the counties, and 6,215 men capable of bearing arms, though
Pynnar suggested that 8,000 was probably nearer the correct
total. Derry had fewest British families, 119, Tyrone most, 447.
Tyrone accounted also for more than one-third of the men. It
is clear that everywhere the settlers were outnumbered by the
original owners. In some parts of the Derry plantation there were
as many as twenty Irish to one British inhabitant.

It will be noticed that Antrim and Down, the two counties
where now the opposition to Ireland's national self-determination
is centred, were not part of the plantation. Many attempts have
been made to identify the six estreated counties of 1610 with
the six Partitioned counties of 1920. They are not only different
but have maintained that difference through the centuries. The
six planted counties had then a majority in favour of Ireland's
independence. They have that majority still. [2]

Thus the present political situation does not derive from the
Confiscations 300 years ago. It has its origin in a contemporaneous influx of Scots and English into Down and Antrim. Some
of that immigration came from the nation which Ireland had
colonised over a thousand years before. The speech, the laws,

---

[1] *Calendar of Carew papers*, 1603-25, p. 75.
[2] The latest census returns (1951) show that in these six planted counties
there are 409,986 Nationalists and 251,584 others.

the polity and the literature of the Highlands of Scotland were what Ireland had established there, and the similarity of race is admitted. It was from these areas of Scotland that part at least of the counties of Antrim and Down were now repeopled. To Down the principal incursion came to the lands of two Scotsmen, Sir James Hamilton and Sir Hugh Montgomery, who brought mainly their own countrymen. The MacDonnells, a Scottish family who for two centuries had been established in Antrim, also brought their countrymen to lands taken by the Crown or inveigled from the remaining Irish chiefs. Recognition is given today by those hostile to Ireland's national claims to the predominantly Scottish origin of these immigrations, for their descendants themselves use the title Scotch-Irish, and though much of the immigration came from the lowlands the Highland Scottish contribution was considerable. Irish-Irish could as well be used to describe these, for racially there was no major divergence—the two-race theory is largely invalidated by history itself.

There were, of course, English settlers as well as Scottish, and the records contain the fact. Of Bangor (Co. Down) a report of 1611 said:

> 80 new houses all inhabited with Scotyshmen and Englishmen.... At Holly Woode, three mylles from Bangor.... there are 20 houses inhabited with English and Scottes. [1]

And of Newtownards the same report said:

> A goode towne of a hundred houses or thereabouts, all peopled with Scottes. [2]

But that the Scots predominated is clear. The influx continued of itself once the Scottish families had taken root on Irish soil. In 1635 William Brereton in passing through Scotland noted that

> Above ten thousand persons have within two years last past left the country wherein they lived, which was betwixt Aberdeen and Ennerness, and are gone for Ireland. [3]

The general effect of the expropriation of the Irish lands in Ulster and the bringing in of Scottish and English settlers had not removed the Irish from their original territories to any marked extent. They remained both on the lands planted by royal decree and on those which private enterprise more successfully took over. The Irish on these lands did not even become a minority,

---

[1] *Two Centuries of Life in Down, 1600-1800*, p. 49.
[2] Ibid., p. 64.
[3] *Chetham Society Publications*, vol. i, p. 119.

for they were in much greater number than the newcomers. The layer at the top had changed, all below remained as it had been, part of the nation. But the process had begun of a powerful outside nation using one section of Ireland's population against the other. The Rev. George Hill sums up his monumental researches into this period:

> The dragon's teeth, so plentifully, and as if so deliberately sown in this Ulster plantation, have, indeed, sprung up at times with more than usually abundant growth, yielding their ghastly harvests of blood and death on almost every plain, and by almost every riverside and in almost every glen of our northern province. [1]

The period after the Plantations was one of dismay for the former ruling Irish families and for the Anglo-Normans who had persevered in the old Faith. To control the new Irish Parliament which King James called in 1613 forty new boroughs were created by the Government. Many of them were in the planted counties. The charters of these new corporations permitted only Protestants to be freemen and so the Irish Parliament was weighted against the older families and the mass of the nation. In the next decade the title deeds by which these older families held their lands, particularly in Wexford and Longford, were attacked by Crown lawyers, and the Anglo-Irish Catholics realised their position was becoming more and more insecure. It was but little mended by the "Graces", never made law, by which King Charles I guaranteed all titles more than sixty years old in return for a substantial sum for his treasury from the title-holders.

To this disquiet among the Irish landholders there was now added the dismay caused by the policy applied by Sir Thomas Wentworth when he was Lord Deputy from 1633 to 1640. His object was to break all opposition to the absolute power of the King and make Ireland subject to England both politically and economically. Irish industries would not be allowed to compete against English manufactures. Anything that interfered with English prosperity must be suppressed. It was put by Sir Thomas into one illuminating phrase:

> All wisdom advises to keep this Kingdom as much subordinate and dependent on England as is possible; and holding them from the manufacture of wool, thus enforcing them to fetch their clothing from thence.... How can they depart from us without nakedness and beggary?

1 Hill, *Plantation in Ulster*, p. 590.

Wentworth, who by this economic policy struck at the merchant and manufacturing classes, and therefore at their workers, struck at the aristocracy by refusing to confirm the "Graces" for which the King had been heavily paid. He also instituted a system of overawing the Juries who were investigating questions ot title. Lands were confiscated, fines exacted, and the old families and all dependent on them were left without redress. For a generation this exploitation had gone on when in October 1641 the Irish struck for freedom again.

It was a remarkable revolution. The memories of Hugh O'Neill's triumphs were not dead, the possibility of foreign alliances was great. Had good fortune lighted the insurgents' banners the insurrection might have succeeded. It failed, and worse than the failure was that the victorious side alone wrote the story of that Rising. That propagandist account has gone into history and it is used to this day as if it were accurate. The Insurrection was represented, as many Irish efforts at freedom have since been, not as a national blow for independence but as an attempt to exterminate the Protestants. It was said that 300,000 Protestants were massacred in Ulster alone, whereas the total Protestant population in that province was about 120,000 in 1641 and there seemed to be as many alive after the "massacres" as before them.

The facts are that this was war: that the families, chiefs and people who had stood by the old faith were on one side and those of the new faith on the other. It happened therefore that every casualty suffered by the eventual victors could not but be a Protestant, who died not for that reason but because men were fighting to liberate themselves and he and his co-religionists opposed them. There were undoubtedly many bitter and dreadful acts in the period. It was a time when wars were to the death; and the fighting continued for eight years. The Protestant historian Lecky thinks that in all Ireland about 8,000 Protestants were killed in the first two years of the insurrection and goes on to write:

> The struggle on both sides was very savage. The quarter the rebels at first undoubtedly gave to their prisoners in Ulster seems very seldom to have been reciprocated, the Lords Justice gave strict orders to their officers to refuse it, and a large proportion of the atrocities committed by the rebels were committed after the wholesale and promiscuous slaughter [by their opponents]. [1]

1 Lecky, *History of Ireland*, vol. i, p. 89.

The facts of this great national effort to restore Ireland as a nation have been established by research, and they show that it was an heroic struggle in which disciplined armies led by commanders of international repute made a well-organised endeavour to free their land.

The Anglo-Irish and the old Irish made common cause in the opening years of the 1641 Rising. The four provinces were combined in the attempt to throw off the yoke. The North, where the insurrection began, was soon joined by Munster, Leinster and Connacht. One of the first acts of the insurgents was to establish a Government and so there came into being the Confederation of Kilkenny, a national Parliament which stood not only for independence but for full liberty of religion and conscience, a remarkable thing in that day. The Armies of the Confederation were led by a famous Irishman. He was Owen Roe O'Neill, nephew of Hugh O'Neill, and he had done long foreign service as General in the armies of Spain. At Benburb he defeated the English General Munroe in a decisive battle in 1646.

When the Royalists were defeated in England, the heart went out of the Anglo-Irish as distinct from the Irish resistance. The effect of this and of the overwhelming strength which the Parliamentary leader Oliver Cromwell had brought with him to Ireland decided the war. On the Irish side it had been a military effort for freedom: that effort was eventually broken, not by military triumphs over the Irish forces, but by the excesses of the Cromwellian soldiery against the civilian population. [1]

There was also a new plantation. When the war ended, the estates of Catholics were confiscated wholesale, over ten million acres being granted to English owners. They were, in the main, adventurers who had supported Cromwell and who now by their possession of land became the power in the country. As in all previous plantations this latest did not change the racial structure of Ireland, but it had one effect which was to remain. It made a religious and social cleavage between the landlords and those who were their serfs rather than their tenants, though the primary division was still of one nation against its oppressors.

Nothing illustrated this so clearly as the almost complete lack of change in Ireland when Charles II was restored. The Catholics, because they were of the Irish nation, remained a dispossessed people, whether they had been lords or serfs. To the single

1 Denis Murphy, *Cromwell in Ireland.*

Parliament held in Ireland during the reign of Charles II only one Catholic was elected. The marked benefit Ireland got from the Restoration in 1660 was eighteen years in which both the Presbyterians and the Catholics were almost free from active persecution. Then came the fabricated plot by which Titus Oates has his place in history, and violent anti-Catholic hysteria swept through Ireland.

These conflicts of the seventeenth century, national and religious, had no lasting effect on the racial composition of the Nation. The population of Ireland in the second half of that century was slightly more than a million. In 1660 the figures collected by Sir William Petty showed that the Irish exceeded the English and Scots in all parts of the country. Despite plantations and confiscations the Irish were in a majority in every county, even in Ulster, and were outnumbered only in or near garrisoned towns where the numbers of British soldiers gave a temporary preponderance. In five of the six counties now cut off from Ireland the Irish were sixty per cent of the population. For Tyrone, the sixth county, there are no figures, but it is strongly nationalist to this day.

The accession of James II in 1685 brought hope of the ending of religious discrimination. The new monarch, two years after he came to the throne, removed all disabilities against both Presbyterians and Catholics. This change of policy frightened the Cromwellian settlers—the holders of land and offices—and to prevent the Presbyterians uniting with the Catholics, rumours were spread everywhere that the Catholics were plotting a massacre of all planters. The rumours were believed, and when William of Orange came to supplant James II, the Protestants and Presbyterians of the North-east of Ireland joined to overthrow the reigning monarch and by the gallant defence of Derry helped eventually to bring King William's cause to success.

Before James was defeated the mass of the Irish had rallied to him as a means of winning back their liberty. A Parliament was called and in it legislation was passed asserting Ireland's independence of the English Parliament and by one statute the Parliament established perfect religious liberty throughout all parts of the country. In an effort to regain the old Irish estates the grants of land made under Cromwell and confirmed by Charles II a generation before were annulled. Despite the Statute guaranteeing religious freedom, this annulment has many times been cited as proof that if the Irish had then secured effective

self-Government they would have acted intolerantly to the Protestant property holders. The facts, however, are that the real
owners of these particular lands were still living and their property
was rightly being restored to them. The Ulster confiscation made
at the beginning of the century was not altered.

The annulment of the Cromwellian settlement was, however,
used to alienate from King James's cause the sympathy of all the
planters. The poor leadership of that King himself and the
stronger foreign aid given to King William decided the war, and
in the defeat of James Stuart another hope of Irish freedom,
fought for by old Irish and new Irish shoulder to shoulder, was
quenched. The final phase of the war was reached at Limerick
where a gallant resistance won for the vanquished honourable
terms of peace and a solemn treaty was drawn up guaranteeing
freedom of religion to the mass of the Irish people. The Irish
armies were given the choice of serving this new master or being
translated to the Continent. As they had really fought for freedom they could not acknowledge the new English King and they
took sail for France.

CHAPTER III

THE EIGHTEENTH CENTURY

As HAD HAPPENED so often before, the undertaking to give toleration to the Irish Catholics, which was so definite a part of the Treaty of Limerick, was not fulfilled. Indeed, the departure of the Irish forces overseas, since it left the nation defenceless, seemed to be the prelude to the introduction of the terrible Penal Laws. Lecky, a Protestant historian of entirely Tory sympathies, has left a description of these Laws which needs no further expansion.

> It was the distinguishing characteristic of the Irish penal code that its victims constituted at least three fourths of the nation, and that it was intended to demoralise as well as degrade.. By an Act of the English Parliament they were forbidden to sit in that of Ireland. They were afterwards deprived of the elective suffrage, excluded from the corporations, from the magistracy, from the bar, from the bench, from the grand juries and from the vestries. They could not be sherriffs or solicitors or even game keepers or constables. They were forbidden to possess any arms.... They could not even possess a horse of the value of more than £5, and any Protestant on tendering that sum could appropriate the hunter or the carriage horse of his Catholic neighbour.. The legislation on the subject of Catholic education may be briefly described, for it amounted simply to universal, unqualified and unlimited proscription.. It was the third great object of the penal code to dissociate the Catholics as much as possible from the soil ... No Catholic was suffered to buy land, or inherit it or receive it as a gift from Protestants.. All Catholic archbishops, bishops, deans and vicars-general were ordered by a certain day to leave the country. If after that date they were found in it they were to be first imprisoned and then banished, and if they returned they were pronounced guilty of high treason and were liable to be hanged, disembowelled and quartered.. The law of 1709 offered a reward of £50 to anyone who secured the conviction of any Catholic archbishop, bishop, dean or vicar-general. [1]

This draconian code was variously operated. Where the local magistrates were zealots it was enforced in full rigour. The civil rights of the majority were annihilated and even those few families whose estates had survived the confiscations of the pre-

---

[1] Lecky, *History of Ireland*, vol. i, pp. 145-60.

vious century were stripped of their lands. The Acts against the clergy were enforced spasmodically. But the common people in some way maintained their sense of neighbourliness. In Armagh a bedridden Catholic priest of ninety years of age was seized by one Walter Dawson in 1712 and thrown into prison and died after four months in Armagh Gaol. Dawson's brother wrote to a cousin in Dublin:

> For God's sake, Cousin, if you have any influence over my brother, persuade him not to do such things for money which brings such an odium on him, and a reflection to his family. For everybody here does cry out upon him for it, and says it is the reward my Lord Anglesey promised to get, put him upon this. [1]

The Penal Laws were not laws against a sect or a troublesome or turbulent group: they were aimed at the Irish nation. Again it was Lecky who put the universality of the code into an oft-quoted phrase:

> It was directed, not against the few, but against the many. It was not the persecution of a sect, but the degradation of a nation. It was the instrument employed by a conquering race, supported by a neighbouring Power, to crush to the dust the people among whom they were planted. [2]

The Penal Laws had a further purpose, to divide the Irish nation on religious lines, all the Protestants on the favourable side of the line, all the Catholics on the other side so that the two might never again unite. The Lord Justices in 1715 urged upon the wholly Protestant Irish Parliament a unanimity among the various Protestant sects as

> may once more put an end to all other distinctions in Ireland but that of Protestant and Papist. [3]

But the ascendancy established by the confiscations was not ready to share its ill-gotten gains with any but those of the Established Church. The other Protestant communities, principally the Presbyterians, even if they had helped King William, were now to be shown their place. As their historian, the Rev. W. T. Latimer, said:

> Presbyterians had won what they thought was liberty but what

[1] W. Burke, *Irish Priests in Penal Times*, p. 282.
[2] Lecky, *History of Ireland*, vol. i, pp. 169-70.
[3] W. Burke, *Irish Priests in Penal Times*, p. 166.

was in reality the privilege of being persecuted by a prelatic aristocracy. [1]

They had hoped, like their Catholic fellow-countrymen, for religious toleration; and in fact a new influx came to Ireland from Scotland with that belief. The Irish Presbyterians and those newcomers were soon to find that the aristocracy set up by the plantations of the seventeeth century and consolidated by the defeat of James II was for the Church of Ireland only.

While the Catholics were excluded by law from Parliament and public office the dissenters were virtually excluded by practice. The British Government of 1701 set the key by refusing to allow a Presbyterian who was elected mayor to take office as he did not belong to the Established Church. In 1704 an Act was passed which excluded from any position under the Crown, civil or military, any person who did not submit to the Church of Ireland.Thenceforward the Presbyterians, like the Catholics, were legally barred from all office. They were also barred from teaching in schools, and even the validity of Presbyterian marriage was denied. The Presbyterians were often not permitted to bury their dead without the funeral service of the Established Church.

The number of Ulstermen who went in the eighteenth century to the United States was proportionately more than from other parts of Ireland, and this has led to the claim that all the Irish emigrants were Ulster Presbyterians. That claim is historically false but here it is well to note what kind of Ulsterman did go to the United States and why. The Protestant Irishman went not as a loyalist or a man who had a homeland other than Ireland; but as an Irish citizen looking for freedom and through his love of it easily moulded into the stout republicanism which soon helped to make America free. With him went many Catholic Irishmen and women from Ulster and from the other three provinces.

An examination of the 1790 census of the United States by the American Council of Learned Societies in 1931 showed that there were 307,000 of Irish descent in the United States at that first count after freedom was established. This was almost a tenth of the whole population. The Council concluded that of these, 191,000 were from Ulster and 116,000 from the other three provinces. It would appear from the basis of their calculations that one-fifth at least of the Ulster group were of Gaelic

1 William Thomas Latimer, *History of the Irish Presbyterians*, p. 217.

rather than settler or planter origin. The Council say in their Report: [1]

> The Celtic Irish thus seem to have contributed about 6.3 per cent. to the population of the United States in 1790 ... The Irish as a whole are estimated at approximately 9.7 per cent of the American population of 1790.

The net result was that the Irish nation contributed more than any other people except England to the white population of the new country, and the contribution would have been higher still if many of the Catholics had not been so completely despoiled as not to have the means of going. It is not surprising, therefore, that having regard to their experience at home the Irish of every province played so important a part in the American struggle for independence.

At the time of the American War the Irish formed as much as fifteen per cent of the population of Georgia and Pennsylvania; and the tenacity and courage of the Pennsylvanian Line won for these soldiers in the War of Independence the tribute of General Henry Lee: "They might have been, with more propriety, called the Line of Ireland." The famous General Edward Hand, from Offaly in the Irish midlands, had among his troops Irishmen from all the four provinces. Other notable Irishmen were General John Clarke of Antrim, General John Sullivan of Limerick, General Walter Stewart of Derry, Colonel Stephen Moylan of Cork, General Andrew Lewis of Donegal, General William Irvine of Enniskillen, General John Shee of Meath and Commodore John Barry of Wexford, Father of the American Navy. It was before a Committee of the British House of Commons that

---

[1] *American Council of Learned Societies' Report;* published at the United States Printing Office in 1932. The Committee which prepared the Report consisted of Walter F. Willcox, Professor of Economics and Statistics at Cornell University, Max Ferrand, Professor of History at Yale, Robert H. Fife, Professor of German at Columbia, Joseph A. Hill, Chief Statistician to the U.S.A. government, and J. Franklin Jameson, Director of the Department of Historical Research in Carnegie Institution at Washington. The method adopted was a statistical analysis of the surnames of the United States given in the Census of 1790. A group of distinctively Irish names was taken and these were then collated with Matheson's *Report on Surnames in Ireland* in 1890. Matheson's *Report* showed what percentage those bearing the selected names made of the total population of Ireland, and from that was deduced the total percentage of the Irish in America's 1790 population. Two counterchecks were applied. A group of names exclusive to each of the four Irish provinces was taken and the result compared with that ascertained by using the wider set of names. Also a similar analysis was made of the contributions of other countries to the American population of 1790.

two witnesses maintained that half the American Army was from Ireland. "We have lost America through the Irish", lamented Lord Mountjoy in the British Parliament.

The freedom for which these Irish fought in America came to mean something for the settlers in Ireland also. It was always in the minds of the old Irish and it slowly became implanted into the thinking of the new Irish. The rise of this acceptance of Nationalism is seen first in the writings of William Molyneux, and in the second half of the eighteenth century many of the ruling aristocracy as well as the Presbyterian tenants in Ulster were influenced by the principles which had led to the American Revolution. Many of the oppressive Acts against Presbyterians and Catholics were repealed, and though others of the Penal Laws remained, it was an era of growing religious tolerance. The Presbyterians were particularly favourable to the cause of the American colonies. The British began to take fright. In 1775 the English Lord Lieutenant commented:

> The Presbyterians in the North (who in their hearts are Americans) were gaining strength every day. [1]

Again in 1779 the Presbyterians were described as

> violently attached.. to republican principles; from thence their strong predilection to the American rebels. [2]

The movement for Irish independence was beginning to get its republican form and the Presbyterians in Ireland were foremost in thus shaping it.

The nationalism of the descendants of the planters took practical expression in 1778 when the Irish Volunteers were founded by Charlemont, Grattan and Flood. At the outset it was an exclusively Protestant and Presbyterian organisation and was ostensibly established to protect Ireland from a French invasion. But it was of Ireland first that these men were thinking, and Lecky has traced the succession:

> The right of Ireland to parliamentary independence had been unanimously asserted by the Irish Parliament of 1641 ... and it was reiterated in emphatic terms by the Parliament of James II, convened at Dublin in 1689. On the ruin of the Catholics, the banner which dropped from their hands was caught up by Protestants. The doctrines of the legitimate independence of the Irish Parliament passed from Molyneux to Swift, from Swift to Lucas,

---

[1] Lecky, *History of Ireland*, vol. ii, p. 163.
[2] *Stopford-Sackville MSS* (Hist. MSS Comm.) vol. i, p. 260-1.

from Lucas to Flood. It was strongly asserted in the writings of Henry Brooke ... It was the first principle of the policy of Charlemont; and the eloquence of Grattan, assisted by the example of America and by the spirit of independence which the sense of power naturally gives, was rapidly preparing its triumph. [1]

On 15 February 1782 delegates from 143 Corps of the Ulster section of the Volunteers assembled in full uniform in Dungannon. They demanded the independence of the Irish Parliament and they demanded also full religious tolerance for their brother Irishmen. These were the words of that famous resolution.

> That we hold the right of private judgement in matters of religion to be equally sacred in others as in ourselves; that as men and as Irishmen, Christians and as Protestants, we rejoice in the relaxation of the penal laws against our Roman Catholic fellow-subjects, and that we conceive the measure to be fraught with the happiest consequences to the union and the prosperity of the inhabitants of Ireland.

It is Lecky who makes the informative comment:

> The assembly at Dungannon had an immediate influence of the most decisive kind. Ulster was the heart of the volunteer movement as it was the heart of the Protestantism of Ireland; and it became evident that no reliance could be henceforth placed on the continuance of those divisions and religious animosities which had hitherto paralysed the political energies of the nation. [2]

Ireland had for the moment shaken herself free of those discords which it was to Britain's advantage to create. Strength came with unity and when Grattan on 16 April 1782 moved a declaration of legislative independence in the Irish House of Commons it was passed unanimously. Britain saw no other course than to accept, and in 1783 there was passed by the Parliament of Britain the Act of Renunciation which declared that the right of the Irish people to be governed only by statutes of the Irish Parliament "shall at no time hereafter be questioned or questionable".

Ireland had begun an era notable for both its harmony and its prosperity. The Parliament, however, remained unrepresentative, because the bulk of the people as Catholics were excluded. The Volunteers after 1782 made attempts to reform the system of election. Progress was slow and it was not until 1793 that Catholics were allowed a restricted vote. The difficulty was that

[1] Lecky, *History of Ireland,* vol. ii, p. 229.
[2] Ibid., pp. 284-5.

the Executive in Ireland was not responsible to the Irish Parliament. It was appointed by the Crown, which in effect meant by the British Government, and was thus responsive in all its critical decisions, and indeed in its whole policy, to instructions from London. The wishes of the Parliament in Dublin had, with it, but a secondary importance. [1]

Meanwhile the more progressive and nationally minded Protestants had founded (1790) the famous Society of United Irishmen of which Theobald Wolfe Tone was the guiding spirit. All the appearances were that Ireland might soon become a nation wholly independent, providing equal status and equal opportunity for all her children.

The British Executive, faced with this uniting of the main sections of the Irish people, used their remaining strength in Ireland to break that reunion. They had retained the power of filling many seats in the Irish Parliament and of influencing others by the distribution of posts, pensions and peerages. By this means they secured a sufficient number of M.P.s to thwart the attempt to make Catholics full citizens. The Society of United Irishmen was decreed illegal in 1794. Its mouthpiece, the *Northern Star,* published in Belfast, was suppressed in 1797 and the proprietors, two brothers named Simms, were imprisoned. In a single swoop two whole United Irish committees in Belfast, numbering almost forty members, were arrested.

This removal or outlawing of the leaders of the unity movement went hand in hand with a policy designed to cause religious bitterness and thus promote disunity. Especially in Ulster armed Yeomanry were allowed to plunder the country, assailing all who stood for liberty. Robert Lowry, a magistrate in Dungannon, Co. Tyrone, described in June 1797 the proceedings of the military:

> For a set of armed men, without any gentlemen at their head, to be permitted at their pleasure day after day, and what is worse, night after night, to scour whole tracts of country, destroy houses, furniture, etc. and stab and cut in a most cruel manner numbers, that, from either private resentment or any other cause, they may take a dislike to, will, if permitted to go on, depopulate and destroy the trade of this country. [2]

[1] "A permanent English administration in Dublin headed by an English chief governor and under the continuous supervision of the English Executive" David B. Quinn in *Irish Historical Studies* (Mar. 1941) describing the outcome of Poyning's Law.
[2] Lecky, *History of Ireland,* vol. iv, p. 96.

Another magistrate in the same county pointed out that such proceedings "if persisted in will in all probability insure a rebellion". In the autumn assizes in Ulster many Irishmen were prosecuted, and sentences of death were frequent for taking part in the movement for freedom. At Monaghan ten men were condemned to execution. The most notable and long remembered trial of 1797 was of a young Presbyterian farmer, William Orr of Ferranshane, Co. Antrim, who was charged with swearing two soldiers into the Society of United Irishmen. He had lain in prison for twelve months before he was tried. A death-sentence was passed on him and on 14 October 1797 he was hanged at Carrickfergus. A contemporary ballad catches the feelings of the Irish people:

> They led him forth from his prison cell!
> They swung him high on the gallows tree!
> And the people wept as the brave man died—
> Died for his faith and counterie.

Universal acts of injustice and terrorism eventually provoked the insurrection which the Tyrone magistrate had predicted. Before it came, however, divisions had entered into the Ulster branches of the United Irishmen. The failure of French aid was one cause. Most potent of all was the success of British propaganda, which represented the devotion of the mass of the Irish nation to freedom as an intention to attack the Protestant minority.

The Rising began in South Leinster on 23 May 1798. A fortnight passed before the faithful Presbyterians took up arms in the North. That fortnight had been employed by Dublin Castle to distort reports of the Rising in the rest of the country till it was made to seem a war against Protestants by Catholics. It was an old trick, but the Ulstermen's ranks were thinned by those fabrications.

Many thousands did rise and they took the field with the battle-cry "Remember Orr". There were several actions of importance. An insurgent force under Henry Joy McCracken, with William Orr's brother as one of his officers, attacked the Garrison town of Antrim, but after a courageous fight it was repulsed with heavy losses. Randalstown and Ballymena were occupied on the same day. However, the defeat of McCracken disheartened the movement in Antrim and the United Irishmen there soon dispersed. In Down the Rising was more substantial and a force of 7,000 under a Lisburn linen draper, Henry Munroe, assembled near Ballinahinch and attacked the troops. Lecky says the insurgents

> showed signal courage, rushing to the very muzzles of the cannon, where many of them were blown to pieces, and where bodies were found as black as coal from the discharge. Once or twice their impetuosity seemed to carry all before it; but at last, superior discipline and greatly superior arms asserted their inevitable ascendancy and dispersed with the loss of 400 or 500 men. [1]

Among those who fought at Ballinahinch was Betsy Gray, who remains to this day one of the heroines of Irish history. She, with her brother and her fiancé, escaped after the battle but were persued by yeomen and killed. A ballad account of their death ends:

> Shame on the cruel, ruthless band
> Who hunted down to death their prey!
> And palsy strike the murderous hand,
> That slew the lovely Betsy Gray!

The insurrection in Ulster, as in the rest of Ireland, was put down with the utmost severity. McCracken, who was executed at Belfast, and Munroe at Lisburn, died in testimony that Ireland's desire for freedom was not local or provincial but national, for on the scaffolds of Leinster, Connacht and Munster hung as noble corpses. A proclamation calling on the Northern insurgents to lay down their arms threatened that if they did not submit

> Major General Nugent will proceed to set fire to, and totally destroy, the towns of Killinchy, Killileagh, Balinahinch, Saintfield, and every cottage and farmhouse in the vicinity of those places, carry off the stock and cattle, and put everyone to the sword who may be found in arms. [2]

In Belfast Colonel Durham issued an order that if anyone harboured an insurgent "such person's house, so offending, shall be burnt, and the owner thereof hanged." So amid scenes of savage repression the cause of Irish independence was subdued in Antrim and Down in 1798 just as it was in the other parts of an Ireland where brave men and women of all faiths and of all origins faced death, torture, imprisonment and exile for love of their nation's liberty.

In other ways, too, Ulster kept her place as part of the nation. Despite the confiscations and plantations, despite penal laws and oppression, Irish literature and the Irish language survived

[1] Ibid., p. 421.
[2] Ibid., p. 423.

even in Ulster. The wandering poets, no longer supported by Irish ruling families, in lamenting the passing of their patrons looked forward in their "vision poetry" to the day when Ireland would rise up again.

These poets in Ulster as elsewhere helped to keep alive the spirit of the nation. One of the greatest of the Ulster poets was Seamus Dall MacCuarta, a blind poet of the late seventeenth and early eighteenth centuries. His songs were sung all over Ulster from Down to Donegal and he was without peer among his contemporaries. His tradition was carried on by Peader O'Doirnin (1704-68), who lived in South Armagh and County Down, and Art MacCubhthaigh (1715-74) of Armagh. As the British historian J. L. Hammond said,

> If in the eighth century Irish civilization was a greater power in the world than English, in the eighteenth century the ghost of that civilization was a greater power in Ireland than the institutions imposed by English conquest. [1]

Despite the settlements the Irish language survived in Ulster and became the language even of some of the settlers themselves, particularly the Scots whose own tongue was Gaelic. The Presbyterians had a dozen ministers able to preach in Irish as early as 1716, and as late as 1835 the Synod of Ulster made the study of Irish compulsory for all the candidates for Holy Orders. Societies for the study and preservation of the language sprang up at the end of the eighteenth century in Belfast and gave an early impetus to a movement which later led to the founding of the Gaelic League, and Irish is today the spoken language in parts of Donegal and there are speakers of it still in North Antrim and the Sperrin Mountains in Tyrone.

[1] J. L. Hammond, *Gladstone and the Irish Nation*, p. 5.

CHAPTER IV

THE UNION AND AFTER

Both catholics and Dissenters, in the Ireland of the eighteenth century, struggled to end the disabilities under which they lay and it was the constant aim of the British Government to prevent any real alliance developing out of this concordance of effort, just as it was the aim of the patriots to bring just such a union about. The British method, as always, was to excite sectarian fears. They whispered everywhere that if the mass of the Irish people won their national and civil rights they would persecute the Presbyterian church and its members.

The religious issue never dominated the minds of the majority. It was in national rights and in national freedom that they were interested, and this freedom they sought, not for themselves as a section, even the predominant section of the Irish people, but for the whole population, Dissenter, Catholic and Protestant alike.

The outlook of the liberals everywhere in Ireland at the close of the eighteenth century was similar. They wished to have liberty for all. The principles of political and civil equality enshrined in the American Constitution and in the new French revolutionary ideas, were reflected in all grades of political thinking. The Irish Parliament was influenced by them and, though representative of the Episcopalian landowners, gradually removed the disabilities of Presbyterians and Catholics.

One of the leaders of the movement for Parliamentary reform was William Todd Jones, deputy for Lisburn, Co. Antrim. He declared his objective in a letter to the Irish Volunteers in Belfast written in March 1784:

> The North disdains partial rights—she contemplates with equal affection her Catholic and Protestant sons. [1]

At that time the northern capital was as alive as Dublin to the danger of British policy. It was the *Belfast News Letter* which in June 1784 said:

> The Machiavellian doctrine of every enemy of Ireland in order to

[1] *Historical Collections Relative to the Town of Belfast* (1817), p. 291

destroy our hopes, by encouraging dissension among the inhabitants would be 'Divide and Govern', but the sound doctrine of every true Irishman, be he of the Church of England, of the Dissenting Church, or of the Catholic, must ever be 'Unite and Conquer'. [1]

The more this spirit spread the more determined the British were to turn it into any channel which later might recreate dissension. Certainly, said William Pitt, British Prime Minister in a letter (October 1784) to the Viceroy in Dublin, let there be Parliamentary reform but a prudent and temperate reform which

> may unite the Protestant interest in excluding the Catholics from any share in the representation or the Government of the country. [2]

But there were, in the Irish view, to be no half measures. It must be true reform. Forty-three prominent citizens of Belfast issued an address on 23 January 1792 urging the extension of the franchise to Catholics:

> We wish to see all distinctions on account of religion abolished— all narrow, partial maxims of policy done away. We anxiously wish to see the day when every Irishman shall be a citizen—when Catholics and Protestants, equally interested in their country's welfare, possessing equal freedom and equal privileges, shall be cordially united, and shall learn to look upon each other as brethern, the children of the same God, the natives of the same land—and when the only strife amongst them shall be, who shall serve their country best. [3]

Not only were the liberal-minded Presbyterians in Belfast ready to ask less for liberty for all—for the desire for reform developed into a vigorous republicanism—they were ready to fight for it; and when the Insurrection of 1798 took place, that section of Irishmen were gloriously involved in it. Their official historian, Rev. W. T. Latimer, shows that in all about thirty ministers and licentiates of the Presbyterian Church were associated with the Risings in Antrim and Down: a considerable figure for a church which numbered 183 congregations in the whole of Ulster. [4] Rev. James Porter, Minister of Greyabbey, Co. Down, and Archibald Warwick, licentiate of the Presbytery of Belfast, were executed for their republican principles. Rev. James Simpson of Newtownards, Rev. John Glendy of Maghera and Rev. Thomas Ledlie Birch of Saintfield had to emigrate to America. Rev. William Steele

1 *Belfast Newsletter*, 28 May-1 June, 1784.
2 *Correspondence between ... William Pitt and Charles Duke of Rutland*, p. 44
3 *Historical Collections Relative to the Town of Belfast*, p. 363
4 W. T. Latimer, *History of the Irish Presbyterians*, p. 399

Dickson of Portaferry, Rev. John Smith of Kilrea, Rev. Samuel Barber of Rathfriland and Rev. Sinclair Kelburn of Belfast were imprisoned. If the proportion of clergymen is an indication of the sympathies of the Presbyterian laymen, the 1798 insurrection had ample support in Ulster.

The failure of the insurrection, the flight of many of the Presbyterian body who took part in it, the propaganda that it was a popish plot, and the rigour of its suppression seemed to break the spirit of those who were left. The Rising was in May. In August 1798 at the Presbyterian Synod of Ulster, meeting at Lurgan, fifty-three ministers and thirteen elders humbly besought the British King "not to impute to the whole the transactions of a part". They contributed £500 to the defence of the Kingdom and ordered the Presbyterians to investigate the political activities of Ministers, elders and probationers. The liberalism of the Presbyterians seemed dead.

Elsewhere the triumph of the British view was having its victories also. The failure to complete Parliamentary reform left the existing House open to corruption, and of this Premier Pitt took full advantage. Votes were freely purchased by money, bribes, and peerages, and then the depths to which the assembly had sunk were used to destroy it finally. Lord Castlereagh's father wrote to his son who was himself organising the destruction of the Irish Parliament:

> Most of those, who were actuated with a strong reforming spirit, entertain such a dislike and antipathy to the present subsisting Parliament of the country that they will not be very adverse to any change that will rid them of what they deem so very corrupt a Legislature. [1]

Castlereagh himself wrote:

> Sometime since, the Presbyterians would have been found most energetic opponents, but they have been long disinclined to the existing system; of late, they are rather tired of the treason in which they had very deeply embarked: perhaps they may be inclined to compromise with the Union [2]

and he expressed the hope that an increase in the Regium Donum from which the Presbyterian ministers were paid would secure for the British the support of their church.

The abolition of the separate Irish Parliament and the substitution for it of a union with Britain under one Parliament in

[1] Lecky, *History of Ireland*, vol. v, p. 199.
[2] Ibid., p. 198.

which the Irish would be in a permanent minority had now become a major aim of British policy. Britain had realised that every group in Ireland — old Irish, Anglo-Irish, the peoples of the plantations, the settlers from Down and Antrim, Protestants, Presbyterians and Catholics — had among them people who were determined to put Ireland above every other thing. In 1782 the British Parliament by a solemn Act had, as we have seen, declared Irish legislative independence to be unquestioned and forever unquestionable. But the Irish had united under that legislative independence and had sought wider freedom: it was not safe to leave them with a Parliament. The Parliament was destroyed: but not without resistance that went far beyond what Britain had anticipated. John Claudius Beresford, himself an Orangeman, wrote to Castlereagh of the "universal disgust nay horror" with which the prospect of union was viewed by the mass of the Irish people. He who had been a British supporter now said:

> Proud of the name of an Irishman I hope never to exchange it for that of a Colonist, or to see my country governed by laws enacted by a Parliament over which she can have no control from the small share she will have in the election of it. [1]

Even the Orange Lodges cried out against the extinction of the Irish Parliament. The Newtownbutler (Co. Fermanagh) Lodge declared that all supporters of the proposal "should be execrated by their fellow subjects and by posterity". One Dublin Orange Lodge passed a resolution:

> We . . . declare as Orangemen, as Freeholders, as Irishmen, in all the several relations in which we are placed, that we consider the extinction of our separate Legislature as the extinction of the Irish nation. [2]

But British ruthlessness with the United Irishmen, the cruel punishment not only of those captured in the Rising but of their relatives and neighbours, terrorised the ordinary people, while their so-called representatives were openly bought and bribed to pass the Act of Union. Lord Cornwallis, who had been defeated by the American insurgents, was appointed Viceroy and placed in charge of defeating the Irish nation by corruption. He records his feelings at this new task:

> It has ever been the wish of my life to avoid this dirty business, and I am now involved in it beyond all bearing.

[1] R. M. Sibbett, *Orangeism in Ireland,* vol. i, pp. 443-4.
[2] Ibid., p. 450

and again:

> I despise and hate myself every hour for engaging in such dirty work. [1]

The Act of Union cost Britain twenty-eight peerages, twenty-six advancements in the peerage, innumerable appointments and promotion in the public service, £1,260,000 paid as "compensation" to owners of borough seats. No record has been preserved of the direct money payments, but they were at the time believed to be many and substantial. Thus was the Union achieved which was afterwards declared to be so sacred a thing that Irishmen must never seek to break it. Its achievement, brought about by the "dirty work" which caused Lord Cornwallis to despise himself, was equated by the British with the voluntary union of the thirteen sisters which created the United States. The day was to come when Lloyd George, using the same methods to maintain the Union as were used to bring it about, was to compare himself with Abraham Lincoln!

Many years were to pass before the Act of Union was accepted even by the pro-British minority. They, who had been freemen, found the new chains irksome. In 1810 the Dublin Corporation, at that time wholly in the control of the Tory party, urged that the Act of Union be repealed and asked citizens everywhere to come together, "to demand a restoration of that Constitution which is our birthright and of which we have been despoiled by fraud and corruption". [2]

In consequence of this call a public meeting was held in Dublin in September 1810 with the High Sheriff, Sir James Riddell, in the chair. One of the speakers was a young lawyer named Daniel O'Connell, then striving for the emancipation of the Catholics. He spoke words, long memorable, in which he denounced the

> religious dissension which the enemies of Ireland have created and continued, and seek to perpetuate amongst ourselves.. they separated the Protestant from the Catholic, and the Presbyterian from both; they revived every antiquated cause of domestic animosity, and they invented new pretexts of rancour.. The Protestant alone could not expect to liberate his country, the Roman Catholic alone could not do it—neither could the Presbyterian—but amalgamate the three into the Irishman, and the Union was repealed. Learn discretion from your enemies—they have crushed your country by fomenting religious discord—serve her by abandoning it forever. [3]

[1] Lecky, *History of Ireland,* vol. v, p. 228.
[2] *Calendar of Ancient Records of Dublin,* vol. xvi, p. 223.
[3] Denis Gwynn, *Daniel O'Connell,* pp. 100-101.

It was as a first step to Repeal of the Act of Union that O'Connell pressed forward his demand for Catholic Emancipation, calling in July 1812 on all Irishmen to support him.

> Let us rouse the Irish people (he said) from one extreme to the other of the island. Let the Catholics combine with the Protestants, and the Protestant with the Catholic and one generous exertion sets every angry feeling at rest, and banishes forever dissension and division. [1]

O'Connell's call was heard by the Presbyterians, and in a resolution of 1813 the Synod of Ulster, while careful to avoid new charges of disloyalty, having protested "unshaken attachment to the principles of the British Constitution", went on to ask emancipation for their Catholic fellow-countrymen:

> Sensible of the blessings of that civil and religious liberty which we enjoy, we cannot be uninterested spectators of the exertions which are made to extend them to all our fellow-subjects.... We consider it our duty to declare that from the abolition of political distinctions on account of religious profession, so far as may be consistent with the principles of the constitution, we anticipate the happiest consequences. [2]

Irishmen, Protestant and Catholic, were drawing close together, but the British Government had another destiny for them. Sir Robert Peel, the new Chief Secretary for Ireland, and later to be Premier, set down the principle on which Ireland should be governed. Referring to the Catholics and Protestants, he wrote:

> I hope they may always be disunited. The great art is to keep them so, and yet at peace or rather not at war with each other. [3]

That was the ghost that haunted Ireland for the next hundred years. Every time the Irish of both great groups were determined to abolish all that divided them, the British, considering themselves secure only when Ireland was weak, used all the arts, influence and patronage at the disposal of a Government to tear the uniting groups apart.

For the first half of the new century the Presbyterians' love for justice showed itself again and again in an endeavour to win civil rights for their fellow-Irishmen. In November 1825 the *Northern Whig* (Belfast) organ of the Ulster Liberals quoted with approval the sentiments of the *Dublin Evening Post*:

[1] Ibid., p. 109.
[2] *Records of the General Synods of Ulster*, vol. iii, p. 397.
[3] British Museum Add. MS. 40287, 16 June 1814.

It was at a meeting principally composed of Presbyterians, at the time of the Volunteers, that the first declaration in favour of the Roman Catholics was made by any public body in Ireland. This should never be forgotten. It is well known that, in the great bulk of that body, the same sentiments still subsist. [1]

There arose, however, at this time within the ranks of the Presbyterian in Ireland a religious quarrel which was to have a lasting effect on the Irish nation. It was a conflict between the liberals in the Church and those who were conservative. The moderates were led by the Rev. Henry Montgomery, Minister of Dunmurry, Co. Antrim; those who stood by the Westminster Confession of Faith were led by the Rev. Henry Cooke, Minister of Killileagh, Co. Down. It happened that Montgomery co-operated with the Catholics in seeking emancipation and appeared on their platforms. This led to Cooke adopting the other side, and it was from September 1828 that the first Presbyterian opposition to civil rights for Catholics was dated. The Presbyterian historian Rev. W. T. Latimer writes of the conflict and its consequences

It is believed that Cooke was as strongly opposed to the political as to the religious liberalism of Montgomery, and was jealous of his influence. In fact the Synod was not large enough for two such great men, and Cooke, supported by the Orangemen without and by the Calvinists within, excluded his great rival in order that he might reign alone. [2]

Whatever the motives that inspired the Rev. Henry Cooke, his religious intolerance and political conservatism drove him away from the mass of the people, who were in all things the natural comrades of the Presbyterians, and drove him towards the exclusive Episcopalians. From October 1834 dates the coming-together of the Conservative leaders of the two Protestant Churches, in a political union designed to oppose the wishes of the Irish people. In that month and year Cooke, at a meeting at Hillsborough, Co. Down, dramatically announced, "Between the divided Churches I publish the banns of a sacred marriage".

Nevertheless, the Liberal movement lived on among the Presbyterians, and many thousands of Protestants throughout Ireland took part in the national movement for freedom. But what Britain had long sought had been brought about through the Rev. Henry

[1] *Northern Whig*, 3 Nov. 1825.
[2] *History of Irish Presbyterians*, p. 443

Cooke: a compact minority inside Ireland which stood first and above all else for the British interest and against national freedom. In the early years of the "sacred marriage" the Liberal movement was still vigorous in the North-east. In the General Election of 1832, of the twelve members of Parliament returned by Down, Antrim and Armagh only four were Tories and the other eight were Liberals.

The success of the Catholic Emancipation movement and the growth of the movement for Repeal gave the British many chances of deluding the minority into believing that these were movements not *for* Ireland but *against* Protestantism. There were two elements that helped to get this view implanted in many minds: Cooke's unity of the Presbyterians and Episcopalians on a basis of anti-nationalism provided the ready audience; O'Connell's methods of organisation and the invective with which he assailed those who disagreed with him, provided much material for misrepresentation. There was no anti-Protestantism in O'Connell: the fact that the oppressed whom he tried to lift up—and did succeed in lifting up—were of one faith and those who oppressed them of another, gave an appearance to what had no substance. In reply to a Protestant Nationalist, O'Connell towards the end of his life wrote in November 1844:

> If the repeal of the Union were to bring about such a state of things as would prevent any one Protestant or Catholic from believing or saying whatever he might think consistent with truth, I would resist that repeal to the uttermost. In point of religion our struggle is to obtain perfect religious freedom for all. This is the principle I have avowed and acted upon for near fifty years of my political life—perfect freedom of conscience for all and for every one. [1]

The Young Ireland movement broke with O'Connell not on any question that O'Connell had become sectarian, but that he was not asking for Ireland that which a nation should demand. The young men, Catholic and Protestant, who made up this new organisation wished Ireland to have true freedom. They wished also that no means of achieving it be neglected. O'Connell stood for self-Government within the British suzerainty to be achieved only by moral force: the Young Irelanders stood for an independent Ireland to be secured by arms if moral force failed.

The Young Ireland group was representative of all Ireland: Munstermen, Leinstermen, Connachtmen and above all Ulster-

[1] Denis Gwynn, *O'Connell, Davis and the Colleges Bill*, p. 25.

men carrying in their bones the traditions of 1798—Thomas Davis of Cork, John Mitchel of Derry, John Martin of Down, John Dillon of Mayo, Charles Gavan Duffy of Monaghan, William Smith O'Brien of Limerick. Those were the new leaders; and among them Mitchel, son of a Unitarian clergyman, traced his nationalism to his grandfather's association with the United Irishmen and Martin to his forebears' connection with the Irish Volunteers of 1782. Davis and Smith O'Brien were Episcopalians, Dillon and Gavan Duffy were Catholics.

The Young Ireland movement, which saw the ravages of the Great Famine in a nation left without self-government or any separate means of organising the people against this calamity, tried in the end to win Ireland's freedom by arms. The attempt failed and most of the leaders who survived were sent as convicts to Van Diemen's Land.

The failure of the '48 Rising and the terrible consequences of the Famine overwhelmed the national movement for a time, and it was an economic question which dominated the third quarter of the nineteenth century in Ireland. The problem of landlord and tenant was for long one of the unsolved Irish difficulties. The previous revolutionary and constitutional movements regarded a just land system as among the first tasks for the native Parliament they were seeking. The problem would give way peacefully to reform.

But there was no native Parliament, and the complete ascendancy of the landlords now made reform impossible. Sharman Crawford, the Liberal representative of County Down, had the case of the oppressed tenant farmers much at heart and spoke of it at Westminster from 1835. The Presbyterian tenant farmers of Ulster and the Catholic tenants throughout Ireland suffered under a system of high rents and insecurity of tenure. In Ulster, to some extent, the tenants were protected by a custom which allowed the departing occupier to sell the goodwill of a holding, but by the middle of the nineteenth century this ancient usage was being infringed. The common danger was reflected in the uprise of a new Liberal movement in Ulster. Its centre was not now Belfast, for this was a rural Liberalism. Under the leadership of James McKnight, editor of the *Banner of Ulster,* the demand for legal protection for tenants increased during the famine.

West Ulster was hit as badly, or almost as badly, as counties in Munster and Connacht. Even in Antrim the description published by Sir Shafto Adair shows how widespread was the distress of 1846 and 1847. [1] Evictions and emigration stalked after the famine, and Ulster, as did the other three provinces, suffered a serious decline in population.

It was in these circumstances that the new unity movement came into being in 1850 when the men of the North stretched their hands across the ruins of the Famine to clasp those of their brother Irishmen. The Tenant Right League was formed. Charles Gavan Duffy, the Young Irelander, was one of the founders and he secured the co-operation of Dr. James McKnight and other Presbyterian leaders, among them Rev. John Rodgers, Rev. William Dobbin, and Rev. David Bell. The General Assembly of the Synod of Ulster, despite the opposition of Rev. Henry Cooke, petitioned Parliament in favour of the tenant cause. Although this movement did not succeed, it led eventually to the revival of the Liberal movement in Ulster. The first to break the Tory phalanx was Samuel McCurdy Greer, a Presbyterian Liberal elected for Derry in 1857. In the 1868 election five Liberals were returned in Ulster, one in Belfast itself. In 1874 in the present Six County area there were seven Liberals, one Home Ruler and fifteen Tories. In 1880 the Liberals won nine seats.

The Home Rule movement had been started in 1870 by Isaac Butt. He had formerly been a Donegal Protestant Tory and he learned nationalism by defending Irish political prisoners at State trials. Many Protestants joined the new movement, but those in Ulster either stood by non-political liberalism or were firm Tories. When the franchise was extended in 1884 the supporters of the former Liberal M.P.s swung towards Home Rule, and this was to have dramatic results.

A young Protestant landlord, Charles Stewart Parnell, had succeeded Butt as Nationalist leader, and in the general election of 1885 the Home Rulers won 85 seats out of 103 in all Ireland. In Ulster there were 33 seats, and of these a majority, 17, were won by the Nationalists. Although they polled 25,799 votes, more than a third of the Tory poll, not a single Liberal was returned, partly because in that year the Tory Viceroy, Lord Carnarvon, was negotiating with Parnell on the question of Home Rule, and where there was no Nationalist candidate the Home Rule vote went to the Tory candidate.

The Home Rule victory was so impressive that Gladstone

[1] A. Shafto Adair, *The Winter of* 1846-7 *in Antrim.*

decided there and then he must as a democrat respond to a national demand so overwhelmingly voiced:

> The Nationalist members (said the *Pall Mall Gazette* Election Supplement) hold nearly five sixths of the Irish seats and, what is more to the purpose, they represent also five sixths of the Irish people. [1]

Gladstone became Prime Minister after the 1885 election and introduced his first Home Rule Bill in 1886. His own following split and Chamberlain and others left him rather than concede self-government to Ireland. This break had a big effect on the Liberals in Ulster. Many of them, too, went against Home Rule and described themselves as Liberal Unionists. Only 5,710 votes were given to Ulster Liberalism in 1886. With the passage of years many returned to the Liberal faith now interpreted in the Gladstonian sense of including self-government for Ireland, and these voted constantly for the Nationalist candidates as a mark that as between British interests and the Irish nation they stood by Ireland.

In the general elections from 1885 to 1910 the Nationalists never had less than 81 of the 103 seats for all Ireland; and in the two elections of 1910 they held 84 seats, leaving but 19 in the whole country for those against an all-Ireland Parliament. On the eve of the Home Rule Bill of 1912 the majority representation of Ulster itself as well as of Ireland was Nationalist. Today six of the constituencies which consistently through generations returned Nationalist M.P.s are in the area cut off from Ireland, and six other seats which occasionally returned Nationalists are cut off too.

The minority which so grievously felt the extinction of Ireland's Parliament were never finally turned against their Nationalist brothers until nearly a century after the Act of Union. They were then organised and incited as described elsewhere and used as part of the British Conservative movement. Their leadership is enshrined in the Ulster Unionist Council made up of 50 nominees of the Orange Grand Lodges, 100 nominees of local Unionist associations and 50 others, mainly M.P.s, Peers and ex-officio members.

The area which in the old days gave to Ireland a long succession of high kings, and thereafter many of her greatest military leaders and finally some of her wisest Nationalist spokesmen, is

[1] *Popular Guide to the House of Commons,* 1886, p. 3

now represented as anti-Irish. It was the Six Counties which provided Ireland with her first republicans and some of the noblest of those who died for an independent Ireland. From the North-east of Ireland and her Presbyterians came leadership in patriotism and tolerance in the nineteenth century, but there now comes from that area a resistance to Irishmen's efforts to unite and enrich their common nation, a resistance which is not native to those people, nor representative of their constructive genius, but reflects only the centuries of British propaganda which by careful arts and for selfish party ends created this problem for both peoples.

The material Britain used for this purpose was a minority to whom was offered the position of ascendancy. The leaders of the minority accepted this offer of a privileged position, and then called on Britain to fulfil her promise to make it permanent. They left in no doubt what it was they wished to have preserved. One of themselves has set it out:

> A Protestant House of Peers, composed of Protestant Lords Spiritual in Protestant succession; of Protestant Lords Temporal with Protestant inheritance; and a Protestant House of Commons elected by Protestant constituents, a Protestant legislature, a Protestant judiciary, a Protestant executive, in all and each of their varieties, degrees and gradations. [1]

That in their eyes was the ideal. It could be realised only in the beginning: the years inevitably blurred its outline and diminished its proportions. But it was striven for vigorously, and today we see it, diminished in size and reduced in numbers, but present still in the partitioned area of Ireland where the Premier of the territory, boasts of the legislature as "a Protestant Parliament for a Protestant people" in an area in which more than a third of the citizens are non-Protestant!

Men with this mind once ruled all Ireland; the reduction of the area of their jurisdiction was not accomplished without overcoming a fierce resistance. The great threat was democracy, the giving of rights to the common people, most of all the right to vote; and so it came about that there was protracted opposition from the ascendancy to every extension of the franchise. As long as the vote was given but could be cast only in public the fear of wider voting was not profound. Lord Anglesey has recorded that so long as the landlords by threat of eviction could

1 J. A. Froude, *The English in Ireland*, vol. iii, p. 53.

control their votes all was well. But when despite the landlords the forty-shilling freeholders elected O'Connell in 1828, their right to vote was "instantly swept out of existence". This disfranchisement reduced the county electorate in rural Ireland from 200,000 to 26,000. It took fifty years to restore so widespread a vote again.

When the 1832 Reform Act increased the number of county voters meagrely to 27,000, the measure was attacked as revolutionary by Thomas Lefroy, M.P. for Dublin University, who said:

> The Reform Bill was a mockery. The representation under such a Bill would also prove a mockery, as it would neither be the Representation of property nor of the established institutions of the country, but that of the numerical force of the people. [1]

This "numerical force of the people" would, all realised, end privilege; and one of the most privileged, Lord Castlereagh, opposed Reform on the ground that it would mean the election of 76 Nationalists among Ireland's 103 representatives, even thus early acknowledging the people's overwhelming demand for the restoration of a National Parliament. Said Mr. James E. Gordon, who was M.P. for Dundalk, a pocket borough with only 32 electors out of a population of 10,750:

> The principal objection which he entertained to the Bill was founded on its certain result in regard to the great question of Protestant ascendancy in Ireland. He confessed that he was one of those old-fashioned bigots who were prepared at all risks to stand up for the interests of Protestant ascendancy in Ireland. [2]

In 1850 Lord John Russell's Liberal government made a further effort to extend the franchise.

Even with these extensions the borough electors in Ireland totalled only 30,700, and in 1868 a reform was introduced which would double that number. Although this reform was proposed by the anti-Home Rule Government which they supported, the ascendancy in Ireland regarded it with dismay and the *Belfast News Letter* of 5 May 1868 spoke of civil war being preferable to it. Then came the Ballot Act of 1872, and, as it introduced secret voting, the Act was applauded in Britain as a practical recognition of the people's right to rule. Every privileged group in Ireland, however, opposed the Ballot Act, and the opposition masqueraded under the very slogans which eighty years later are used to perpetuate Partition.

[1] Hansard, 25 May 1832, vol. xiii, col. 128-9.
[2] Ibid., col. 159.

The Ballot (said the *Belfast News Letter*) is .... objectionable to all who love our good old Constitution; and it is particularly so in Ireland because it will increase the power of the Ultramontane party. [1]

A great enfranchisement was proposed under the reform of 1884 when every householder in both England and Ireland was given a vote. There had been 224,018 Irish electors in 1882; the new Bill raised this to 741,913. Instantly the ascendancy were in arms. The representation of the Irish constituencies before this extension of the franchise was 63 Nationalists, 26 Conservatives and 14 Liberals. For the province of Ulster there were 18 Conservatives, 8 Liberals and only 3 Nationalists. The Irish minority saw in the increase of the popular vote a grave threat to privilege everywhere. The Ulster Constitutional Club passed the following resolution:

That this meeting, representative of the Constitutional Associations of the Ulster Counties and Boroughs, hereby strongly protests against and condemns the Redistribution Bill at present before Parliament on the grounds that its adoption would virtually hand over the representation of Ireland to the avowed enemies of the British connection.... [2]

The result of the first election fought under the Redistribution Bill was that of 103 members the Nationalists numbered 85 and the Unionsts 18. 17 Nationalists were elected in Ulster and only 16 Conservatives, and a by-election soon afterwards made the Nationalist total 18 to 15. Compared with the previous year, the result of widening the franchise was dramatic; the Conservatives came down from 26 to 18; the Nationalists went up from 63 to 85.

The foregoing examples all relate to Parliamentary Government. Local Government remained still almost entirely in the hands of the ascendancy. It was controlled by unrepresentative Grand Juries which struck rates, gave contracts, provided employment, made appointments and governed the whole local county administration. The broadening of the local-Government franchise by the Reform Act of 1840 was opposed bitterly by the ascendancy, one of whom at a Dublin meeting on 22 February 1839 spoke of "that Popish and idolatrous Municipal Reform Bill". [3] Although over eighty per cent of the Irish people of

1 *Belfast News Letter*, 20 Feb. 1872.
2 Ibid., 6 Dec. 1884.
3 *Epitome of the case of Irish Corporations*, p. 35.

that time were not of the Protestant faith, the meeting passed
a petition asking of the British House of Commons

> That in whatever bill you may pass for the reform of the Irish
> Municipal Corporations you may be graciously pleased carefully to
> provide for the maintenance of their Protestant integrity. [1]

Nearly fifty years later, in 1898, reform of the county administration came. That there should be elective Councils was
regarded by the Tories as a betrayal of the "loyalists". The
measure came from a British Conservative Government and the
wing of that party in Ireland was therefore unable to vote against
it, but their speeches made plain that they submitted only
because there was no alternative. They spoke with contempt of
the Nationalists, to whom the wider electorate would give the
power. Col. Saunderson, Irish Tory leader, admitted that with
the Grand Juries gone

> the party which up to the present time had had the Government
> of Ireland in its hands.... would disappear almost universally all
> over Ireland and in the place of the Gentlemen who had hitherto
> done the work so admirably would be found others such as they
> saw on the Poor Law Boards of Ireland. [2]

We have seen the minority in Ireland first dominant over the
whole land, maintaining their ascendancy by plantation and by
organising settlers to take Irish land, later upholding their pre-
dominance by such savage measures as the Penal Laws; then,
when the national ideal came to be accepted by the descendants
of those planters and settlers, the leaders of the minority acquiesc-
ed in the destruction, planned in London, of their own Parliament rather than let the majority have one. Thereafter, when
the mass of the people were still debarred from any share in
Government, the minority spokesmen and M.P.s fought every
extension of rights to them for the whole breadth of a century.

When the question arose of giving to the Irish nation the
self-Government it had long demanded peacefully and with
extraordinary consistency, the minority, worked upon by British
conservatives, rose in revolt, arming themselves and threatening
civil war. In the end self-Government was given only to a partitioned Ireland, the last of the Ascendancy taking refuge in an
area cut by Britain for them from the body of Ireland. There
today, they still deny to the Nationalists what they so long
denied to the whole people, equal electoral and civil rights, as
is told in a later chapter.

[1] Ibid., p. 115.
[2] *Belfast Newsletter,* 22 Mar. 1898.

CHAPTER V

THE IDEA OF PARTITION
(1833-1912)

IT IS EASY to trace the coming of the idea of partition into English politics. It was first put forward as a suggestion more than a hundred years ago and was often repeated. But almost always it was Englishmen or British leaders who put it forward and it was Irishmen and Irish leaders who rejected it. It was rejected by the majority in Ireland as a matter of course but it was no less roundly rejected by the minority.

Lord Macaulay was the first to propose, as a minor point of argument, that Ireland ought to have not one Government but two. He was replying to Daniel O'Connell's plea for Repeal of the Union. "I defy the honourable and learned member", Lord Macaulay said in the British Parliament on 6 February 1833, "to find a reason for having a Parliament at Dublin which will not be just as good a reason for having another parliament in Londonderry". Macaulay apparently forgot that Derry and the whole wide area of which it acted as the capital, namely the North-west of Ireland, had as Dublin had a Nationalist majority.

The subject was not seriously referred to again until October 1843 when the question of a separate Parliament at Belfast was raised anonymously in the Belfast Newspaper *Northern Whig*. [1] There was no popular backing and no official approval and the idea lapsed. The Home Rule movement proper began in the 1870's and under its first leader, the Protestant Isaac Butt, it grew to national importance, the support for it increasing with every extension of the franchise. Startled by the strength of this support English politicians spoke of there being two nations in Ireland, which apparently was meant to explain why Ireland as a whole could not have Home Rule. The Presbyterian historian Rev. James P. Woodburn answered this "two nation" theory. He said:

There were not two races in Ireland; the whole population is a

[1] *Northern Whig*, 17 Oct. 1843.

mixture of Celtic and Teutonic and the Ulsterman has probably as much Celtic blood as the Southerner. [1]

The proposal to partition Ireland lay dormant for many years and did not again arise until after the extension of the franchise in 1884. It was only by limitation of the number of electors that the minority was able to rule in Ireland. As has been shown each extension of the voters lists was stoutly opposed, and the 1885 general election proved why. The Nationalists won eighty-two per cent of the seats, and Gladstone was to say, after another dramatic election in 1892:

> By the largest majority, perhaps, ever returned in these islands for any purpose whatever — in the last and in the present Parliament the only elections since this great franchise has been given — the Irish people have pressed upon you in a respectful and Constitutional manner that you should make them this great final concession (Home Rule). [2]

The 1885 result was so emphatic that the British Tory Party themselves, as told in more detail elsewhere, thought that Ireland must be given some form of self-government. Gladstone had intended to propose Home Rule but felt that the demand for it was so clear it should not now be a controversial measure. He wrote to the Marquess of Hartington:

> I consider that Ireland has now spoken; and that an effort ought to be made *by the government* without delay to meet her demands for the management by an Irish legislative body of Irish as distinct from Imperial affairs. Only a Government can do it and a Tory Government can do it more easily and more safely than any other. [3]

The Tory Government in fact undertook the first steps but changed direction and went out to use the "Ulster Question" to destroy Gladstone's party.

So instead of proposing Home Rule they declared that the Nationalists were lawless and that the Home Rule movement must be suppressed. They themselves faced northward to light the Orange fires. Carnarvon was forced to resign and Irish self-government became the plaything of British politics.

It was from this period that the partition proposals really date, always being put forward not as a practical solution but to make any solution impracticable and thus drive the Liberals

1 *The Ulster Scot*, p. 17.
2 Hansard, 6 April 1893, vol. x, cols. 1601-2.
3 J. L. Hammond, *Gladstone and the Irish Nation*, p. 458.

out of public favour. This method of using Ireland as a pawn in the British party game had its roots in what the London *Spectator*, itself a Tory journal, writing of the abandonment of the Parnell-Carnarvon talks, said was:

> the most barefaced dereliction of principle of which the political history of the century shows us any trace. [1]

On 26 January 1886 the Tory proposal of coercion for Ireland was defeated in the British House of Commons. Salisbury's Government resigned. Gladstone took office and set out a plan for Home Rule for Ireland. Rumours of an actual Bill got around, and the Conservative leader, Lord Randolph Churchill, realised he must organise a counter to Gladstone's popular strength. It could be done best, he felt, by raising a religious issue. He visited Belfast and launched what became in the end a movement of pogrom and anarchy. Joseph Chamberlain, who had broken with Gladstone on Ireland and was to become the biggest man amongst the later leading British Conservatives, said at Birmingham on 21 April 1886:

> I would be glad if there could be conceded to Ulster a separate assembly. [2]

That was to be the basis of the fight against Gladstone, the Liberals and Home Rule. Demand something that cannot be conceded so that nothing at all will be conceded. Make that demand so vague that in any case it ceases to be practical. Those who used partition as a weapon in the British party struggle were never agreed on the area to be cut away. In the Gladstonian days the whole nine counties of Ulster was the Tory minimum. Gladstone himself referred to that small portion of Ulster "where there was an Orange majority". Subsequent efforts to define the area were Winston Churchill's three counties (Down, Antrim and Derry) in April 1912; Bonar Law's four counties in June of the same year, adding Armagh to Churchill's three; and the Tories in September 1912 demanded the whole nine counties again: a few days later a new proposal of three counties and part of three others, the Chief Liberal whip's "roughly five counties" in June 1914. Then the Buckingham Palace Conference of July 1914 broke down on the question of whether Tyrone and Fermanagh should be added to Bonar Law's

1 *Spectator*, 17 Jan. 1886.
2 Chamberlain, *Home Rule and the Irish Question*, pp. 89-90.

four; in May 1916 Lloyd George suggested six and eventually the area was arranged as "the largest... which would give an overall Protestant majority over the largest possible Nationalist minority". [1] There was in all this no request from any party in Ireland for partition. The British Conservative leaders even while they put it forward themselves declared against it:

> It seems to me equally impossible (said the Rt. Hon. G. J. Goschen in June 1886) to include Ulster in the Legislative Body at Dublin or on the other hand to give it a separate legislature. [2]

The anti-Home Rule leaders in Britain actually used the absurdity of Partition as an argument against Gladstone's Government. The Marquess of Hartington, who also had broken with Gladstone in the question of Irish self-government, said to his Scottish audience at Paisley on 28 June 1886:

> Supposing it had been proposed to endow Scotland with a new Constitution, a new Parliament and a new Government, a complete system of autonomy such as that which was proposed by the Government for Ireland, and supposing for some local reasons or other it had been admitted by the Government that the question of the exclusion of Lanarkshire and Renfrewshire, the city of Glasgow, and the burgh of Paisley, was a subject which might be well worthy of consideration, I should like to ask you what would have been thought of such a proposal in connexion with such an exception. What would anyone think of a scheme for conferring autonomy upon Scotland which should exclude from Scotland the city of Glasgow and the burgh of Paisley, and the counties in which they are situated, and what are we to think of a proposal for conferring a new system of autonomy upon Ireland in regard to which its author contemplates, although he does not exactly suggest it, the exclusion of that portion of Ireland which is, at all events, as important to the prosperity of Ireland as Lanarkshire and Renfrewshire are to the Kingdom of Scotland. [3]

The reply to this British policy of cutting Ulster away from the rest of Ireland came from the Ulstermen themselves and there was no doubt of the tone in which the reply was made. At a Synod of the Church of Ireland held on 23 March 1886, Sir Francis William Heygate announced:

> We in the North have no desire to separate ourselves from the rest of Ireland. On the contrary we feel that we have one Church,

1 E. Strauss, *Irish Nationalism and British Democracy*, p. 240.
2 Hansard, 7 June 1886, vol. cccvi, col. 1151.
3 Hartington, *Speeches.... during....* 1886, pp. 52 - 3.

one faith, and our only desire is to identify ourselves with the whole Church of Ireland. [1]

The Irish Tory leader, Colonel Edward Saunderson, M. P. said in the debates in the Home Rule Bill:

> It is proposed that Ulster should be excluded in some way from this Bill... On the part of Ulster and every loyal man in that Province I repudiate that suggestion. We are prepared and determined to stand and fall, for weal or woe, with every loyal man who lives in Ireland. [2]

Mr. C. E. Lewis, M. P. for Derry, put in a sentence what all his colleagues were saying:

> We do not want any tinkering or exceptional legislation; we do not want to be invited to form for ourselves a separate Parliament. [3]

The defeat of Home Rule, by all means: the defeat of it by Partition, by no means. That was the reaction of the Irish minority to the campaign of the British Tory leaders.

Gladstone had studied the question inside-out. When he introduced his first Home Rule Bill he gave his considered opinion of this form of solving the Irish problem:

> Various schemes short of refusing the demand of Ireland at large have been proposed on behalf of Ulster. One scheme is, that Ulster itself, or, perhaps with more appearance of reason, a portion of Ulster should be excluded from the operation of the Bill we are about to introduce. Another scheme is that a separate autonomy should be provided for Ulster or for a portion of Ulster. Another scheme is that certain rights with regard to certain subjects — such, for example, as education and some other subjects — should be reserved, and should be placed, to a certain extent, under the control of provincial councils ... There is no one of them which has appeared to us to be so completely justified either upon its merits or by the weight of opinion supporting and recommending it as to warrant our including it in the Bill, and proposing it to Parliament upon our responsibility.[4]

The Home Rule Bill was defeated. Gladstone resigned: a Tory Government took its place. Chamberlain and other Unionist leaders went to Ulster to keep its people roused against Home Rule. It was their speeches which, according to Mr. R. C. K. Ensor in *The Oxford History of England,* went far to alienate

[1] *The Church of Ireland and the present crisis,* (1886), p. 15.
[2] Hansard, 12 April 1886, vol. ccciv, cols. 1395-6.
[3] Ibid., 10 May 1886, vol. cccv, col. 678.
[4] Ibid., vol. cccvi, cols. 1053-4.

the Belfast area from the rest of Ireland. But on the day after Chamberlain, his tour over, left Belfast in 1887, Dr. Kane, the Orange leader, said:

> The word 'Ulster' has too much prominence given to it in the speeches of Mr. Chamberlain and his friends. It is most important that it should be understood by all concerned that geographical Ulster — loyal Ulster — has no intention in the wide world of ever separating her fortunes from Loyal Munster, Leinster and Connaught. [1]

And a supporting chorus of Irish-Tory M.P.s re-echoed Dr. Kane. W. E. Macartney, M. P. for South Antrim, Sir Thomas Lee, M. P. for South Derry, Col. Waring. M. P. for North Down, spoke with the same voice and vehemence: No treatment but the treatment administered to the rest of Ireland. Gladstone himself summed it up on 18 June 1892:

> In the year 1886.... I declared in the strongest terms that the minority ought to be protected... I named, among other methods that had been suggested, one of cutting off from Ireland all that small portion of Ulster in which the Protestants are so concentrated as to form a great majority... That particular plan has not been desired in Ireland and much to their credit, the Ulster Protestants... have entirely and vehemently protested against that plan.

The Protestant spokesmen of the North-east were against Partition: so was the Protestant who happened then to be the spokesman for the Irish majority. Charles Stewart Parnell had in the debate on the first Home Rule Bill stated national policy:

> No Sir; we cannot give up a single Irishman. We want the energy, the patriotism, the talents, and the work of every Irishman to insure that this great experiment shall be a successful one. The best system of Government for a country I believe to be one which requires that that Government should be the resultant of all the forces within that country. We cannot give away to a second Legislature the talents and influence of any portion or section of the Irish people.[2]

Through the period in which Gladstone's second Home Rule Bill, that of 1893, was being discussed, the leaders of the Irish minority made it quite clear that if they put forward amendments to the Bill it was not to change it but to defeat it:

> We moved amendments (said Col. Saunderson) not because we believed the Bill could be made acceptable but in order to show

---

[1] J. J. Clancy, *Mr. Chamberlain in Ulster,* p. 22.
[2] Hansard, 7 June 1886, vol. cccvi, col. 1180.

up the corpse we have been dissecting during the last five months. [1]

It was at a press conference the previous May that Col. Saunderson had asserted that the loyalty to the British Crown under guise of which Home Rule was being resisted had nothing to do with democracy. The *Pall Mall Gazette* representative asked him whether by his resistance to majority rule he did not

> throw over the theory of Representative Government. Your loyalty to the Crown is loyalty to the Crown of an absolute monarch, not to the Crown of a monarch acting through representative institut- ions!

Saunderson:

> Exactly, that defines our position precisely. [2]

As the British Conservatives had anticipated, the Home Rule Bill, for which a majority in the British Parliament no less than that of Ireland's representatives had voted, was rejected by the House of Lords. The Conservatives took office and held it till 1906. In that period many amongst the Tory leaders felt that there should be some kind of Irish control over Irish af- fairs, and the British Under-secretary in Dublin Castle, Sir An- tony MacDonnell, discussed with Lord Dunraven a proposal for the most meagre devolution of some financial control to an Irish- elected Council. [3] By the storm that followed the discovery of these talks is to be measured the determination of the minority in Ireland and their backers in Britain to allow no diminution of their ascendancy.[4] The Irish people must be allowed not the smallest share in the administration of any part of their own national affairs. It is told in the most recent life of George Wyndham, published in 1952, that when the Orange leaders heard of the talks:

> Edward Carson, the Solicitor General, threatened Balfour with his resignation. The Dunraven-MacDonnell scheme was a vile betrayal.[5] trayal. [5]

George Wyndham, who was then Chief Secretary for Ireland, was forced to resign and his political career was ended: Sir

[1] Ibid., 1 Sept. 1893, vol. xvi, col. 1781.
[2] Quoted in *Belfast News Letter*, 3 June 1893.
[3] Earl of Dunraven, *The Outlook in Ireland*.
[4] See F. S. Lyons in *Irish Historical Studies*, Mar. 1948 "The Irish Unionist and the Devolution Crisis of 1904-5".
[5] John Biggs-Davidson, *George Wyndham, A Study in Toryism*, p. 160.

Anthony MacDonnell was disowned and this over a scheme preposterously hedged round with every form of Imperial restriction.

The first hint that the British Tory Party, whether the Irish Tories agreed or not, would use Partition to defeat any form of Home Rule was put forward in the *Spectator* on 24 December 1910, after the second Liberal victory of that year. This Tory journal was aware of the opposition of the minority in Ireland even to discussing such a way out as Ireland's dismemberment, and it made a heartfelt appeal to them to adopt it as the only real way of killing Home Rule altogether:

> We appeal to the political sense of the people of Ulster to let these questions come before the United Kingdom even though it may seem as if to do so will involve some neglect of the minority in the South of Ireland. We are convinced that if these questions are placed before the people of the United Kingdom they will defeat the scheme of the Government for destroying the Union. [1]

The British Tory Party eventually did make Partition the basis of their effort to defeat the British Liberals, as is told in detail in the next chapters. Some of the Liberals were not averse to this way of evading their responsibilities to Ireland, and one of them so stated at the Kilmarnock by-election in September 1911. It was the *London Times* which wisely commented:

> His solution is impossible for two excellent reasons: it would not be accepted by the Nationalists and it would not be accepted by Ulster ... No man could draw the frontier between Ulster and the South, and any attempt to separate them would only substitute for the present problem two others, each more difficult. Instead of a strong Unionist minority ... we should have two weak minorities. [2]

[1] *Spectator*, 24 Dec. 1910, p. 1121.
[2] *The Times*, 25 Sept. 1911.

CHAPTER VI

THE ART OF CREATING DISSENSION
I

ALL THROUGH THE period from the first invasion of the Normans to the Union, and through the century and a half that followed, to today, the imperialist art of "Divide and Conquer" ran as the woof through Britain's Irish policy. One section of the people — not always the same section — was incited into opposition to the others, and that opposition was stimulated and aided by all the influence and material strength that could be given. Francis Bacon, in the sixteenth century, praised the zeal of the English Queen in pursuing this course. In *Pacata Hibernia*, which is an account of the "pacification" of Ireland in the sixteenth and seventeenth centuries by English troops, appears this passage about General Sir George Carew, English President of Munster:

> Now the President discerning this Warre in Mounster to be like a Monster with many heads, or a Servant that must obey divers Masters, did thinke thus; that if the Heads themselves might bee set a variance, they would proue the most fit Instruments to ruine one another . . . [1]

And General Carew himself wrote

> Of the natives of Munster I make no reckoning, having means sufficient, by such instruments as I have found, to set division amongst them.

For centuries every pretext for "setting division" amongst the Irish people was used — clann against clann, Norman against Gael, Anglo-Irish against Irish, and after the Reformation, Protestant against Catholic. These last terms will recur throughout this book. They are to be understood for what they were and are — political, not religious, terms. The Protestants were accounted the pro-British minority, the Catholics were regarded as the Nationalist majority. It was Lady Gregory who said, "The Church of Ireland is not so much a religion as a side in politics." Many Protestants were, as many still are, Nationalists

---

[1] *Pacata Hibernia*, p. 36.

and worked and wished for Irish independence. [1] Some Catholics are pro-British and work and wish for Ireland's subordination to and dependence upon Britain. In both cases, therefore, the description of the supporters of one view as Protestant and the other as Catholics is neither apposite nor accurate.

The period from Carew to Castlereagh is over two hundred years. Yet the same method of exploiting division is described by Lecky as operative in the eighteenth century. Lecky himself approved of British Sovereignty over Ireland. His description in his History of Ireland of the administration in the eighteenth century is therefore all the more interesting:

> its method of managing Ireland was the worst of all expedients, that of endeavouring to inflame the animosities and deepen the divisions between the Protestants and Catholics. This was the policy of Cromwell, and it was the policy which was systematically pursued for a long period after the Revolution. The exclusion of Catholics by an English Act from the Irish Parliament; the lament of Bishop Burnet that the division of Whig and Tory was beginning to appear in a country where the sole divisions had hitherto been those between Protestants and Papists; the habitual employment by the governors of Ireland, in the early years of the eighteenth century, of the terms 'common enemy' and 'domestic enemies' when speaking of the Roman Catholics clearly indicate a policy which was steadily carried out.

It is in this light that the British attitude to the United Irishmen is to be viewed. This organisation was created out of the Protestant minority. Its leaders were either of the Protestant Church of Ireland or belonged to the Presbyterian Assembly. The aims of the United Irish Society were set out by Theobald Wolfe Tone:

> To subvert the tyranny of our execrable government, to break the connection with England, the never-failing source of all our political evils, and to assert the independence of my country — these were my objects. To unite the whole of Ireland, to abolish the memory of all past dissensions and to substitute the common name of Irishman in place of the denominations of Protestant, Catholic and Dissenter, these were my means. [2]

It is not realised today how much these aims were accepted by the once pro-British minority, but it was very plain in the

[1] "In Ulster the Nationalist Party was now in a majority. There were 900,000 Roman Catholics as against 400,000 Presbyterians, of whom many had become Nationalists, and 300,000 Church of Ireland". Sir Arthur Hardinge, The Fourth Earl of Carnarvon, vol. iii, pp. 193-4.
[2] William T. Tone, Life of Theobald Wolfe Tone, vol. i, p. 55.

The unsought boundary

Gormley, Enniskillen

KING RANDOLPH CROSSING THE BOYNE.

LORD RANDOLPH CHURCHILL, having failed to retain office by negotiating for an Irish Parliament himself, is about to visit the North, like another King William, "to rouse the Orangemen."

1886 — A contemporary cartoon

1790's. At its meeting in July 1793 the General Synod of Ulster rejoiced at the success of the new movement in lessening religious persecution and expresed the Synod's

> earnest Prayer that the time may never more return, when Religious Distinctions shall be used as a Pretext for disturbing Society, or arming man against his neighbour. [1]

The British power was seriously alarmed at all this. Lord Castlereagh recognised and admitted that the two most closely "settled" counties were for the new ideal. Referring to the United Irish Society he wrote in August 1796:

> Belfast is its centre, it is very general towards Lisburn, the County of Antrim has been largely infected, and the County of Down is by no means exempt. [2]

The creation of division was regarded as essential if British domination was to survive; and Premier Pitt in London and Lord Castlereagh in Dublin set about it with a will. They used every method. An author previously referred to, Rev. W. T. Latimer, official historian of the Presbyterian Church in Ireland, speaks of what he calls the "Episcopal aristocracy"

> raising the animosity of Protestant farmers against their Roman Catholic fellow-sufferers ... while at the same time they excited the Catholics against their Protestant neighbours. We have a trustworthy witness to the truth of this, in the Rev. Dr. Campbell (Presbyterian Minister at Armagh) who states that the authorities went so far as to even encourage the Defenders (a violent agrarian association of Catholic tenants) in order to strengthen the animosity of religious rivals in the North. [3]

This throwing of religious groups into conflict was not merely the work of a section of the ruling few; it was the governing plan. Lord Grenville, when he was British Minister for Foreign Affairs, wrote to the English Lord Lieutenant of Ireland, the Earl of Westmorland, in 1791:

> I cannot help feeling a very great anxiety that such measures may be taken as may effectually counteract the union between the Catholics and Dissenters, at which the latter are evidently aiming. I may be a false prophet but there is no evil that I would not prophesy if that union takes place in the present moment. [4]

[1] *Records of the General Synod of Ulster,* vol. iii, p. 157.
[2] Lecky, *History of Ireland,* vol. iii, pp. 464-5.
[3] William Thomas Latimer, *Ulster Biographies,* p. 4.
[4] Lecky, *History of Ireland,* vol. iii, p. 37.

The Earl of Westmorland wrote to Pitt as to what had been achieved in this regard and what in his view should continue to be the principle shaping all British policy towards Ireland:

> The present frame of Irish government.... is particularly well calculated for our purpose. That frame is a Protestant garrison.... in possession of the land, magistracy and power of the country; holding that property under the tenure of British power and supremacy, and ready at every instant to crush the rising of the conquered. [1]

Whether the instruments used to promote dissension were in themselves worthy of support was in the British view of no consequence. In 1795 the Orange Order was established, first in Armagh. It was an exclusively Protestant Society and was made up of violent men steeped in sectarian prejudice. It soon had instituted a widespread persecution. Lord Gosford, British Governor of Armagh, declared at a meeting of County Magistrates on 28 December 1795:

> It is no secret that a persecution, accompanied with all the circumstances of ferocious cruelty, which have in all ages distinguished that dreadful calamity, is now raging in this country.... The only crime which the wretched objects of this ruthless persecution are charged with is a crime, indeed of easy proof; it is simply a profession of the Roman Catholic faith, or an intimate connection with a person professing that faith. [2]

This new Order was regarded by British officialdom as a heaven sent means to an end. "If I am permitted" wrote General Knox, Commander of the British Army in Ulster, "as I am inclined, to encourage the Orangemen, I think I shall be able to put down the United Irishmen." He got the permission, although those who gave it knew the base character of the organisation. Thomas Pelham, English Chief Secretary, wrote to Gneral Knox that his plan was endorsed to "increase the animosity between the Orangemen and the United Irishmen". Pelham went on to say that he considered the destruction of the United Irish Society so necessary to British interests that "one can hardly object to any means of gaining it". Soon this sectarian terror was openly approved, when General Lake, Commander of all British Forces in Ireland, and General Knox both took part in an Orange demonstration in Lurgan, Co. Armagh. Knox in reporting his designs to London said:

1 Ibid., pp. 48-9.
2 R. Barry O'Brien, *Thomas Drummond*, pp. 96-7.

I have approved a plan to scour a district full of unregistered arms, or said to be so.... and this I do not so much with a hope to succeed to any extent, as to increase the animosity between the Orangemen and the United Irishmen, or liberty men as they call themselves. Upon that animosity depends the safety of the centre counties of the North. [1]

These and the similar steps Britain took in other parts of Ireland bore bitter fruit but the purpose was achieved. The Irish people were set against one another, and in their weakness Britain crushed them mercilessly. They lost not only those societies that united them but, as told in the previous chapter, they also lost the Parliament that dared in some measure to assert Ireland's will to independence.

In the later years every sign of unity among the Irish people was met by similar incitements to the extreme elements among the pro-British minority.

Although the excesses of the Orangemen were such that the British Judge Fletcher at the Wexford Assizes in 1814 declared "they poison the very fountains of justice", [2] Sir Robert Peel, British Chief Secretary for Ireland, encouraged them with faint condemnation. "Their only fault", he said, "was an exuberance of loyalty". [3]

After the Reform of 1832 the British parties turned to Ireland for extra seats and carried their bitter political warfare to the Irish hustings. Irish problems, Irish needs were forgotten, as the English political quarrel was fought out in the Irish constituencies. This neglect led to the more disastrous consequences of the Famine, and though the decimation of the Irish people caused rejoicing in London, in Ireland it drew men of all groups together; and in 1848 another attempt in arms to give Ireland a free Government was made.

It was defeated and to make that defeat of more lasting benefit to British policy the British Viceroy armed and used the Orangemen to achieve it. Other supporters of the British régime in Ireland offered themselves for the task, but the offer was rejected in favour of the most undisciplined and ruthless organisation, and the arms were given only to that one section whose use of them would create the deepest cleavage among Irishmen.

The centripetal force which drew Irishmen together now acted

---

[1] Lecky, *History of Ireland*, vol. iv, p. 52.
[2] R. Barry O'Brien, *Thomas Drummond*, pp. 124-5.
[3] Hansard, 18 July 1814, vol. xxviii, Col. 743.

along economic lines, and in 1850 the Tenant Right Movement arose. It has already been described and is recalled because it illustrates how if left to themselves the Irish people would normally unite in their search for the common good. The only way to break this unity was to stir up a new wave of sectarianism. That was done. Lord John Russell, the British Premier, had in a later-regretted mood, introduced a Bill which roused much religious controversy in England. It was the Ecclesiastical Titles Bill, which penalised Catholic prelates who included British placenames in their titles. Whatever pretences could be made to justify the Bill in Britain, where the Catholic population was a small percentage of the whole, there was nothing to justify its extension to Ireland. Yet it was so extended even after the riotous unrest aroused by it across the Channel. The historian of the Tenant Right League commented:

> The suspicion was widespread that this extension of the measure was designed to break up the union of parties in Ireland. [1]

Dr James McKnight, editor of the official Presbyterian organ, *The Banner of Ulster,* speaking about this time at Newtownards, Co. Down, recorded this effort to end the League:

> Parties have tried to break us up by arraying Protestant against Roman Catholics and Orangemen against the industrial rights of both classes of their countrymen.... [2]

The Tenant Right League momentarily weathered the storm, but the seeds of discord had been sown and these eventually led to the failure of the movement.

More than a decade later there was to be a dramatic example of how, if there were no outside Power interested in creating dissension, Irishmen would peacefully accommodate themselves to necessary changes even of the most vital kind.

In 1868 the British Government proposed to disestablish the Church of Ireland as the State Church. The extreme wing of the Protestant minority took fire and the Disestablishment Bill was met by the same oratorical opposition as later expressed itself against the Bills for Irish Home Rule. Rev. John Flanagan said in a famous speech at Newbliss, Co. Monaghan, on 20 March 1868 that if any steps were taken towards disestablishment

> 200,000 Orangemen will tell them it shall never be.... It appears wonderful that there is one thing upon which we can confidently

---

[1] Charles Gavan Duffy, *League of North and South,* p. 123.
[2] W. T. Latimer, *Ulster Biographies,* p. 100.

throw ourselves and which has been overlooked by nearly all speakers—I mean the Queen's Coronation oath. She should be reminded that one of her ancestors, who swore to maintain the Protestant religion, forgot his oath, and his crown was kicked into the Boyne.... We must tell our gracious Queen that if she break her oath she has no longer any claim to the crown.... Put your trust in God, my boys, and keep your powder dry. [1]

If any Bill should have led to a spontaneous uprising among the Protestant extremists, this Disestablishment Bill was such a measure. It abolished some of the privileges of the minority: it ended the financial support forced from eighty per cent of the Irish people to a Church to which they did not belong. Some of the minority leaders issued the call to arms. At Portadown, Rev. Thomas Ellis said:

> We will fight as men alone can fight who have the Bible in one hand and the sword in the other. We will fight—nay, if needs be we will die—die as our fathers died before us, as our sons will die who succeed us. [2]

But there was no fighting and no dying, and it is of great importance to realise the reason for this peace. It was that the British parties did not wish for conflict over the Disestablishment Bill. The British Tories under Benjamin Disraeli had reached agreement with the British Liberals under Gladstone on the Bill, and thus the question did not become the subject of English party intrigue. Without outside support for violent opposition in Ireland the problem was solved in a democratic manner, without disorder, despite furious speeches and predictions of chaos.

This fortunate occurence for both nations was all but repeated on two later occasions: in 1885 and in 1910. The Tory leader in 1885 was the Marquis of Salisbury. He was on intimate personal and political terms with the fourth Earl of Carnarvon, who had piloted Federation through in Canada and had sought a similar solution for South Africa.

Ireland in 1885 was in the midst of the Land Wars, evictions were of daily occurrence often accompanied by conflict between the people and the Crown forces. Many leading Englishmen began to feel that some change would have to be made in the government of Ireland if full scale insurgency was to be prevented. That was Lord Carnarvon's own feeling, when Sir Charles Gavan Duffy, then Speaker of the Legislative Assembly of Vic-

---

1 *Northern Whig*, 21 Mar. 1868.
2 *Belfast Newsletter*, 27 April 1868.

toria, visited him at his home at Highclere in October 1884. [1]

Sir Charles put before Lord Carnarvon a plan which included four local assemblies, one in each of the Irish provinces, these assemblies to have strictly limited functions, and one central Parliament of two Houses for Ireland as a whole, with wide powers. Protection would be given to the Protestant minority by a special system of election and by the necessity of a two-thirds majority for any alteration of the fundamental charter, which would contain safeguards for them.

Lord Carnarvon, though not sure of its workability, thought well of the proposal and promised to consult leaders of his party about it. Meanwhile, if Sir Charles would write a general article on it in the *National Review,* it could be discussed on the basis of that article. Gavan Duffy's article appeared in the *National Review* for February 1885. The scheme, Lord Carnarvon's biographer says, "might open the way to an Imperial and agreed settlement. The general election would soon be upon them and Ireland was the crucial question." [2]

Lord Carnarvon wrote "very confidentially" to Lord Salisbury on February 5:

> For my own part I have little doubt that in the general interests of the country and of Irish loyalists—whose safety is the great difficulty and the principal consideration to which we are bound in point of honour and policy—our best and almost only hope is to come to some fair and reasonable arrangement for Home Rule with their protection guaranteed as strongly as constitutional charters and fundamental laws can guarantee it.... I quite recognise the very great difficulty of your own position but I have put all this before you partly because I desire to say what has long been in my mind and of which indeed we have spoken more than once.... [3]

Lord Salisbury on 10 February answered this letter; and, considering that it is the Tory leader who is writing, the answer contained some remarkable phrases:

> It is possible that such a scheme as you hope for may be devised which would give us all the requisite guarantees for the interests which we are bound in honour not to abandon, and yet would satisfy Separatist feeling.... The Irishmen who offer it must represent a majority of the Irish members; and the Englishmen who

[1] Sir Arthur Hardinge, *The Fourth Earl of Carnarvon,* vol. iii, 1878-1890, p. 148.
[2] Ibid., p. 151.
[3] *The Fourth Earl of Carnarvon,* vol. iii, pp. 151-2.

accept it must command a majority in Parliament. We will talk the matter over more fully when we meet. [1]

These sentences, however surrounded by phrases such as "I am not hopeful", indicate an acceptance of the possibility of Home Rule for a united Ireland.

In the light of them is to be considered what followed. In June the Liberal Government was defeated and, as a new election under a greatly extended franchise was to be held at the end of the year, the Tories formed a caretaker's Government to bridge the period. It then became one of the Tory objectives to secure in the coming election the support of the Irish Nationalists, which they believed would give them a secure majority in the next Parliament.

In forming the Government Lord Salisbury brought Lord Carnarvon in as Lord Lieutenant of Ireland, with a seat in the Cabinet. A short period as head of the Irish administration confirmed Lord Carnarvon in his Home Rule views and convinced him of the advantages to both countries of a policy of Irish self-government.

As a demonstration of the Tory party's willingness to broaden their policy Lord Carnarvon suggested to Lord Salisbury that he meet Parnell. Lord Salisbury agreed but advised that as little as possible be put in writing. Lord Carnarvon communicated, through Mr. Justin MacCarthy, with Parnell, and a date and place was arranged. Informing his chief of this, Lord Carnarvon wrote from the Vice-regal Lodge in Dublin, and the opening passage of his letter anticipates similar phrases on a similar occasion in 1910: [2]

> This is only for your own eye and if you feel after reading it that you do not need it for reference, it may be perhaps best to destroy it. [3]

Then he discusses from several angles what he believes will be Parnell's attitude and writes: "lastly I have some reason to believe that he would agree to an actual alliance if such were desired", adding: "an alliance would mean on his side the support of every Conservative Candidate at the elections and on our side an undertaking to make a very large measure, though not an extreme one, a Cabinet question in the new Parliament

[1] Ibid., p. 153.
[2] See Chapter 7.
[3] *The Fourth Earl of Carnarvon,* vol. iii, p. 175.

if we got a majority." He asks Lord Salisbury to "tell me what you think and wish". If Lord Salisbury replied, the letter is not extant.

The interview took place on 1 August at 15 Hill street, London. The two men, Queen's Viceroy and Irish leader newly out of prison, spoke frankly to each other, agreeing that a large measure of self-government would be best for Ireland. There was no question of any special difficulties over Ulster. Both men— for there was no third party present—left records of the conversations. Carnarvon's was written immediately afterwards in a report to Lord Salisbury and is to be found in Sir Arthur Hardinge's *Life*. [1] Parnell's was published in the press of 12 June 1886 following references to the interview made in the Commons and in the Lords on the previous days. The meeting was referred to many times in subsequent months and years, and John Morley in his *Life* of Gladstone summarises one reference of Parnell's to it:

> "Was I not justified", he asked long afterwards, "in supposing that Lord Carnarvon, holding the views that he now indicated, would not have been made viceroy unless there was a considerable feeling in the cabinet that his views were right? Could he imagine that the viceroy would be allowed to talk home rule to him.... unless the prime minister considered such a solution to be at any rate well worth discussing". [2]

But Lord Carnarvon was not the only member of Lord Salisbury's Cabinet to have private talks with Parnell. He was seen also by Lord Randolph Churchill, though few details are known as to what occurred. But apparently Lord Randolph told the Irish leader that the Government of which he was a member would rule Ireland without coercion.

"It is certain that he had more than one conversation with the Irish leader", his son, Winston Churchill, says and makes clear that at least one of the meetings was in Lord Randolph's own home at Connaught Place, London. In the *Life* of his father, Sir Winston records a conversation Lord Randolph had with a friend in which he relates that "Parnell when he sat on that sofa" promised him "the Irish vote at the election". [3]

On November 20 Lord Randolph, speaking in Birmingham three days before the poll, made a public declaration that the

1 Ibid., pp. 178-81.
2 Morley, *Life of William Ewart Gladstone*, vol. iii, p. 231.
3 Winston Spencer Churchill, *Lord Randolph Churchill*, vol. i, pp. 394-5.

Tory party would govern Ireland without coercion and without abridging the liberties of the people. [1] Next day Parnell issued the manifesto calling on the Irish in every constituency to vote for the Tory candidates. All these talks were carried out under a secrecy so profound that Sir Arthur Hardinge says in relation to Carnarvon's meeting with Parnell:

> It was settled that the Cabinet should not be informed of the meeting with Parnell, Lord Carnarvon holding it was fairer to their colleagues not to tell them after the event. Lord Carnarvon proposed that the Queen be informed, but this Lord Salisbury held to be inexpedient. [2]

The result of the election of 1885 was a triumph for Parnell, but it did not give the Tory Party the clear majority they sought, the 86 Nationalist members barely bringing them three seats above the Liberals. Thereupon, without a moment's delay, the Tory party reversed engines, decided they would split the Liberal party quickest by opposing Home Rule, plumped for the immediate coercion of Ireland, and initiated the policy of inciting the Ulster Orangemen to revolt.

Lord Randolph wrote to Lord Salisbury three days after the election was over (22 December 1885):

> If the Government went out and Gladstone introduced a Home Rule Bill, I should not hesitate, if other circumstances were favourable, to agitate Ulster even to resistance beyond constitutional limits. [3]

Lord Randolph had also been engaged a few weeks earlier on another mission which he kept secret, arranging with the Catholic Hierarchy for concessions in educational matters. Now with the swift change of policy he threw all these negotiations into the wastepaper basket, and launched himself on a deliberately anti-Catholic campaign. His son, Sir Winston Churchill, writes:

> Christmas found him planning his visit to Belfast. By the New Year the arrangements were completed. The Ulster Hall was prepared and the Orange drums were beating. 'I decided some time ago', he wrote bluntly to Fitzgibbon on 16th February 1886, 'that if the G. O. M. went for Home Rule, the Orange Card would be the one to play. Please God it may turn out the ace of trumps and not the two'. [4]

---

[1] London *Times*, 21 Nov. 1885.
[2] *The Fourth Earl of Carnarvon*, vol. iii, p. 181.
[3] Winston Spencer Churchill, *Lord Randolph Churchill*, vol. ii, pp. 28-9.
[4] Ibid., p. 446. (G.O.M. = Grand Old Man, i.e. Gladstone).

In Belfast this British Tory leader whipped the Orangemen into a fury and suggested to them that they arm against what secretly his leaders had been discussing with Parnell. "Ulster", he told this excited audience at the Ulster Hall, "at the proper moment will resort to the supreme arbitrament of force".

Thus a campaign was launched which for the English Tories proved that the Orange Card was trumps, but for Ireland it had dire consequences. Sir Winston Churchill, in the biography already quoted, tells of the riots his father's speeches caused:

> So savage, repeated and prolonged were the disturbances, breaking out again and again in spite of all efforts to suppress them, that they became in the end the subject of a Parliamentary Commission the evidence and report of which are not pleasant reading and proved, when finally published, damaging to the Orange party. [1]

Thus deliberately and after mature consideration the Irish question was fashioned by the Tories into a weapon to defeat their opponents, the Liberals. If it gravely injured all Ireland and prevented the natural union of the Irish people in the promotion of their own national needs so much the worse for the Irish people!

In the succeeding years that weapon was not allowed to rust or lose its fine edge. English politicians frequently visited Belfast and its neighbourhood to keep alive the violent antagonisms they had created there. Joseph Chamberlain and the Marquess of Hartington, men of Cabinet rank, were among them.

In the general election of 1892 the Tories again used the Irish minority in an effort to unseat the Liberals. "Ulster is our trump card", wrote Edward Dicey, a Tory journalist, in *Nineteenth Century*. It had succeeded in 1886, driving Gladstone from office after only less than one year. It failed in 1892, for the Liberals were returned at the election of that year; but Gladstone was soon turned out again and by then the Tories had introduced a new principle into democracy, the right of the minority to revolt in arms against the majority's will.

Lord Salisbury, the Tory leader, decided to visit North-east Ireland; but as he fell ill, he sent his lieutenant, Arthur J. Balfour, who was later to be Prime Minister himself.

> I will not say (Balfour affirmed at Belfast in April 1893) and I do not think any rational and sober man will say—that what is justifiable against a tyrannical king may not under certain circum

₁ Ibid., p. 450.

stances be justifiable against a tyrannical majority.... You have
behind you.... the great majority of the English people. [1]

That was to be the guiding principle of British political leaders
until Ireland was partitioned nearly thirty years later. In their
own nation they would insist with all the forces of the State
that majority rule be obeyed by all, but in Ireland the forces
of the State would be used to elevate the minority above the
will of the nation. It is significant that the Tory campaigns of
violence in North-east Ireland coincided with the periods in
office of the Liberal party: 1886, 1893 and 1912-14.

The House of Commons defeated Home Rule in 1886, but in
1893 the Home Rule Bill was passed in the representative
House and was defeated only in the House of Lords. This Upper
House, dominated by the wealthy Conservative families, was
looked upon by the Tories as the instrument of their will and
as their protector even when they advocated unconstitutional
action against Parliament itself.

Shortly after the defeat of the Home Rule Bill in 1893, the
Tories, under Lord Salisbury, again took office, and they held
it until 1906. They had closely linked themselves with the Ulster
Tories during that period, and, when they lost power, it was
arranged that an English Tory, Walter Long, [2] should take over
the leadership of the Irish Tories. His task was to organise among
the pro-British elements in Ireland a recalcitrant minority which
could be used at times of political tension to prevent the growth
of those unifying forces which, had Ireland been left to herself,
would, as in the past, have taken deep root and prospered.

---

[1] *Belfast News Letter,* 5 April 1893.
[2] "Walter Long represented the best tradition of what Lord Salisbury once
described as 'pure conservatism'.... Long, the representative of old
rural England...." (Robert Blake, *The Unknown Prime Minister: The Life
and Times of Andrew Bonar Law,* p. 73).

CHAPTER VII

THE ART OF CREATING DISSENSION

II

THE BRITISH TORY party's control of the Irish minority was not rigorous or overpowering. It was more in the nature of assuring that, when there was need for it, that minority would uphold British rather than Irish interests and would take directions from London. In 1910 came the chance to exploit this carefully prepared position to the benefit of the Conservatives.

To understand the incitement to the Irish minority which came from Britain in the four following years we have to recall the political situation in Britain in those years.

The Tories had been in power for most of the preceding generation. They were the party of the aristocracy, the land-owners and many of the rich. They had many privileges, not least that of being accepted as the ruling caste. They were in fact that; for though the elected house of the British Parliament was opened, by the gradual extension of the franchise, to the representatives of Liberalism and Labour, no such danger threatened the hereditary House, the House of Lords. Gladstone's second Home Rule Bill, for which the British people had voted and which the House of Commons had passed, was rejected by the House of Lords. As long as the Tories knew they could thus use the Lords to block the popular mandate, they need not think of unconstitutional action to defeat the wishes of the Commons.

But in 1906 the Liberal party came into office with a majority bigger than any that had been known for nearly seventy-five years. [1] The majority was so large that the Liberals could afford to go their own way in the Commons, independent of allies; and for four years they did so. In 1910 the situation changed. The Liberal party's majority was reduced so much in the General Election of January 1910, that the votes of the eighty Irish Nationalist representatives then sitting in the Commons were

[1] The strength of the parties after the Election was: Liberals 377, Labour 53, Nationalists 83 and on the Opposition side of the House, Conservatives 132, Liberal Unionists 25.

necessary to keep the Government in office. The Liberals felt the need, therefore, to fulfil the promises which so often and for so long had been given to Ireland; that the democratic demand of the Irish people for self-government would be fulfilled.

The reduction in the Liberal majority gave renewed hope to the Tories. If they could find a good enough cry now they might win the next election. It was the Liberals, however, who made the next move. They introduced the Parliament Act, by which the power of the House of Lords was so curtailed that if the Commons in a period of not less than two years passed an Act three times over the Lords' rejection of it, it would thereupon become law.

This was a fatal blow at Tory rule in Britain. It meant an end to that power which had survived all other Parliamentary reform and which had given the Tory party an ascendancy over the popular will whenever it desired, through the House of Lords, to exercise it. The anger of the Tories was increased by the fact that the House of Lords was compelled to pass this destruction of its own veto. The Liberal Government had made it known that it had the consent of King George V to the creation of 400 peers and could thus give itself a majority in the House if the Parliament Bill failed to go through. The Lords submitted and passed the Bill; but from that moment the Tories were determined to destroy the Liberal party.

It was in that situation, with English politics at white heat and with the heads of the English parties looking upon each other as public enemies, that the Tories chose the Irish issue as that on which the Liberals might most easily be smashed. The chance came soon. The Home Rule Bill was introduced in 1912. It could go to the Lords three times by the middle of 1914. Within that period, if the Tories could launch a sufficiently powerful campaign, they might, if not unseat the Liberals, at least overawe them.

What was to be the nature of the compaign? That was obvious from the beginning. Lord Randolph's phrase had marked out the course: "The Orange Card would be the one to play". From the Tory point of view it was an excellent choice, for the English masses had been reared with both a fear and a contempt of the Irish. It is not necessary to go into the reasons: enough to say that the whole Irish people had been so deeply injured by centuries of misgovernment, that the English feared (quite unreasonably but no less understandably) what they might do if they once wrested themselves free. In that atmosphere the giving of Home Rule to Ireland by a Government dependent on Irish votes could be made to seem a betrayal of English interests and the fruit of a corrupt bargain. And to this could be added, if the Orange Card were well played, a useful appeal to that barely submerged sectarianism which so much influenced mass-thinking in Britain forty years ago. Indeed the Tories were openly to exploit it.

All the campaign needed, before it could plumb those depths, was a cry for help from Ireland. That cry took some careful organising and many visits by British politicians to Belfast and its environs before it had really any volume. For the individual Ulster Unionist knew his brother Irishman and, left to himself, would not have anticipated a denial of justice at his hands. But without the Orange card there could really be no Tory assault on the Liberals, so the minority in the North-east of Ireland had to be roused again and filled with hatred of their own countrymen and then blooded, in an effort to make the chasm unbridgeable.

That was done. As Lord Randolph Churchill had gone in 1886 to the North-east and there excited sectarian passions which expressed themselves in horrible assaults on the Nationalist minority, so now the leaders of the Tory party went in 1912 and drove the Orangemen to fury and to violence with inventions as to the humiliations and persecutions the Nationalists would heap upon them if they once got Home Rule.

It must be remembered that these were not ordinary mob orators who were thus inflaming the North. They were among the highest in English political life: F. E. Smith, M. P., afterwards Lord Birkenhead, Lord Chancellor of England; Walter Long, M.P., afterwards Lord Long, Secretary of State for the Colonies; Lord Londonderry; Mr. Bonar Law, Leader of His Majesty's Opposition and afterwards British Prime Minister; Lord Claud Hamilton, Lord Willoughby de Broke; Mr. Duke, M.P., afterwards Chief Secretary for Ireland in the British Cabinet; Lord Allington; Mr. Joynson-Hicks, M.P., afterwards British Home Secretary; Mr. Austen Chamberlain, afterwards British Foreign Secretary; Lord Milner; Lord Robert Cecil and many others.

The Orangemen, filled with fear by these men's predictions, were induced to form a volunteer army (the first private army in modern Europe), and British political leaders and British ex-Generals organised the running of arms from Germany to equip that army.

As in all such campaigns it needed newspaper publicity on a big scale really to frighten the public. That need was fulfilled, pressed down and running over; for the same Tory party who played the Orange card also influenced some of the most widely circulating newspapers in Britain. Those newspapers depicted for the Orangemen the destruction of all they held sacred once the Irish people became self-governing.

For two years this hurricane of propaganda swept from Britain into the North-east of Ireland. It created fear and a sense of helpless doom among the Orange rank and file. Naturally they cried to their "Protestant brethren in England" for aid and protection. That cry, represented as the spontaneous plea of the threatened Northmen, was sent echoing through England by newspapers and politicians who cared little for Orange fears but everything for an English anti-Liberal response to them. Before the third passing of the Home Rule Act the Tories had the Liberals on the run. The game did not quite end as they intended it; for the Liberals, to save themselves, jettisoned the Irish to whom they were trebly pledged. To keep themselves in office they surrendered to the British-led Orange minority, now armed, and agreed to partition Ireland.

The promised Home Rule Bill was not introduced into the British Commons until 1912, but ever since 1910 the British Tory campaign had been in motion. Scores of British Members of Parliament who had nothing whatever to do with Irish affairs visited the Belfast area. A House of Commons Committee set up in 1835 to enquire into the proceedings of the Orange Order had reported:

> It is notorious that the Orange Lodges exist under the patronage of men high in rank in England, Ireland and Scotland: and the countenance given, in consequence of all the orders of the Orange institution being issued by and under the authority of such men as His Royal Highness, the Duke of Cumberland, as Imperial Grand Master, and of His Grace the Duke of Gordon, Deputy Grand Master for Scotland, will be found to have a greater effect on the poor and ignorant — of which the Orangemen chiefly consist — than might be expected. [1]

It was men in similar positions who were influencing the Orangemen in 1912. No less than seventy came to Belfast and its environs on one occasion and among these and others who followed as the campaign developed were two former British Prime

[1] *Report of the Select Committee on Orange Lodges*, p. xxv.

Ministers, two former British Chancellors of the Exchequer, a former Secretary for War, a former Secretary for Foreign Affairs, a former Secretary for the Colonies, a former President of the Local Government Board, a former Postmaster-General, two ex-Lords Chancellor of England, several former Lords of the British Treasury, an ex-Governor General of India and of Canada, an ex-First Lord of the Admiralty, a Field Marshal, a retired Commander-in-Chief of the Mediterranean Fleet.

Since then, there have been examples in other parts of Europe of the highly placed politicians of one country inciting a minority within a neighbouring country to revolt and defy the will of the Parliament. The British Conservatives were, however, the pioneers of that form of activity. The note of mounting hysteria heard in the speeches on the Continent in the 20's and the 30's was the same as that in the British Tory oratory which in 1910—14 drove the Irish minority to rebellion in order that they themselves might get to office.

From Liverpool came one of the first orders to that minority to sectarianise their politics and make religion the issue. The speaker is an Englishman, Mr. F. E. Smith, M. P. for Liverpool, who, in the outcome, became Lord Chancellor. On 19 July, 1910, Mr. Smith, announcing his devotion to the Orange cause, said:

> No matter what the rest of the country shall say we in Liverpool shall fight under the Protestant watchwords, 'No surrender: no compromise.'

Later that year, on 6 December, 1910, Mr. Walter Long, M.P., who was to be rewarded with the Colonial Secretaryship, was one of the first to envisage even Civil War "if the Liberals tried to force Home Rule on Ireland". Lord Londonderry stressed the "Civil War" aspect in the British House of Lords, exonerating from guilt the minority who were being incited to revolt. On 20 July 1911, he said:

> If blood was shed it would be the fault of His Majesty's Government. Those were strong words to use but he wanted to warn the Government of what would occur. They would ruin Ireland and bring about Civil War... They (the Orangemen) declared if the worst came to the worst they would fight. [1]

As the campaign proceeded, the Tory speeches became wilder,

[1] *The Complete Grammar of Anarchy*, p. 3.

and the Orangemen were informed that they could go to any lengths in defying majority rule.

> He for one (said Mr. F. E. Smith, M. P. at Liverpool on 22 January 1912), speaking with a full sense of responsibility went further and said there was no length to which Ulster would not be entitled to go, however desperate and unconstitutional... [1]

This threatening note soon came into all the Tory leaders' speeches. At Larne, Co. Antrim, Mr. Bonar Law said on 9 April 1912:

> I have only one word more to say and that is that if this Home Rule Bill should by any chance be forced through then God help Ulster, but heaven help the Government that tried to enforce it. [2]

The Orangemen were sufficiently roused by this time but hesitant as to the protection and support they might receive for unconstitutional acts.

They received from Mr. F. E. Smith this promise made at Nottingham on 18 April 1912:

> They will have the full support not only of the Unionists of Ireland but of the whole of the Unionist members of the House of Commons in all risks, at all hazards, and in every extremity. [3]

But might not the British army put down armed revolt against an Act passed in Parliament, asked the now eager Orangemen? The British Conservatives decided that even if it took the encouragement of mutiny to get office they would not baulk at that, and future Prime Minister Bonar Law answered from the British House of Commons on 18 June 1912:

> If Ulster is in earnest, if Ulster does resist by force, there are stronger influences than Parliamentary majorities... The Government which gave an order to employ troops for that purpose would run a great risk of being lynched in London. [4]

A month later, on 27 July 1912, this leader of the British Conservative party made a statement showing that the real inspiration behind the Tory campaign was not any concern for the position of Orangemen in a Home Rule Ireland, but the desire to compel the Liberal party to face an election, in the hope that it would be driven from office:

[1] Ibid, p. 5.
[2] Ibid, p. 6.
[3] Ibid, p. 7.
[4] Ibid, p. 9.

> We regard the Government as a revolutionary Committee which has seized by fraud upon despotic power... We shall not be restrained by the bonds which would influence us in an ordinary political struggle... We shall use any means to deprive them of the power which they have usurped, and to compel them to face the people they have deceived. I can imagine no length of resistance to which Ulster will go in which I shall not be ready to support them, and in which they will not be supported by the overwhelming majority of the British people. [1]

That speech and those of two outstanding contemporary witnesses have left on record the real purpose of this mass-inflamation of the minority in Ireland.

Mr. Winston Churchill, in a letter to the President of the Dundee Liberal Association, said in August 1912: "They (the Tories) have always been straining after some short cut to office and they now seek to utilise the fanaticism of the Orangemen" for that end. [2] Speaking again on the same subject a year and a half later, Mr. Churchill accused the Tories of hypocrisy in their "concern" for minority rights in Ireland. Behind every sentence of Bonar Law's speeches on the Ulster Question, there was the

> whisper of the party manager, "We must have an election.. Ulster is our best card. It is our only card. This is our one chance". [3]

To the English public Mr. Churchill gave the warning:

> Let me say this: we must be careful that the honest necessities of the Ulster case do not suffer from this entanglement with Tory party interests and intrigue.

But the most significant comment of all came from Sir Edward Carson, the Orange leader, who had thought that the Tories were doing all this for him. On 14 December 1921 he, as Lord Carson, surveyed in a speech in the House of Lords the effects of the Tory use of the Irish question as its ladder to office:

> I was in earnest. I was not playing politics. I believed all this. What a fool I was: I was only a puppet and so was Ulster and so was Ireland in the political game that was to get the Conservative Party into power. [4]

Indeed the Tories were as willing to get into power by giving

---

[1] Earl of Oxford and Asquith, *Fifty Years of Parliament,* vol. ii, p. 137.
[2] *London Times,* 15 Aug. 1912.
[3] At Bradford, 14 Mar. 1914.
[4] Hansard, House of Lords, 14 Dec. 1921, vol. xlviii, col. 44.

all Ireland Home Rule as they were to get there by refusing to give all Ireland Home Rule.

Just before they launched their plan for rousing the Orangeman to unconstitutional opposition, they were secretly trying to dish him. The story has come out piecemeal only over the last two decades, and it was not until the publication in April 1953 of a *Life of Lord Carson* by Captain Montgomery Hyde, M. P. for South Belfast, that the jig-saw came fully together.

The story has the quality of the best fiction. In the autumn of 1910 the Tory and Liberal leaders met in a Constitutional Conference to find a way of lessening political tension for the new King, George V, who had just succeeded Edward VII. Under the cover of this conference, negotiations of the most secret kind were inaugurated. [1] Lloyd George, then Chancellor of the Exchequer, and Winston Churchill, then Home Secretary, acted for the Liberals with the knowledge and approval of Asquith. Austen Chamberlain, F. E. Smith (Lord Birkenhead) and Bonar Law acted for the Tories. The proposal was that a Coalition Government be formed and that its policy include Home Rule for Ireland.

> Balfour (writes Lloyd George) was by no means hostile: in fact he went a long way towards indicating that personally he regarded the proposal with a considerable measure of approval. [2]

He felt too committed by his anti-Home Rule speeches in 1886 and 1893 to participate himself, but he left the field open for the younger Tory leaders: "Younger men less involved in the controversies of '86 and '93 might be free to contemplate what he could not accept." [3] F. E. Smith fully approved and was enthusiastic: Austen Chamberlain was hesitant but ready. "As far as Austen

---

[1] "This Conference like so many similar gatherings was less remarkable for what took place at its formal sessions than for what went on behind the scenes. In this instance it was no less than a proposal by Mr. Lloyd George for the formation of a Coalition administration. The suggestion was never discussed in the Conference itself and it was first made by the Chancellor of the Exchequer to Mr. Balfour in terms of such secrecy that the latter did not at first mention it to his colleagues... Before the negotiation finally broke down its existence had been disclosed to the other five members of the Conference as well as to Mr. Winston Churchill, Mr. F. E. Smith, Mr. Akers-Douglas (the Tory Chief Whip), Mr. Bonar Law and Mr. Gerald Balfour." (Sir Charles Petrie, *Life and letters of Rt. Hon. Sir Austen Chamberlain*, p. 258).

[2] Blanche E. C. Dugdale, *Arthur James Balfour*, p. 73.

[3] Austen Chamberlain, *Politics from inside* (1936), p. 293.

was concerned" says his biographer, Sir Charles Petrie, "the negotiations serve to show his lack of rigidity in the matter of Ireland." [1]

The discussions took the participants so far towards a Coalition Government that the offices were being allocated: Asquith to remain Premier but to go to the Lords; Lloyd George to remain Chancellor of the Exchequer, if Austen Chamberlain did not covet that office; Balfour to be Leader of the House; Lord Lansdowne to be Foreign Secretary; Chamberlain, First Lord of the Admiralty; even Ramsay MacDonald, the Labour Leader, who had been drawn into the secret, was to have a post. [2]

The Tory leaders communicated with one another on the proposal with great circumspection. "Please burn this ... I burned your letter as it dealt with very private matters", wrote F. E. Smith to Chamberlain. Chamberlain failed to carry out the injunction and Smith's letter was found among his papers. [3] It certainly would have surprised those who listened to his platform speeches. It argued eloquently for the Coalition. It described Home Rule as "a dead quarrel for which neither the country nor the party cares a damn outside of Ulster and Liverpool." He assessed the position of the Tories if the acceptance of Coalition was discovered and then the Liberals reneged:

> We should still be a united party with the exception of our Orangemen and they can't stay out long.

They could not carry the Coalition project through without losing some friends, he said, "but I think we should lose very few and those temporarily." He told Chamberlain that the Liberal Chief Whip, the Master of Elibank, estimated that the Liberals would lose about "40 Radical dissidents but says he will carry the party machinery and of course the Irish".

The steps taken to keep the negotiations secret were extraordinary. Austen Chamberlain in one of his books says:

> No word as to these secret and extraneous negotiations was ever spoken in the Conference by any of the eight who sat there ... In the Conference we all acted by common accord as if nothing of the kind were in progress. [4]

[1] Petrie, *Life and letters of Rt. Hon. Sir Austen Chamberlain*, p. 262. See also Harold Nicolson, *King George V*, p. 131.
[2] M. A. Hamilton, *Arthur Henderson*, p. 74.
[3] *Frederick Edwin, Earl of Birkenhead by his son*, pp. 205—6.
[4] Sir Austen Chamberlain, *Politics from Inside*, p. 293.

Nevertheless at the last moment the whisper got out that a Coalition was being discussed, and the rank-and-file of the Tory party revolted. The scheme evaporated, and, though all the participants have left memoirs of other things in their lives, there has been a general playing-down of this important episode in British politics. But the incident was and remains momentous. It shows that the Tory leaders' opposition to Home Rule was a fabricated thing, and their rousing of the Orangeman to protect his liberties was a cynical playing of a party game of their own. If the game could have been more advantageously played by abandoning the Orangeman, F. E. Smith and the others would have played it no less heartily. Chamberlain wrote of it all: "What a world we live in and how the public would stare if they could look into our minds and our letter bags". [1]

Had the public seen into the Tory minds, they would have seen, also, into the insincerity of the arguments for partition. This "settlement", which the Irish majority repelled with indignation, which the Irish minority did not seek, the Tories, though championing it, did not believe to be necessary. Because it is easier to inflame passions than to control them, the incitements of 1886, 1893 and 1910—14 had baneful effects which continue even to this day. Incitements led to pogroms, which, even as they did on the Continent, resulted in weeks of uncontrolled arson and murder in Belfast, in which hundreds have been slain and thousands have had their houses and business places destroyed by incendiarism or damaged by mobs, while they themselves have been pitilessly driven from their homes and their places of employment. [2]

The rank and file of Irishmen of every group and party can at least take comfort that these pogroms and orgies of destruction were not truly of Irish origin. They have occurred only in response to incitements which, directly or indirectly, came from outside. Their real origin, as has been set out in this chapter, is to be found in a struggle where the contenders used Ireland as a pawn in a party game with office as the prize. The English Tories counted on victory by inciting a minority and arming it against the national will, but the Liberals outman-

[1] Sir Charles Petrie, *Life and Letters of Rt. Hon. Sir Austen Chamberlain*, vol. I, p. 258.
[2] "Virtually the whole of the Catholic working population were driven from their employment" (Dr. J. Dunsmore Clarkson, *Labour and Nationalism in Ireland* (Columbia University, New York) p. 369 et seq.)

oeuvred them at the last moment by dismembering Ireland themselves.

Britain based her partition policy on divergences she herself created and fostered among the Irish people. Other democratic nations have had similar problems to those of Ireland. These have been solved, with justice to all concerned and within the framework of the national units in question, because no powerful neighbour set out to prevent a settlement by exploiting internal differences.

CHAPTER VIII

THE UNITY WHICH ALL ACCEPTED

THE ACTUAL DECISION to partition Ireland was taken by the Liberal Government in England in 1914. It was not carried out then mainly because the proposal caused such violent reactions among the Irish people. It was implemented in 1920 when Ireland was under full-scale military repression.

The idea of detaching from the national unit an area occupied by a majority hostile to self-government had, as we have seen, been previously voiced. Until 1912, the proposal had, however, never been put forward as anything more than a tactical manoeuvre whose real object was to defeat the grant to the Irish people of self-government. [1] The minority, as is shown in another chapter, had ruled the country for centuries. To them belonged as of right both the power and the patronage of government which in days before Public Accounts Committees and Civil Service Commissions were valuable perquisites. Many of the politically powerful families provided for their households and their friends through this system and any alteration in it could well mean grave personal losses.

Whenever it was proposed that the people as distinct from the privileged few should be given the right to rule, the minority who held that right exclusively to themselves naturally opposed the proposal. They were not always conscious that what they were really defending were their own privileges, and it would be unjust to charge them with wholly selfish motives. As is the way with human nature, they had come to regard themselves as alone having the attributes essential for government, which in their minds the mass or its leaders had not. They were, therefore, able, not without sincerity, to claim that for the good of Ireland their powers must not be taken from them or be lessened in

---

[1] "The Home Rule issue from 1886 to 1912 was invariably discussed on the assumption that partition was impractible and that, whatever solution was ultimately adopted, it must embrace the whole of the island". (Robert Blake, *The Unknown Prime Minister: The Life and Times of Andrew Bonar Law*, p. 124).

any vital way. "After us the deluge" is an illusion among rulers not restricted to any part of Europe in the eighteenth or indeed any other century.

Because the minority had so successfully and, let it be said, ruthlessly, resisted any diminution of their power, it came all the harder after centuries of overlordship to envisage a wholly different kind of Ireland. Exclusive political and economic privileges had created deep class distinctions. These were reinforced by the efforts of the minority leaders to exploit differences of faith among the mass of the people in order to buttress their own position. Those minority leaders did not hesitate to sectarianise their politics when they regarded that as the best way of deepening the divide between them and the majority. All through the eighteenth and nineteenth centuries Protestants, Presbyterians and Dissenters had almost unbrokenly been chosen to lead the Nationalist majority, and they had been welcomed and honoured by the mass of the people. But the minority movement, in whose hands power rested, never once permitted the leadership to go outside a narrow circle of sectaries. It was more logical of them to act in this way, since it fitted in with their fundamental thesis that the majority were incapable of ruling themselves, and from that it was an easy transition to say that any who held the faith of the majority was incapable of leadership. This openly sectarian attitude of the minority suited British policy perfectly; indeed it was the fruit of British policy in the past; and, as it tended now by dividing the Irish to keep them weak, it had the support especially of the British Conservatives.

The result was that in Ireland the minority contested every movement to extend the franchise, to establish local councils, to transfer to ordinary Irishmen any form of authority over any phase of national activity. Above all, they contested what they feared would completely dismantle their position of supremacy — the grant of Home Rule to Ireland.

They fought Home Rule with many weapons. One of these was the proposal to partition Ireland. Whenever it was put forward in the early days of the Home Rule controversy, there was, as told elsewhere, no intention that partition should become operative. It was put forward merely as a form of blackmail. To the mass of the people of all grades and faiths a dismembered Ireland was so hateful a prospect that it was hoped to defeat the demand for liberty itself by insisting that even the most modified form of self-government might bring dismemberment.

The British Government of 1912 was itself conscious of this all but unanimous concern for a united Ireland. When the separation of part of Ireland from the operation of the Home Rule Bill of 1912 was put forward in an amendment, the members of Mr. Asquith's government rejected it as indignantly as the Irish people. Mr. Asquith himself said:

> You can no more split Ireland into parts than you can split England or Scotland into parts ... You have, in Ireland, a greater fundamental unity of race, temperament and tradition. (Hon. Members 'Oh!') I am expressing my own opinion which I believe to be justified by experience. You have an essential unity of race and temperament ... The more Irishmen are encouraged and empowered to co-operate in the great works of governing their own country, the more convinced am I that these differences will disappear ... in that common sense of fundamental and overpowering unity which I believe to be the centre of Irish nationality. [1]

He repeated that assertion of the essential unity of Ireland in a speech a few weeks later in Dublin:

> Ireland is a nation; not two nations, but one nation. There are few cases in history, and as a student of history in a humble way, I myself know none, of a nationality at once so distinct, so persistent, and so assimilative as the Irish. [2]

Three others who were to become Prime Ministers of Britain expressed the same conviction; Churchill, Lloyd George and Ramsay MacDonald. Winston Churchill, in proposing the Second Reading of the Home Rule Bill, dealt with this unity of Ireland and the limitations of minority right:

> It would be a great disaster to Ireland if the Protestant population in the North stood aloof from a national Parliament ... No man can measure in words, or can tell, the blessing that Ulstermen have it in their power to bestow on their fellow-countrymen or the benefits they would confer on the State or the fame and honour they would reap themselves, if they would lead a united Ireland home. [3]

Referring to the minority's use of the threat of partition to defeat the proposal to give Ireland self-government, he said:

> On one point I think there will be very little dispute: Whatever

[1] Hansard, 11 June 1912, vol. xxxix, col. 787.
[2] *Irish Times*, 30 July 1912.
[3] Hansard, 30 April 1912, vol. xxxvii, cols. 1720-21.

Ulster's right may be, she cannot stand in the way of the whole of the rest of Ireland. Half a province cannot impose a permanent veto on the nation. Half a province cannot obstruct forever the reconciliation between the British and the Irish democracies and deny all satisfaction to the united wishes of the British Empire. [1]

Mr. Lloyd George, who was to succeed Mr. Asquith as Prime Minister, said:

Take all the great questions through years of controversy in Ireland and in this country, during the last twenty or thirty years, or even beyond that, and in regard to all those questions it will be found that Ireland has been treated as a whole, as a separate unit, and there has never been a demand from any county in Ireland or from any part of Ireland or from any party in Ireland that Ulster should be treated separately. [2]

In the same speech he described the proposal to exclude part of Ireland from the operation of Home Rule as

a gigantic demand which would be a serious departure from every precedent.

Later, a fourth speaker who was also to become Prime Minister of England, Ramsay MacDonald, emphasised the essential unity of Ireland. He, too, questioned the right of a minority to impede the progress of a nation:

The first question is: Is Ulster to deny the rights of the rest of Ireland to self Government? We say "No, emphatically not!" Arising out of that, and a somewhat narrower question, is this: Is Ulster going to deny the right of Ireland ever to speak and act and govern itself as a united nationality? We say "No, emphatically not!" [3]

The Irish minority leader himself, Sir Edward Carson, in those Home Rule debates, more than once stressed the fact that Ireland was an indivisible unit, though he wanted to keep it under the Imperial Parliament. On the same day on which Mr. Augustine Birrell had emphasised that to omit Ulster from the operation of the Home Rule Bill would be to destroy the measure, Sir Edward said:

[1]   Ibid. Ten years later Churchill still stressed the passionate desire for unity on the part of the majority in Ireland, when he said: "What is their (Irishmen's) heart desire more than anything else. . . . I say really what the Southern Irish most desire and what Irishmen all over the world most desire is not hostility against this country but the unity of their own." (Hansard, 16 Feb. 1922, vol. cl, cols. 1278-9).

[2]   Hansard, 13 June 1912, vol. xxxix, col. 1121-4.

[3]   Hansard, 9 Mar. 1914, vol. xlix, col. 938.

I think he (the Chief Secretary for Ireland — Mr. Birrell) did say that
without Ulster Home Rule would be incomplete and ineffective;
I do not remember his exact words.
The Chief Secretary for Ireland: Truncated.
Sir Edward Carson: I agree with him. I believe it would be almost
impossible ... the only way you can treat Ireland, having regard
to her special conditions, is to treat her as one entity by the
Imperial Parliament, and the moment you try to alter that, the
idea of governing Ireland with anything like peace falls away. [1]

Carson continued to show that partition was asked for merely to
kill the demand for Home Rule. Quoting a speech he had made
a little earlier in Dublin, he said:

'Ulster asks for no separate Parliament. She never has in all the
long controversy taken that separate course ... and you need fear
no action of Ulster which would be in the nature of desertion of
any of the Southern provinces. If Ulster succeeds Home Rule is
dead.' What I said there (continued Sir Edward) is exactly what I
am saying now, that Ulster will ask for no separate Parliament [2].

This stand on Ireland's unity was maintained by Mr. Asquith,
Mr. Lloyd George, Mr. Churchill and Mr. MacDonald and by
the Ulster Tories themselves in all the public debates on Home
Rule until March 1914.

Between June 1912, and March 1914, the situation had changed in one aspect only. The leadership of the British Conservative party had observed a weakening of Asquith's Government
on the question of Home Rule. They intensified their effort and
co-operated in securing weapons for the private army the minority
had raised and themselves set about raising another private army
for the same purpose in Britain, where, said Lord Willoughby
de Broke at Norwich on 13 November 1913,

We are enlisting and enrolling and arming a considerable force
of Volunteers who are going to proceed to Ulster to re-inforce the
ranks of Captain Craig and his brave men.

At the same time, the Conservatives, as told more fully later,
were negotiating with the highest officials in the British War
Office to secure from them a pledge of non-compliance by the British Army with any order which might be interpreted as enforcing
Home Rule. These negotiations soon bore fruit; the War Office
chiefs were more than co-operative.

The British Liberals saw this situation developing and, instead

---

[1] Hansard, 13 June 1912, vol. xxxix, cols. 1074-5.
[2] Ibid., col. 1076.

of restraining those who defied Parliament, decided to strive for a compromise. The Irish Parliamentary Party, whose votes, given in return for a pledge of self-government for all Ireland, had kept the Liberals in office for more than four years, were not informed of any change of policy until Mr. Asquith had secretly seen the Opposition leader Mr. Bonar Law in November 1913. [1] The fact that Asquith did see him without any conditions was itself extraordinary, for Bonar Law had pledged himself a little while before to assist the Irish minority in armed resistance. He had also, in a speech in the Commons on 1 June 1913, recorded with approval the determination of the Belfast Tory leaders to hand over that part of Ireland to "the Government of a foreign country" (Germany) rather than submit to Irish majority rule.

There is no record of the views exchanged at this secret meeting between Asquith and Bonar Law, but it is clear from similar negotiations Asquith held with Carson a few weeks later that his offer to Bonar Law still asserted the unity of Ireland, though it envisaged some form of autonomy within a self-governing nation for an undefined portion of Ulster. Redmond, the Irish national leader, had an interview with Asquith on 2 February 1914, and he dictated an account [2] of it immediately afterwards in which he summarised:

> Mr. Asquith informed me that he and his colleagues were all firmly opposed to the exclusion of Ulster or any part of Ulster even temporarily. They had come to the conclusion that a temporary exclusion on the part of Ulster would have the most disastrous results on Ireland.

As the interview progressed, it was clear that Asquith was panicking in face of the Tory encouragement of armed resistance. He told Redmond that both the Navy Estimates and the Army Bill (which latter had to be passed each year to keep the British Army in being) were threatened with defeat, and he pleaded with him for his consent to

> an offer to Ulster of such a character that in the event of their

[1] "Asquith wrote confidentially to Mr. Bonar Law suggesting they should meet. Meet they did with elaborate precautions for secrecy at Sir Max Aitken's house near Leatherhead on 14 Oct. 1913 and the first meeting was followed by a second" (J. A. Spender and Cyril Asquith *Life of Lord Oxford and Asquith*. See for details of these meetings and of a third, Robert Blake, *The Unknown Prime Minister: The Life and Times of Andrew Bonar Law*, pp. 161-6).

[2] Denis Gwynn, *The History of Partition*, p. 78.

Walter Long, later British Colonial Secretary, Lord Londonderry, former British Viceroy in Ireland, Bonar Law, British Conservative leader and later Premier, and Sir Edward Carson, later British First Lord of the Admiralty—on the reviewing stand at a parade of the Ulster Volunteers in April 1912.

Two of the many famous national leaders which the minority gave to Ireland:

Thomas Davis (1814-1845)

Theobald Wolfe Tone (1763-1798)

Yours sincerely,
William S. O'Brien

refusal of it — and he thinks at this stage any offer he makes short of the exclusion of Ulster would be rejected — it would deprive them of all moral force.

Redmond sensibly replied that any such concession now would be interpreted as "an abandonment of his Bill' and urged him and his Cabinet to stand their ground. But the ground had practically been given away. Carson and Bonar Law had perceived that Asquith had come to care more for retaining office than for his pledges to Ireland and that they had but to keep up their pressure to secure from him a concession which both sides had now admitted would wreck the value of Home Rule to Ireland — the exclusion of part of the country from the operation of self-government.

From 2 February Governmental pressure, which ought to have been used to restrain the armed defiance of democracy by the Tory minority, was turned instead against Redmond and his colleagues. They were told by the British Cabinet that unless they yielded to some form of exclusion, Ireland might get no self-governing powers at all. Eventually, Redmond gave way to save what he could of the jettisoned cargo. The concession asked of him was stated by the British Premier to be strictly temporary, and he received from the whole British Cabinet a guarantee of that. The counties of the North-east were to be permitted to vote on whether they would remain in or out of a Home Rule Ireland, but the return of the excluded counties was to be automatic after six years. Redmond's acquiescence in that bargain was to cost him his leadership. It was clear, the morning after the terms of the compromise were announced, that even the most temporary partition horrified the Irish people and not the Nationalists only.

The announcement came on 9 March 1914. Asquith, in proposing the amendment to the Home Rule Bill which the proposals involved, spoke as one who was himself dismayed at them. He put them forward, he said, as the maximum concession which it was possible to make to the Opposition. He would have preferred other solutions, which he named. One was that after a period of years in an all-Ireland Parliament Ulster would have the right to withdraw. This he said "has the great merit that it starts from the beginning with a wholly representative and fully developed Irish legislature." Another proposal was that the Ulster members would have the right of veto over any legislation passed by an all-Ireland Parliament, and would also have local

autonomy in educational matters and in factory legislation.
These alternatives to exclusion he put forward, Asquith said,
because

> There are obvious and formidable objections to exclusion in what-
> ever guise it may be clothed and I believe they are felt quite
> as much by men of all parties and opinions in Ireland as they are
> by more detached critics outside... No one, I believe, either in
> Ireland or here, is in love with exclusion for its own sake. I do
> not expect the proposals I have outlined will be received with
> enthusiasm in any quarter. [1]

As a term of the proposals he insisted that

> Nothing is to be done — and I call particular attention to those
> words — which will erect a permanent or insuperable barrier in the
> way of Irish unity.

Subject to that condition, areas opposed to Home Rule would
be permitted to decide by a vote of each county whether to opt
out or remain within the jurisdiction of the Irish Parliament.
They would remain out for six years and then the Home Rule
Act would come into operation for the whole country.

Asquith had already pledged himself to Redmond that he
would not go beyond this concession. Lloyd George repeated
that pledge on 27 February to the three Nationalist leaders,
Redmond, Dillon and Devlin. This would be the Government's
last word, and Redmond, in a Memorandum dictated after the
meeting, records Lloyd George's emphatic declaration thus:

> No pressure whatever would be put upon us to accept any enlarge-
> ment of it... that the scheme in substance would be the last
> word of the Government. If it was rejected the Government were
> determined to proceed with the Bill as it stands forthwith and to
> face any consequences in Ulster that might result. [2]

Churchill repeated that pledge later, in his celebrated speech
at Bradford. Having referred to the "awful sacrifice", agreement
to temporary exclusion meant for the Nationalist leaders, he said:

> In principle — I do not speak of detail — in principle this is the
> last offer (great and prolonged cheering) which His Majesty's Go-
> vernment can make or ought to make (more cheering). Consider
> what that offer is. Any Ulster county upon the requisition of a
> tenth of its electors can by simple vote stand out for six years of
> the whole operation of the Home Rule Bill and remain exactly
> as they are. [3]

[1] Hansard, 9 Mar. 1914, vol. xlix, col. 917.
[2] Denis Gwynn, *Life of John Redmond*, p. 264.
[3] *Irish Times*, 16 Mar. 1914.

The British Tory reaction to this fatal concession by Asquith was characteristic. To them it was proof that their policy of threatening Civil War if the majority did not yield had over-awed the Liberal Government and that a little more of the same pressure might bring about what had all along been desired, the destruction of Home Rule altogether, and with it of the Liberal Government.

Indeed, they did not wait for the outcome of their own negotiations with Asquith to speed up their preparations for a wider use of force. While Carson was in communication with the British Prime Minister in the interests of peace, he and his fellow Tories were secretly organising the purchase of weapons and munitions from Germany for use, if necessary, against the British Army. At the same time, the other Tory participant in the peace talks, Bonar Law, was in secret communication with Sir Henry Wilson at the War Office as to how best the British troops might be got to disobey their own Government's orders to Tory advantage.

In the early days of February, Carson was in conference at his home in London with an adventurer named Crawford, whose main business at that time was illegal traffic in arms. Carson authorised him to go to Germany, purchase thirty thousand rifles (among them German army weapons) and millions of rounds of ammunition, and smuggle the lot into Ulster. Judging from the account given in Colvin's *Life of Lord Carson* money was no object and in the course of the operation not only were the arms bought but also two ships in which to transport them. The funds apparently came from Tory organisations in Britain and in Belfast and most of the high-ranking Conservative leaders in London were in the plot.

Bonar Law and Lord Milner had come to an understanding with the heads of the British Army. Lord Milner's objective had been stated in a "very confidential" letter to Carson from London on 9 December 1913. The Ulster "rebellion", he said,

> must fail unless we can *paralyse the arm* which might be raised to strike you. How are we to do that? That requires forethought and organisation *over here*. [1]

The Director of Military Operations at the War Office, General

[1] Colvin, *Life of Lord Carson,* vol. ii, p. 241.

Sir Henry Wilson [1] records in his Diary how Milner and Bonar Law were in constant touch with him and set about inducing this paralysis by winning him over even to the dissolution of the Army as a Tory manoeuvre against Asquith. The House of Lords would refuse to pass the Annual Army Bill, without amending it in favour of the Six County majority.

> We (i.e. Bonar Law and Wilson) had an hour's talk, and he entirely persuaded me to his side ... We discussed it all backwards and forwards, the handle it will give against the Lords, the possibility of no army remaining after April 30th, the effect abroad, and I am convinced that Bonar Law is right. Desperate measures are required to save a desperate situation. [2]

After the resignation, over the Curragh mutiny (now to be described) of Sir John French, Chief of Imperial General Staff, and Sir. J. Ewart, Adjutant General, Lord Milner got Wilson to sound out their successors:

> I talked the situation over with Douglas and Sclater without of course saying anything about Milner. I was pleased with the result. They have no intention at all of moving.... [3]

But all this was very secret, disclosed only to Bonar Law, Carson, Milner and other top-ranking Tory leaders. The British Government were about to find out where the higher officers in the Army stood.

Rumours of possible gun-running, and the consequent danger to military stores in the area, impressed upon the Asquith Cabinet the need for strengthening the British forces in the Northeast of Ireland. Orders were sent to the Commander-in-Chief in Ireland, Sir Arthur Paget. He gave his directions, and promptly there was a mass-refusal by officers to carry them out. On 20 March 1914, he wired the War Office in London:

> Regret to report Brigadier General Gough and fifty seven other officers of the 3rd Cavalry Brigade prefer to accept dismissal if ordered North.

Three days later, on 23 March, in a debate in the Commons, Bonar Law approved the mutiny. "In our view, of course, it is

---

[1] "Unrest in the army was being actively fomented from within the War Office itself by one of its own principal officers, Sir Henry Wilson, the Director of Military Operations." J. A. Spender and Cyril Asquith, *Life of the Earl of Oxford and Asquith*, vol. ii, p. 40.
[2] Sir C. E. Callwell, *Field-Marshal Sir Henry Wilson*, vol. i, p. 138.
[3] Ibid., p. 148.

not necessary to say it", he said. "Any officer who refuses is only fulfilling his duty".

At the War Office the news of the mutiny was received with deep pleasure. In his diary under the date 24 March 1914, Sir Henry Wilson describes preparations being made for naval intervention by the Government to strengthen the Crown forces vis-à-vis Carson's army in the North-east and adds:

"This was frustrated by our action in the Army."

Lord Milner's desire for paralysis had been completely fulfilled. Meanwhile the arms were on their way from Germany, and they were successfully landed on the night of 24 April at Larne. To protect themselves in this open treason the Tory leaders needed something as well as a complacent Army. They needed also a complacent Press. Lord Milner, who had suborned the army, turned his attentions to Fleet Street; and on 26 March 1914, Walter Long, M. P., wrote from London to Carson:

> George Gibbs gave a luncheon on Tuesday to the Editors of all the leading London papers with the exception of the *Times* to meet Milner and myself. We had a most interesting discussion with thoroughly satisfactory results. The effect of it was this. I put the question to them straight: 'Supposing Sir Edward Carson has to move suddenly without notice and adopt the offensive, what will be the attitude of the London press?' They carefully considered the situation and unanimously decided that they would support you whatever you did. [1]

It was the green light given by the British Press even for an offensive against their own Army.

What was the real objective of these revolutionary actions in which the British Conservative party played the major part? It was now clear that it was not really to secure separate treatment for the minority in Ireland. It was to defeat a Bill to which the prestige of the Liberals was so closely tied that they might fall with it. It was *after* they knew the British Government was ready to concede separate treatment to Ulster (November 1913) that the Tory leaders conspired most eagerly with the Army chiefs, arranged for the gun-running and nobbled the London Press. After the mutiny at the Curragh the *Morning Post,* leading Tory organ in London, rejoiced on 26 March:

> The Army has killed the Home Rule Bill and the sooner the Government recognises the fact, the better for the country.

[1] Colvin, *Life of Lord Carson,* vol. ii, p. 353.

The objective was to render the British Liberal Government impotent as the first step to a general election. A series of successes in British by-elections had convinced the Tory leaders that a whirlwind campain against a party weakened by frustration and compromise might put the Government back into Tory hands. It was from that point of view that the biographer of Carson records the joy in the Tory camp and the mutual congratulations after the gunrunning.

> There was cause for those congratulations (he writes). If we consider these two groups of events of the Curragh and the Larne in March and April 1914, it will be seen that *before* them the British Government was armed and the Loyalists of Ulster unarmed, and that *after* them the British Government was disarmed and the Ulster Loyalists were armed. [1]

The first reaction of Sir Henry Wilson to Asquith's proposal to give the option to "Loyalist Ulster" to exclude itself from Home Rule was not that the cause of separate treatment had been won but that Home Rule for any part of Ireland was now dished.

For despite themselves all through this campaign, and for long afterwards, British Tory and Irish minority alike thought, spoke and acted subconsciously on the same basis as the British Liberals and the Irish majority—that Ireland was a unit. [2] The difference was that, in the majority view, that unit was to be given self-government, and, in the minority view, to be denied it. "We don't want Home Rule for Ireland" was one of the most popular slogans at the Orange meetings and parades in Belfast all through this campaign. Carson the more readily rejected the "exclusion" offer of 9 March 1914, because his objective was an undivided Ireland not separated from the United Kingdom. The Tories rejected Asquith's proposals because to have agreed would have strengthened the Liberals in office, whereas the whole point of backing the Irish minority was to loosen the Liberals' hold, bring down their prestige and drive them out of Downing Street.

The fate of "county option" (by which term this proposal for temporary exclusion by county vote became known) is soon told. The Liberal Ministers had emphatically pledged themselves that this was the last word, and that if it were rejected, the Home Rule Bill would go through as it stood. But again

[1] Ibid., p. 376.
[2] "There is no one in the world who would be more pleased to see an absolute unity in Ireland than I would...." (Sir Edward Carson at Torquay, as reported in *The Times*, 31 Jan. 1921).

they took fright after the Curragh Mutiny and the Larne gun-running and resumed their pressure on Redmond and the other Nationalist leaders to yield something more. The method adopted was, as before, to impress upon them that without further concessions there might not be any Home Rule at all, to isolate them as if they were the only obstacles to a peaceful settlement, and finally to overbear them in conference. We see these three methods being applied, as the Tory campaign of lawlessness reached new heights of incitement and defiance in Britain and Belfast.

The guns were landed at Larne on 24 April. When Parliament next met, this act of lawlessness was denounced by Asquith in the House of Commons in the sternest terms. It was "a grave and unprecedented outrage" and he promised a cheering House that

> His Majesty's Government will take, without delay, appropriate steps to vindicate the authority of the law. [1]

Instead of taking any action on the side of the law, the head of the British Government wrote to "my dear Carson" on 4 May inviting him to a conference which was kept completely secret from the country, the Parliament and the Nationalists. Indeed, it would never have been known of had it not been accidentally disclosed in the House of Lords on 16 June by Lord Crewe, who next day received pained letters of protest from both Asquith and Carson. From that moment forward the Prime Minister of England negotiated furtively with the author of the "unprecedented outrage". The subject of their talks was how the Irish nation might, at the behest of a minority armed with German rifles, be denied the self-government her people had constitutionally demanded by overwhelming majorities in nine successive general elections.

The British Tory leaders pressed forward with a plan to establish in Belfast a "Provisional Government" which would defy the British Government. Asquith sent the friendliest letters to the proposed head of that "Government" and the Attorney General, whose special function it was "to vindicate the authority of the law", also wrote to Carson on 28 May.

> I should be so proud and pleased if — for old sake's sake — you found it possible to come to my King's Birthday dinner on June 22nd. [2]

1 Hansard, 27 April 1914, vol. lxi, col. 1348.
2 Colvin, *Life of Lord Carson*, vol. ii, p. 399.

The Tories were no longer so much interested in the fate of Home Rule, whose doom they felt was sealed; out of the chaos they had created, they hoped, however, to force a General Election and get to power themselves. If they could only get Asquith to attack! Walter Long, M.P., wrote to Carson on 28 May:

> If we can avoid a row in Ulster and force the Government to begin I believe we shall sweep the country and be able to do as we like.

On 30 May he wrote again:

> If you stick to 'Ulster as a whole and no time limit' I think we are safe as I feel sure Asquith will never consent to this or rather he won't be let. [1]

Asquith for his part thought solely of avoiding an election. In this game that was being played out, only the rights of Ireland were not to count. When, at the end of June, Redmond was called upon to take part in consultations, it was to face a situation in which the Liberal Government, the Tory Opposition and the minority leader in Ireland were leagued against him.

On 23 June the Amending Bill containing the proposals agreed upon between Redmond and Asquith came before the House of Lords; and Lord Crewe, Asquith's representative in the House, told their Lordships (who were predominantly Tory) that the Government invited amendments to it. On 24 June the Speaker of the House of Commons, no doubt at the instigation of the Government, began negotiations for some new Conference, inviting Redmond and Carson to see him. Both refused, Carson because the tide was running strongly with him, and Redmond because he stood on what Asquith, Lloyd George, Churchill and himself had agreed was to be the last and final concession.

Practically the entire British daily Press was by this time whipping public opinion into a fury at the prospect of Civil War, when Lord Murray of Elibank, former Chief Liberal Whip and colleague of Asquith, called on Redmond on 30 June. He brought proposals no longer for exclusion by county option for a six-year period but for an area of "roughly five counties" [2] to be fabricated into a State. This area was to vote on exclusion as a bloc, thus allowing the concentration of Tories in Belfast

---

[1] Colvin, *Life of Lord Carson*, vol. ii, pp. 400-401.
[2] Denis Gwynn, *The History of Partition*, p. 106.

to outvote Nationalist areas. There was to be no automatic inclusion, but a vote of the same bloc after every six years. In his talks with Redmond on this and subsequent days, Lord Murray disclosed that the King was ready to use his influence for a settlement if Redmond would agree to extend the area and abandon the time limit. On 2 July, Lord Northcliffe, owner of *The London Times,* came with Lord Murray; and now the proposal changed again. This time, the area to be excluded was more clearly defined. It was to consist of three full counties, Antrim, Derry and Tyrone, and part of three others, Armagh, Fermanagh and all except the Nationalist districts of Down. Their inclusion in an indefinite future under an all-Ireland Parliament was to depend on a bloc vote in the separated area. Redmond rejected these grave extensions of the "Government's last word" and called on the Liberals to fulfil their pledges.

Then Lloyd George took a hand. He saw another of the Nationalist leaders, T. P. O'Connor, on 10 July and "hinted that the King might possibly refuse to sign" the Home Rule Bill if the Nationalist leaders would not concede something more to the Tories' liking. On 16 July, after he had failed to get Redmond's consent to further concessions, Asquith decided to call in the King. His Majesty invited "representatives of parties British and Irish" to a conference at Buckingham Palace.

The membership of the Conference, which was weighted heavily on the side of further concessions to the armed minority, included the Speaker of the House of Commons, Asquith and Lloyd George for the Liberals, Lansdowne and Bonar Law for the Tories, Carson and Craig representing twenty per cent of the Irish people, all seven of whom were determined to squeeze the Nationalists further. Redmond and Dillon alone represented the Irish majority.

The conference failed. Carson returned to his original demand for the total exclusion of the nine Ulster counties "in the interest of the earliest possible unity of Ireland", though he might settle for six if he got good terms. Redmond held to the understanding of 9 March against pressure from every side. Within a united self-governing Ireland he would, however, he told the Conference "favourably consider very large concessions" to the Irish minority.

In describing Carson's demand for a clean cut of the nine Ulster counties his biographer declares:

Carson, as we have seen over and over again had no faith in half

> measures between union and separation, and if he supported the
> exclusion of Ulster from the Home Rule Bill it was only as a
> means to wreck that measure.[1]

Later he says:

> The Unionists (at the Buckingham Palace Conference) stood for
> the 'clean cut' that is to say, the exclusion of the Province of Ulster
> without a time limit. Carson, as we have seen, adopted that course
> as his deliberate policy, hoping thereby to wreck the Home Rule
> Bill. [2]

Nothing could be clearer than that all through this period,
neither of the Irish parties desired to destroy the unity of Ireland.

To save his régime Asquith, supported by Lloyd George,
himself decided on applying Partition. As fate decreed, this
abandonment of principle was to destroy the Liberal party,
which has never seen office in the forty years that have since
passed and is now but a handful of members in the House it
once dominated. Those who organised Civil War and initiated
mutiny completely triumphed.

This rather squalid drama was acted on a world stage where
the clouds of war darkened everything. Germany was encouraged
and France dismayed by the Curragh mutiny. [3] Those in other

[1] Colvin, *Life of Lord Carson,* vol. ii, p. 398.
[2] Ibid., p. 416.
[3] Speaking on Ireland at Penmaenmawr, 9 Sept. 1924, Lloyd George said:
"Let us remember that this dispute was one of the causes responsible for
the great world conflict in 1914. It is very problematical if war would have
been declared if Britain had not been believed on the Continent of Europe
to be so completely absorbed in serious civil dissension over the Irish
Question that she could not intervene in a European struggle. To the world
we looked at that time to be a nation on the brink of civil war with the
army in full mutiny".

James W. Gerard, American Ambassador in Berlin from Sept. 1913 to Feb.
1917, writes in *My Four Years in Germany* (p. 63): "Undoubtedly the
German Foreign Office believed that Great Britain would remain out of the
war. The raising of the Ulster army by Sir Edward Carson.... was reported
by the German spies as a real and serious revolutionary movement and,
of course, it was believed by the Germans that Ireland would rise in
rebellion the moment war was declared."

Dr. Alice Stopford Green, the historian, says in *Ourselves Alone in Ulster*
(p. 16): "With Europe on the edge of war the Ulster Volunteer army was
reviewed by Sir Edward Carson under remarkable conditions. Among the
forty reporters said to be gathered in Belfast there were three or four
Germans watching the poceedings, and Baron von Kuhlmann of the
German Embassy, now the German Secretary for Foreign Affairs, arrived
quietly, without information given to the Press, as an honoured guest to
view the stirring scene, and the magnitude of the Protestant preparations
for Civil War."

nations who looked to the British Government for determined leadership against armed might saw it shivering and surrendering at the orders of political parties with arms—German arms—in their hands. The Liberal leaders' reaction to the war situation was typical. Asquith used it as the excuse he needed to abandon Home Rule, as his first step in the "war for the freedom of small nations". The Home Rule Bill unamended did reach the British statute book but was immediately negatived by a Suspending Bill and never came into operation.

CHAPTER IX

THE 1916 PROPOSALS

THE SUSPENSION OF the Home Bill had an effect on Irish public opinion which eventually was decisive. Already, it had been clear to many that there was little sincerity in the British Government's pledges to concede self-government to the people who for a generation had asked so consistently for it.

As part of the organisation of the resistance to Home Rule, the Solemn League and Covenant was signed by 219,000 men in the Province of Ulster on 28 September 1912. Mr. Ian Colvin tells in his *Life of Lord Carson* the origin of this Covenant. The idea originated as a means of relieving a desperate situation for the leaders. Their incitements were bearing bitter fruit. The Catholic minority in Belfast were being set upon in their homes and in their work places, and so brutal and so continuous were the attacks that the directors of Harland and Wolff's decided to close those great shipyard "in view of the brutal assaults on individual workmen and the intimidation of others". The mob had got out of hand, and the bigotry of the movement to which the highest British Conservative leaders had tied themselves was being bloodily advertised to the world. Carson, his biographer says, saw "the necessity for a diversion" if he was to avoid "an explosion, cruel, bloody and premature, disastrous both to peace and to the cause." [1]

The "diversion" was the Solemn League and Covenant. It was modelled on the Scottish Covenant, but its purpose was very different: for it was drawn up specifically to deny to the Irish nation its democratic liberties. It did not come into being by any spontaneous action of the people of Ulster or any other section of the Irish people. It was drafted in a London Tory Club— ironically "the Constitutional"—and the leaders of the campaign to work up the Six County people into signing it were, besides Carson, almost wholly British. In an important passage, Mr. Colvin names them. Having said of James Craig that he organis-

[1] Ian Colvin, *Life of Lord Carson*, vol. ii, p. 135.

ed the meetings and of Carson that he was to be the principal orator, Mr. Colvin goes on:

> There were others—Lord Charles Beresford, Lord Salisbury, Lord Willoughby de Broke, Lord Hugh Cecil, Mr. F. E. Smith [1]

all Englishmen.

These leaders of British Conservatism were naturally interested in the Covenant only in so far as its signatories would aid them in ejecting Asquith and his Liberals. When four years later it became convenient for a British Government dominated by Tories to tear up the Covenant and get some of its signatories to abandon others, its solemnity did not prevent them from successfully urging this course. Carson, when pressing the Covenant on his supporters at the Derry Guildhall on 20 September 1912, said:

> They were going to make mutual pledges one with the other, and any man who, having made that pledge, went back on it or failed at the critical moment was a betrayer of his brother.

Carson himself in June 1916 "failed at the critical moment" and, at the behest of Lloyd George, figured in painful scenes, as he urged his supporters in six of the nine Ulster counties to abandon his supporters in the remaining three. But that was four years ahead. Meantime, 219,000 loyalists in the Province signed the Covenant in which they

> do hereby pledge ourselves in Solemn Covenant throughout this our time of threatened calamity to stand by one another.... in using all means which may be found necessary to defeat the present conspiracy to set up a Home Rule Parliament in Ireland.

Two months later the signatories of the Covenant were asked to take a further step in overawing Parliament and to enrol in an army which Carson and the Tory opposition leaders alone would control.

The establishment of this force was viewed from many different angles in the rest of Ireland. Some saw in it a nationally-valuable assertion by Irishmen of the right so long denied them to bear arms. Hitherto any attempt to organise an armed force on Irish soil had met with death and other dire penalties. It was decided to put the matter to the test. Would the same indifference by the British Authorities be shown to the organisation of a force to defend majority right? If so, Ireland might have an armed force to support her demand for freedom. It took a

[1] Ibid., p. 138.

long time to put the idea into operation, for there was no mighty British party to provide both the means and the incentive. But on 25 November 1913 the Irish Volunteers were established at a public meeting in Dublin.

The establishment of this force has been misrepresented as a "reply" to the Ulster Volunteers. Its aims show that it was not. It envisaged its service to be for all Ireland and for all her people. The enrolment form made plain that the rights of every section of the people would be defended. It read:

> I, the undersigned, desire to be enrolled in the Irish Volunteers, founded to secure and maintain the rights and liberties common to all the people of Ireland without distinction of creed, class or politics.

The British response was almost immediate. On 4 December, within ten days of the founding of this national body, the Government issued a decree prohibiting the importation of arms and ammunition into Ireland.

The mass of the Irish people clearly understood what was behind this discrimination: the minority unhindered could organise at British Tory instigation to defeat Irish self-government: the majority must, however, be kept unarmed and helpless lest they become too strong to be denied their democratic right.

If there was any lingering belief among the Irish people in the sincerity and impartiality of the British Government, it was soon extinguished. As we have seen, guns were run into Larne, on Belfast Lough, in April 1914, and all officialism, including the British Government, looked the other way while 30,000 rifles were being disembarked and distributed. But when, in July 1914, the Irish Volunteers landed 1,000 rifles at Howth, troops and police were mobilised and the day ended with fire being opened on an unarmed crowd in the centre of Dublin city. Killed and wounded numbered 43, with no casualty among the British forces. The Irish people were preparing to assert their rights with arms in their hands.

The Great War was raging when they did so. It had been declared from every allied Chancellery to be a war for small nations and peoples "rightly struggling to be free". The Irish people were asked to contribute men to the British forces on the express declaration of the British War Office that when the war ended Ireland would receive the same freedom as Belgium. Three hundred thousand Irishmen out of a total population of 4,250,000 served voluntarily in the war. [1] The years were to bring to this multitude of the brave a cruel disillusionment.

Other Irishmen understood Britain's Government better and knew that once the war was over Ireland's sacrifices would be forgotten and, because these very sacrifices had weakened the nation, Ireland's rights would be the more easily denied. These men appealed to the young who were enlisting in British regiments to think of their own unfree land first and stay to fight for liberty on Irish soil. But in a tidal wave of self-immolation the youth poured out of Ireland to die for small nations at Mons, at Messines, at Ypres, on the shores of Gallipoli, in the mountains of Serbia, along the deserts of Mesopotamia. Ireland's casualties in the First World War were higher than those of invaded and occupied Belgium whose population was twice as great.

Persuasion having failed, there was only one way remaining by which Irishmen could be inspired to the sacrifices necessary if their country was to recover its freedom. A Rising had been planned for some time during the war. The date had not been fixed but soon after August 1914 an understanding was reached between the leaders of the Irish Volunteers and the leaders of a parallel force, the Irish Citizen Army, organised by the trade union movement during the great strike in Dublin in 1913. Both agreed that there must be an insurrection. It was felt that to allow a war declared to be for the liberation of small nations to pass by without themselves striking a blow for freedom would doom the Irish to generations of future subjugation with the taunt that when others were asserting their right to independence they were mute. When at last the date, Easter 1916, was fixed the insurrection was to be nation-wide. Weapons were to come from Germany to equip 40,000 men and from Ulster to the coast of Cork, Irishmen would assert in arms that they too were a "nation rightly struggling to be free".

[1] Estimate of General Sir William Hickie, K.C.B., Commander of the 16th (Irish) Division in the 1914-18 War. On 4 Aug. 1924 the London *Daily Mail* published a geographical analysis of the casualties in the First World War. It showed that France suffered a casualty for every 14 of her population, the United Kingdom 1 in 23, Australia 1 in 25, Canada 1 in 40, Belgium 1 in 750 etc. Next day the *Irish Times* published a letter from Sir William Hickie which said: "From statistics which I believe to be correct I compute that, without counting Irish casualties in the Dominion Forces or in the American Army the proportion of Irish casualties to total population of our island was just one in twenty." (See *Irish Times*, 5 Aug. 1924).

As things fell out a chapter of accidents prevented a national Rising, and the insurrection, which began on Easter Monday, was confined to Dublin and to two or three other localities. During a week of brave resistance the Irish capital was shelled from the river and the heart of the city was set on fire. Faced with the decimation of the civil population the insurgents surrendered unconditionally.

The first act in the rising had been the Proclamation of an Irish Republic from the steps of the General Post Office which was made the headquarters of the insurrection. That Proclamation, which has since become one of the great documents of Irish history, contained these passages:

> We declare the right of the people of Ireland to the ownership of Ireland and to the unfettered control of Irish destinies, to be sovereign and indefeasible. The long usurpation of that right by a foreign people and government has not extinguished the right, nor can it ever be extinguished except by the destruction of the Irish people. In every generation the Irish people have asserted it in arms. Standing on that fundamental right and again asserting it in arms in the face of the world, we hereby proclaim the Irish Republic as a Sovereign Independent State, and we pledge our lives and the lives of our comrades-in-arms to the cause of its freedom, of its welfare and of its exaltation among the nations.
>
> The Irish Republic is entitled to, and hereby claims, the allegiance of every Irishman and Irishwoman. The Republic guarantees religious and civil liberty, equal rights and equal opportunities to all its citizens, and declares its resolve to pursue the happiness and prosperity of the whole nation and of all its parts, cherishing all the children of the nation equally, and oblivious of the differences, carefully fostered by an alien government, which have divided a minority from the majority in the past.

A Provisional Government of the Republic was set up and the Proclamation was signed by seven leaders on behalf of that Government.

Those seven leaders were among those who surrendered. One was an old man, one was severely wounded, one was maimed. The British shot them all and with them the commanding officers of other insurgent forces. Hundreds of volunteers were sent as convicts into British prisons. Thousands were deported to British prison camps.

At first the effect of British propaganda—for the Press was immediately controlled—was to make the Irish people at home and abroad look askance at the insurgents and their aims. But as the truth spread from mouth to mouth of the chivalry they had maintained in the unequal fight and the nobility with which the doomed men died—among them poets, orators, artists, journalists—the Irish people understood that this was in line with the great insurrections of the past, and they gave their passionate devotion to the dead and the living who had participated in it. [1]

This change of public feeling was so compelling and the fervour of it passed with such rapidity to Irish populations abroad that the British Government found itself everywhere condemned for the ruthlessness by which the Rising had been crushed and its leaders slain.

> The hurried vengeance of the military authorities for which the Government is responsible (said the *New York World*) has written a chapter that will forever stand to Great Britain's discredit. [2]

The fear that this discredit might damage Britain's prospects and keep America out of the war drew from Asquith an announcement on 11 May that Ireland was to get self-government and that he was about to visit the country to arrange the details. He said:

> The Government has come to the conclusion that the system under which Ireland has been governed has completely broken down. The only satisfactory alternative, in their judgment, is the creation, at the earliest possible moment, of an Irish Government responsible to the Irish people.
>
> The Government has determined, therefore, to address itself forthwith to the task of endeavouring to make such arrangements as will enable it, by agreement between different parties in Ireland, to put the Government of Ireland Act into operation at the earliest practicable moment.

A week after his return from Dublin the British Premier told the

---

[1] "The rising of 1916 was one of the greatest events of Irish history, not for what it immediately achieved but for what it symbolized. Physically, practically, it was a wretched failure. Morally it was a glorious triumph. The men who led it knew it was going to be a failure. They did not face the risk of death. They faced the certainty of it. And by their deaths they intended to raise up a nation, to create a new kind of dignity and self-consciousness, to accomplish a release of moral power and fortitude.... when the news of the executions came out, there was a shock of horror through Ireland and there was a moment of stillness in which people reflected on what had really happened. In that stillness they understood. In that stillness was born that terrible beauty of which Yeats wrote.... The Irish people understood as a nation, and however much they may deviate or have deviated from the inspiration of that moment, they will never quite forget". (Dr. Hugh Shearman, *Not an Inch: A Study of Northern Ireland and Lord Craigavon*, pp. 146-7).

[2] Quoted from Dorothy Macardle, *The Irish Republic*, p. 199.

Commons on 25 May that the task of putting the Cabinet's
decision into operation and of securing agreement with it from
the Irish leaders had unanimously been entrusted by himself and
his colleagues to the Minister for Munitions (Lloyd George).

Lloyd George was not slow in taking up his task. He invited
the Nationalist leaders, Redmond, Dillon and Devlin to see him.
They told him

> that unless two fundamental principles were accepted it was no use
> going on with the negotiations at all.... the Irish party should
> remain in the House in undiminished numbers and.... that all
> the arrangements should be temporary and these two conditions
> were accepted by the Secretary of State for War (Lloyd George)
> and were incorporated in the heads of agreement. [1]

After several meetings Lloyd George put before them proposals
which, he told them, had the approval of the Cabinet. These were
that the Home Rule Act was to be brought into immediate
operation subject to an Amending Bill which would, "as a
strictly War Emergency Act to cover only the period of the War
and a short interval after it" [2], exclude six of the nine Ulster
counties. These six would remain under the Imperial Parliament
for this emergency period. Meanwhile the representation of
Irish members in the Imperial Parliament would remain at full
strength.

Lloyd George begged the Nationalist leaders in view of the
grave war situation and the disquiet among the Allies which the
situation in Ireland was causing to go to Ireland and get the
consent of their followers to this solution.

Redmond had had experience of Lloyd George as a negotiator.
Realising the magnitude of what the British Minister asked
(for to the four counties for which county option had been
proposed in 1914 the British were now adding the Nationalist
counties of Tyrone and Fermanagh), he demanded an assurance
that the British side of the bargain would be kept, if his followers
made the sacrifice demanded by the temporary exclusion of six
counties. After his death there was found among Redmond's
papers dealing with this period the following note in his own
handwriting:

> Before proceeding to Ireland to ask the consent of our friends to
> the agreed proposals, we specifically asked Mr. Lloyd George whether,
> if we obtained that consent, we could rely upon him and the

[1] Mr. Dillon in the Commons: Hansard, 31 July 1916, vol. lxxxiv, col. 2120.
[2] See the terms of the proposals in the Appendix to this Chapter.

Prime Minister not to tolerate any further concession being sprung upon us.

He gave us the most emphatic assurance, saying he had 'placed his life upon the table, and would stand or fall by the agreement come to'. He assured us also that this was the attitude of the Prime Minister. We said on that assurance that we would go to Ireland and ask the consent of our people, but not otherwise. Dillon, Devlin and myself were present. [1]

But before Lloyd George had seen the Nationalist leaders he had had a conference with Sir Edward Carson and to him also he made proposals and he gave guarantees. There was no "temporary" clause in what was offered to Sir Edward. There was to be a "clean cut" of six counties from Ireland forever.

The minority leader, as Redmond, Dillon and Devlin had done, asked for an assurance from Lloyd George. Would he stand by his terms if his (Carson's) following agreed to permit the Home Rule Act to operate, though still bound by the Solemn Covenant against any Home Rule for Ireland or any separation from their brothers in the three other Ulster counties? Carson had since the outbreak of the War become a fellow Minister of Lloyd George's in the British Cabinet. He knew him more intimately than the Nationalist leaders did, and he asked for Lloyd George's assurance *in writing*. It was given in the form of a letter attached to the proposals. Its wording confirms the temporary nature of the proposals themselves, but completely alters their provisional character. The letter was:

Whitehall Place, S.W.
May 29th, 1916.

My dear Carson,

I enclose Greer's draft propositions.

We must make it clear that at the end of the provisional period Ulster does not, whether she wills it or not, merge in the rest of Ireland.

Ever sincerely,
D. LLOYD GEORGE.

Will you show it to Craig?

With this letter in his pocket, Carson went to Belfast. Redmond, Dillon and Devlin, with Lloyd George's passionate assurance of the strictly temporary character of the proposals still ringing in their ears, went to Dublin.

Nothing illustrates so well the horror with which the Irish

[1] Denis Gwynn, *The History of Partition*, p. 150.

people in every part of the country viewed the dismemberment of their nation as the difficulties that now met Carson and Redmond. They both had promised Lloyd George to do their best to secure the acceptance of his proposals by their supporters. Both almost failed, although they used to the utmost their influence and prestige and called to their aid the spectacle of a world war lost by Britain.

Carson laid the terms before the Ulster Unionist Council on 6 June 1916. "It was plain from his speech", says his biographer, "that he had no liking for his task." He had to ask them to agree first to permit the Home Rule Bill to operate: then to submit not only to the dismemberment of Ireland but to the partition of the province of Ulster, abandoning three counties to which they were bound by one of the most solemn pledges ever publicly made. He succeeded only by telling them that the war might be lost if they did not accept. Half-way through his speech he read to them a telegram announcing the disaster which caused the death of Lord Kitchener and his staff. By such methods was the separation of six counties from the body of Ireland made acceptable even to those most bitterly opposed to Home Rule.

A week later, Carson reported to the British Conservative leader Bonar Law:

> I have had a very painful and difficult task in trying to induce the six counties to accept the terms the Government have offered.... I had no alternative but to do my best, especially as I was told the necessities of war imposed this duty upon me. [1]

One of his colleagues has left on record a description of the scene:

> His (Carson's) task was an extremely difficult one for the advice he had to offer was utterly detestable to himself and he knew it would be no less to his hearers.... It was the saddest hour the Ulster Unionist Council ever spent. Men not prone to emotion shed tears. [2]

If it was painful and distressing for Carson, it was not less so for Redmond. In pleading for asquiescence in the temporary exclusion of six counties the Nationalist leaders were asking for even more than what Churchill had described as the "appalling sacrifice" of 1914. It required the combined threat by Redmond, Dillon and Devlin to abandon their leadership, before a gloomy

[1] Colvin, *Life of Lord Carson*, vol. iii, p. 172.
[2] Ronald McNeill, *Ulster's Stand for Union*, p. 247.

and grudging assent was wrung from a Convention in Belfast. [1] They went to Belfast, Dillon told the House of Commons later, thinking one

> very probable result of the whole of these negotiations would be to break up our party and drive us permanently from political life in Ireland. [2]

They secured acceptance of the terms but only

> by straining our influence to the very uttermost. We were very near to being defeated. I am not ashamed to admit that. I see no reason to be ashamed. Our people were against us. We went to our supporters and only by straining our political influence to the breaking point did we succeed in getting these terms accepted. [3]

It is clear from subsequent events that there was an understanding between Carson and Lloyd George that the letter would remain secret; for, though as will be seen, a most bitter controversy flowed from the consequences of Lloyd George's deceit, the letter was never published nor its terms referred to directly. It did not see the light until 1924. Carson then published it [4] in a letter to the Press, designed to influence the Boundary Commission which was sitting to delimit the border of the separated area in accordance with the Treaty of 1921. [5]

The British Government were fully aware of Redmond's interpretation of what he had been offered. Indeed, all through the period in which these proposals were under consideration, the fact that the Nationalists regarded them as wholly temporary was widely publicised in British newspapers. At a meeting of the members of his party on 10 June 1916, Redmond described the proposals as a "war emergency measure" strictly confined to the period of the war "and a short specified interval after it". He was quoting the document he received from Lloyd George, which stresses the temporary nature of the proposed settlement five times in six clauses. [6]

In his address to the Ulster Unionist Council which sat in secret session, Carson in recommending the same proposals stated that the exclusion of the Six Counties would be permanent, and he disclosed to a few colleagues that his authority for that was

---

[1] The proposals were never submitted to an Irish national convention even of the Irish Parliamentary Party's supporters.
[2] Hansard, 31 July 1916, vol. ixxxxiv, col. 2119.
[3] Hansard, 24 July 1916, vol. lxxxiv, cols. 1459-60.
[4] See *Belfast Newsletter*, 3 Oct. 1924.
[5] See Chapter XII.
[6] See Appendix to this Chapter.

an undertaking from Lloyd George himself. This statement swiftly found its way into print and caused anxiety among the Ulster Nationalists who were then choosing delegates to the convention in Belfast at which Redmond and his colleagues would seek a decision on the proposals. The Nationalist leaders already knew that it would be difficult to get an acceptance of any form of exclusion, however temporary. Permanent exclusion was certain beforehand to be unanimously rejected. Lloyd George became aware of these difficulties and took steps to reassure the Nationalists. The reassurance came from no less a person than the Prime Minister of England himself. Speaking at Ladybank in his constituency on 14 June 1916, Asquith said:

> I will say nothing about the negotiations which are going on under Mr. Lloyd George except that I am certain that all of us wish to those negotiations a successful issue.... what is desired now is a provisional settlement.

The effect of this statement was immediate. The Nationalist leaders regarded it as a public declaration from the highest authority in Britain underscoring the emphatic pledges of Lloyd George that the proposals were temporary. Among the Ulster Nationalist rank and file its influence was felt at once.

The London *Daily News* said:

> Following Mr. Asquith's definite statement at Ladybank in connection with the Irish negotiations when the Prime Minister made it clear that the present basis of settlement was provisional.... there has been a marked change of feeling amongst the Ulster Nationalists.... The Prime Minister's speech has undoubtedly relieved an awkward situation and it is expected will smooth the way to an ultimate agreement to the terms of settlement by the Ulster Nationalists. [1]

Carson made no public statement in reply to Asquith of whose Government he had been made a member in May 1915 when a Coalition was formed. [2] He merely privately reassured his colleagues that exclusion would be permanent. He showed to the more important of them the reason why he could afford to remain silent. Thus the rumours of an undertaking persisted and led to a sharp comment by the *Church of Ireland Gazette*. In an editorial condemning the proposed dismemberment of Ireland, this journal of the Protestant minority, whose traditions were predominantly pro-British, said:

[1] *Daily News*, 16 June 1916.
[2] He resigned in Oct. 1915.

It is not at all unlikely that into a settlement which involves such a variety of betrayals a little deceit has been imported as well. Mr. Lloyd George may well have told Sir Edward Carson that the 'settlement' is to be permanent and Mr. Redmond that it is to be temporary. [1]

On 23 June the fateful conference met at Belfast. It was drawn from representatives of Nationalist organisations and societies in the six counties threatened with exclusion. They were to be asked to deny themselves self-government so that the rest of the nation could have it.

It was a painful demand on their chivalry and sacrifice, for of all parts of Ireland the Northern Nationalists most needed self-rule. Under the Tory Ascendancy they were daily discriminated against and were denied many rights, and they were in constant danger of some new pogrom. These Nationalists would never agree to permanent exclusion from a self-governing Ireland. But if they could be convinced that by remaining themselves three or four years longer under the harrow they could liberate the majority of their fellow countrymen, their agreement might be secured, particularly as their sympathies were deeply stirred by the spectacle of that majority suffering stern military repression after the Insurrection.

The importance, therefore, of the temporary and provisional nature of the proposals was supreme in the eyes of those Northern Nationalists. They sought and were given by their leaders, and Asquith's own statement was there in living proof of it, the most emphatic guarantees that all they were consenting to was a provisional separation which would automatically end in "the shortest possible period".

This question of the nature of the proposals was in everybody's mind as the Convention assembled in the North-eastern city. The *Irish Times,* which also opposed dismemberment, now declared in a strong editorial that what Asquith said was false and that Carson was silent because he held a written guarantee. The editorial appeared on the morning of the Belfast Conference. [2] It said:

> Did he (Lloyd George) lay the same proposals or two different sets of proposals before the Ulster Unionist Council and the Nationalist Party? Will the Nationalist Conference at Belfast to-day be asked to vote on the same scheme which the Ulster Council has accept-

1 *Church of Ireland Gazette,* 17 June 1916.
2 *Irish Times,* 23 June 1916.

ed?..., The Ulster Unionists have been told that the exclusion of the Six Counties is to be permanent. The Nationalists are assured by Mr. Redmond that it will be provisional and the Prime Minister says Mr. Redmond is right. One might have supposed that the Unionists of Ulster who are hard men in the matter of business would have demanded an immediate explanation of this contradiction in terms. We shall tell the public why they have not demanded it. Sir Edward Carson possesses a written promise from Mr. Lloyd George that the exclusion of Ulster is to be permanent. There is no doubt about the terms of this document. It is clear and explicit. It means, if words mean anything, that Ulster is to be excluded from Home Rule *saecula saeculorum,* unless and until of her own free will she makes another choice.

The report of the Conference showed the anxiety this editorial caused. Redmond, putting the terms of settlement to the gathering, referred to the *Irish Times* statement that exclusion was to be permanent. A shout came from the hall "Never!" Redmond went on:

> I entirely re-echo that cry of "Never". That statement is an absolute lie. There were never proposals in which there was such a time limit as in the present ones.... the proposals are temporary and provisional. If they were not, I would oppose them. If at any time or in any quarter an attempt is made to turn them into permanent proposals my colleagues and I are determined to oppose them in every way. [1]

He added that neither he nor his colleagues would regard any settlement as satisfactory based upon the permanent exclusion of Ulster or any part of it. "I tell you if you give us fair play that is an absolute impossibility. We want a United Ireland". Many of the delegates were reassured by such emphasis, which Dillon reinforced by asking did any of the delegates think that it was without pain that the leaders of the Party had agreed to the "shortest temporary division of Ireland".

Despite this reiteration and positive assurance, the conference was still hesitant. Many suggestions from the platform that the delegates were being selfish in denying immediate self-government to the rest of Ireland were not even sufficient to secure a majority, so deep was the reluctance to divide Ireland for any length of time.

In the end it needed a threat by Redmond to resign the leadership and end his life's work—a threat delivered with all the emotional power of Irish oratory at its best and supported by his colleagues—it required that to compel even from this carefully

[1]   *Irish Independent,* 24 June 1916.

selected convention of Redmond's own followers a favourable vote. The delegates from Tyrone and Fermanagh opposed the proposals from beginning to end by a two to one majority, but they were outvoted by the representatives of the other counties.

The terms of the resolution on which the vote was taken expressed once more the nature of what was being accepted and why:

> That this Conference of representatives from the counties of Antrim, Down, Derry, Armagh, Tyrone and Fermanagh and from the cities of Belfast and Derry having considered the proposals of Mr. Lloyd George for the temporary and provisional settlement of the Irish difficulty is of opinion that they should be accepted and that in view of all the circumstances of the present situation in Ireland they offer the best means of carrying on the fight for a United self-governing Ireland. [1]

What Lloyd George had asked the Irish leaders for had been accomplished. Both the Nationalists and the Unionists had accepted his proposals. The next step should have been their prompt implementation. But now followed events which suggested that acceptance by the Nationalists was not what the British Coalition Cabinet wanted. [2]

The proposals, as we have seen, had their origin in the British desire to undo the disastrous effect of their military repression on American opinion. [3] The British Cabinet, or Lloyd George who was acting in their name, had apparently hoped that this result might be achieved without any concession to Ireland—if only one or other of the sections to whom the terms had been offered would reject them. Evidently Lloyd George was more anxious that this rejection should come from the Nationalist side, for he had, by his secret letter, taken special steps to get

[1] *Irish Independent,* 24 June 1916.
[2] "Now what the great Unionist leaders said to themselves, I am sure, was this: 'We don't believe a settlement is possible. We don't want one because it would dish our party game after the war. We are perfectly certain however that, if the Nationalists accept the proposals which Lloyd George puts forward, Carson's Ulstermen will reject them and if Carson's Ulstermen accept them that the Nationalists will reject them. The chances are that both independently will reject them and then all will be well'." (*The Anvil of War:* Letters between F. S. Oliver and his brother, 1914-1918, p. 150).
[3] "He (Carson at the Ulster Unionist Convention) spoke of difficulties with America which a settlement might tend to allay". (Colvin, *Life of Lord Carson,* vol. iii, p. 168).

Tory acquiescence. To his or, at all events, to his colleagues' embarrassment, both sides said "Yes". Had either said "No" British war propaganda in the United States would no doubt have taken the line that the British Government had been ready to settle but the Irish could not agree among themselves. In the new circumstances, it was now the British Cabinet's turn to produce the Bill implementing the terms and putting the Home Rule Act into operation.

Instead, Britain repudiated her own proposals. As we have seen, the vote of the Nationalist conference was taken in Belfast on 23 June. The first hint of what was about to happen came within three days. A delegation of prominent Irish Tories from outside Ulster was received in London on 26 June by British Tory leaders, several of them members of the Cabinet. A spokesman of the Irish Tory delegation, Mr. J. W. Maddock, said after the interview that "he had received assurance that the Government are not committed to the proposals." [1]

The next day the London *Daily News* and the London *Daily Chronicle* urged that as Irishmen had agreed the Cabinet must now go forward.

> Certainly (added the *Daily Chronicle*) no one anticipated that when Mr. Redmond, Sir Edward Carson and Mr. Devlin had come to terms their agreement would be repudiated from the British side. [2]

The repudiation had, however, already begun. Lord Selborne, Lord Lansdowne and Walter Long made clear to their colleagues in the Government that they could not agree either to the provisional nature of the terms or to permitting the Irish members to remain in full strength in the British Commons until the excluded counties had returned under an All-Ireland Parliament. These were the two fundamentals on which the Irish leaders insisted at the start of the negotations. The retention of Irish M.P.s at Westminster was an important feature of the settlement, since it gave the Irish Party a lever for securing the completion of the bargain after the first part (temporary exclusion) had been operated. A few days later, Lord Selborne resigned from the Cabinet to give an earnest of Tory determination. Once more Asquith and his Liberals surrendered to Tory pressure, though it again meant a breach of the most solemn

---

[1] *Irish Independent,* 27 June 1916.
[2] Quoted in the *Irish Independent,* 28 June 1916.

pledges to Irishmen—this time within a few weeks of their being given. [1]

The Amending Bill to give legal enactment to the Lloyd George proposals was already drafted, containing all that the Cabinet had promised Redmond, Dillon and Devlin. On 11 July Lord Lansdowne announced that that Bill instead of being a "strictly temporary war emergency measure" would "be permanent and enduring in its character", and it was hurriedly redrafted in that sense. [2] Redmond made an immediate protest and called for the introduction of the Amending Bill forthwith that its true character might be seen.

The Government reply was an insolent message from Ministers who only a few weeks before had been pleading with Redmond to save them from the consequences of their own ruthlessness in Ireland. On 24 July 1916, Redmond in a debate in the House of Commons thus described this British change of front and the gross discourtesy with which it was conveyed to him: [3]

> I ask the House to mark what I am now going to say. On July 20th I received a most extraordinary message from the Cabinet to the effect that the consideration of this draft Bill had been postponed and that a number of new proposals had been brought forward. When I asked what the nature of these proposals was, I was informed that the Cabinet did not desire to consult me about them at all, and that they would not communicate with me in the matter until they had again met and had agreed upon what new proposals they would approve of . . . I asked was any new proposal submitted on the question of the provisional character of the Bill? I was told it was quite impossible to answer my question. The next communication I received was on Saturday last when the Minister for War (Mr. Lloyd George) and the Home Secretary (Mr. Herbert Samuel) requested me to call and see them at the War Office. They then informed me that another Cabinet Council had been held and that it had been decided — mark you, decided — to insert in the Bill two entirely new provisions, one providing for the permanent exclusion of the Six Ulster Counties and another cutting out of the draft Bill the provision for the representation of the Irish members in full force at Westminster during the transitory period, and I was given to understand in so many words that this decision was not put before me for the purpose of discussion or

[1] "I went to Ireland in 1916 and the hon. Member for the Falls Division (Mr. Devlin) knows something of what he went through and what I went through. . . . both of us having done our best we were both thrown over when we came back to England." Sir Edward Carson (Hansard, 31 March 1920, vol. cxxiii, col. 1294).

[2] William O'Brien, *The Irish Revolution*, p. 295 et seq.

[3] Hansard, 24 July 1916, vol. lxxxiv, cols. 1432-3.

consultation, that the decision was absolute and final and the
Right Hon. Gentlemen described themselves to me as messengers
without any power or authority to discuss these questions in any
way whatever with me, and they informed me that it was the
intention of the Government to introduce a Bill containing these
provisions, practically whether we liked it or not.

There is little more to be told of this squalid story, except
that the British Premier and his Cabinet, having tricked the
Irish Nationalist leaders, sought in the same spirit to put upon
those they had deceived the responsibility for the break-down
of negotiations now inevitable because of the British repudiation
of their own terms. America must at all costs be convinced that
it was the Irish who could not agree.

Lloyd George's reply to Redmond's speech was a model of pre-
varication. He admitted the proposals as made to the Nationalist
leaders were provisional: "a purely temporary and provisional
arrangement" were his words. But after the terms had been
accepted, the Tories in the Cabinet "found it impossible to support the proposal". With much labouring he explained the
changes that had been made in consequence. Every one of them
was substantial. The greatest of them was the conversion of the
temporary arrangement into the permanent exclusion of the six
counties. The whole basis of the agreement had been altered,
but this in no wise prevented Lloyd George's attempt at the end
of his speech to put upon the Nationalists the responsibility for
the break. Both Redmond and Dillon had said they could not
support anything less than what they had got their followers to
accept:

> If that is the view of the Irish members (said Lloyd George) of
> course it would be idle for the Government to bring in a Bill for
> bringing Home Rule into immediate operation under any con-
> ditions. If that is the view of hon. Members for Ireland I deeply
> regret it.... They know their own country, they know its diffi-
> culties, they know the conditions. It is for them to decide. The
> Government ought not and will not force this proposal upon them. [1]

In their speeches in this debate, both Redmond and Dillon
showed that they knew their leadership had been gravely shaken by
what had happened. With the Cabinet's unanimous delegation
of the task of an Irish settlement to Lloyd George, with Lloyd
George's pledge of "his life upon the table", that he would
stand by the terms he gave them, with Asquith's knowledge and
approval of those terms, and with his own personal intervention

[1] Hansard, 24 July 1916, vol. lxxxiv, cols. 1443-4.

at a critical moment to emphasise that the settlement sought was solely provisional—with all that to reassure them of British sincerity the heads of the Irish Parliamentary Party had gone to their supporters and themselves pledging their honour that this was the final concession, asked for and got approval of what they held in writing from Lloyd George. Then the British abandoned their own proposals and left the Irish leaders empty-handed and stultified before an angry following and an angrier nation. It was the real end of the Redmond period in Irish politics. The rest was merely the epilogue to a story already told.

But before they left the positions of trust and influence they had held in Ireland, Redmond and Dillon placed on record the fact that they had been deceived. In the debates on the failure of the negotiations Redmond said:

> We never for one moment contemplated the idea that this great question was to be foreclosed and settled now ... They (the British Government) have disregarded every advice we tendered to them and now in the end having got us to induce our people to make a tremendous sacrifice and to agree to the temporary exclusion of the Six Counties, they throw this agreement to the winds ... [1]

Later in the same House he said:

> It was put before us as a temporary emergency war measure intended not to settle any of these grave problems which could not be settled in existing circumstances, but merely to bridge over the period between now and the permanent settlement. As such it was accepted by us and as such it was submitted to our followers. [2]

Dillon said:

> We have the written document and the pledge of Ministers. We stand by that pledge. We hold it in our hand and we hold them to our meaning on which we obtained the consent of our people in Ireland ... Then we came back to London and we were told that Ministers were prepared to break their word — that forsooth the Marquess of Lansdowne will leave the Cabinet if they adhere to their pledge. The Prime Minister ... knew all the terms and pledged himself to them. [3]

Dillon went on:

> I am bound to say that the consequences of this breach of faith with us puts an end to all prospect of a settlement on these lines during the war ... You have struck a deadly blow at the whole

[1] Ibid., col. 1434.
[2] Hansard, 31 July 1916, vol. lxxxiv, col. 2150.
[3] Hansard, 24 July 1916, vol. lxxxiv, cols. 1459-60.

future Government of Ireland. How will you ever get the Irish
people to have confidence in the terms and words of British
Ministers?

A week later Dillon said, "What must be the opinion of the Irish
people of a Cabinet that does that kind of thing?" [1]

Carson had said that he had been given assurances. Dillon
commented:

> Whatever may be the secret assurances given behind our backs
> to the right hon. and learned member for Trinity College (Sir
> Edward Carson) the words of the document remain and in all
> its provisions this proposal was to be, according to the under-
> taking of the Minister on the faith of which we went to Ireland,
> a strictly provisional war-emergency measure in all its details...
> When the Cabinet drafted the Bill last week.... the Bill in all
> its clauses and details was strictly temporary and provisional
> and acceptable to us. That in my opinion, disposes absolutely of
> the statement of the right hon. gentleman. I do not challenge the
> accuracy of his statement unless it be true which I shrink from
> believing that the Minister for War (Lloyd George) was telling the
> right hon. gentleman one story behind our backs and quite a
> different story to us. [2]

Both Lloyd George and Carson knew, as these words were being
spoken, that what Dillon shrank from believing *was* true, but few
others knew the extent of the undertaking until the letter was
published more than eight years later.

Britain did not entirely forget the 1916 proposals which col-
lapsed in such seamy circumstances. Grudging assent to them
had been secured from one section in Ireland by deception, an
assent which cost Irishmen who had trusted Britain their position
as leaders of the Irish people. That grudging assent Lloyd
George was later to use with deadly effect against the territorial
integrity of Ireland.

[1]   Hansard, 31 July 1916, vol. lxxxiv, col. 2124.
[2]   Hansard, 24 July 1916, vol. lxxxiv, col. 1462.

APPENDIX to Chapter Nine

THE 1916 PROPOSALS

The proposal which Mr. Lloyd George submitted to the Irish Leaders in the negotiations of May-June, 1916, were published on 12 June 1916 and are given here as from the London *Times* of that date:

(1) To bring the Home Rule act into immediate operation.

(2) To introduce at once an amending Bill as a strictly war emergency Act to cover only the period of the War and a short specified interval after it.

(3) During that period the Irish members to remain at Westminster in their full numbers.

(4) During this war emergency period six Ulster counties to be left as at present under the imperial Government.

(5) Immediately after the war an Imperial Conference of representatives of all the Dominions of the Empire to be held to consider the future government of the Empire, including the question of the Government of Ireland.

(6) Immediately after this Conference, and during the interval provided by the War Emergency Act, the permanent settlement of all the great outstanding problems, such as the permanent position of the six exempted countries, the question of finance, and other problems which cannot be dealt with during the War, would be proceeded with.

CHAPTER X

THE CONVENTION OF 1917

By THE BEGINNING of 1917 the international position of Britain compelled her again to do something about the Irish question. The large Irish populations in the United States, Canada, Australia and New Zealand, as well as the great number of people of Irish birth or descent in Britain itself and in the British Army and Navy, had taken a very simple view of the Easter Week Rising. To them it was their own nation striking for her freedom.

In America, even outside the ranks of the Irish, the insurrection was viewed as not unlike their own attempts to win independence from the same power. In consequence, the execution of the Irish leaders after the Rising had a continuing impact on American thinking. As week followed week and the readiness with which the leaders met death for liberty became known, British propaganda against them was brushed aside; and under distinguished patronage funds were opened for those who had suffered and were bereaved, while memorial services, attended by many leading Americans, were held to honour the dead.

Britain's diplomatic representatives had already warned their Government that America was turning away from her as the result of "recent events in Ireland". Sir Cecil Spring-Rice, the British Ambassador in Washington, wrote that the executions made it impossible now to conciliate the Irish there. "They have blood in their eyes when they look our way."

Britain, with a view to retrieving this position and eventually to bringing America in on her side, had initiated the 1916 proposals in an attempt at conciliating American opinion generally. The attempt, as we have seen, failed because of the double-dealing of Lloyd George, who succeeded Asquith as Prime Minister in December 1916, and other members of the Government. Sir Edward (now Lord) Carson said on 8 October 1924, in the House of Lords:

> In 1916.... the whole settlement broke down because of the duplicity of those who were negotiating the settlement. [1]

[1] Hansard, House of Lords, 8 Oct. 1924, vol. liv, col. 616.

Through German action America came into the war on 6 April 1917. As a result the importance of the Irish question temporarily grew. Britain regarded her own survival as dependent on swift American intervention on the Continent, and this might be delayed if her good faith in this "war for small nations" remained suspect. President Wilson was announcing war aims whose application must free Ireland. Britain, her Ambassador in Washington urged again, must do something to remove the barrier to confidence raised by her treatment of Ireland's demands:

> The fact that the Irish question is still unsettled (wrote Sir Cecil Spring-Rice after the American declaration of war) is continually quoted against us as proof that it is not wholly true that the fight is one for the sanctity of engagements or the independence of small nations. [1]

At the same time the British Premier was being pressed to the same purpose by the American Ambassador in London. In the *Life and Letters of Walter H. Page,* there is quoted a letter to him from President Wilson sent towards the end of April:

> If (said the President) the American people were once convinced that there was a likelihood that the Irish question would soon be settled, great enthusiasm and satisfaction would result and it would also strengthen the co-operation which we are now about to organise between the United States and Great Britain. Say this in unofficial terms to Mr. Lloyd George but impress upon him its great significance. [2]

The first reaction of Lloyd George, now Prime Minister, to this communication was typical. He denounced Carson and his Tory colleagues to Page as the opponents of a settlement although, knowing of the intransigeance of Carson and such colleagues as Walter Long, he had taken them into his Cabinet to fill the important posts of First Lord of the Admiralty and Colonial Secretary. To Page he now called them "madmen" and declared to him later in Carson's presence:

> I've been telling the Ambassador, Carson, that we've got to settle the Irish question now—in spite of you. [3]

The American Ambassador was not deceived as to where the reluctance to settle the question lay. And Lloyd George now felt the necessity for action.

[1] *Letters and Friendships of Sir Cecil Spring-Rice,* vol. ii, p. 393.
[2] *Life and Letters of Walter H. Page,* vol. ii, pp. 255-6.
[3] Ibid., p. 260.

Thus it came about that within six weeks of America's declaration of war, John Redmond received on 16 May 1917 a letter from Lloyd George. It made these proposals:

> 1. Britain would establish Home Rule immediately for Twenty Six Counties; the Six Counties to remain part of the United Kingdom and be governed direct from London for five years after which Parliament would reconsider the question. A Council of Ireland would be set up on which the Six Counties and the Twenty Six would have equal representation to deal with questions common to the two areas.
> 2. Alternatively, that a Convention of Irishmen of all parties be assembled 'for the purpose of producing a scheme of Irish self-government.... for the purpose of drafting a Constitution for their country'. [1]

Redmond rejected the first on the grounds that the time for even the temporary division of Ireland had passed. He accepted the proposal of an Irish Convention, asking for an assurance that what the Convention decided would be made law. Lloyd George gave the following pledge on 21 May 1917, in the House of Commons:

> The Government are prepared to say this: that if substantial agreement should be reached as to the character and scope of the Constitution framed by the Convention for the future Government of Ireland within the Empire, they will accept the responsibility for taking all the necessary steps to enable the Imperial Parliament to give legislative effect to the conclusions of the Convention. [2]

It seemed that at last something sincere was being done to achieve an Irish settlement. That appearance of sincerity did not last.

The Convention was not to be an elected body. In Ireland a series of by-elections was taking place as the Convention personnel was being decided upon. The results of these by-elections plainly indicated that the Irish people had turned away from the Irish Party and now supported those who had participated in the Rising, the policy of whose political organisation, Sinn Fein, was complete Irish independence. It was decided, nevertheless, that the Convention would be made up of 100 members, only 5 of whom were to be drawn from the now dominant national movement, while 95 other members were to be taken from minority groups. This result was achieved by careful selection and nomination.

The membership of the Convention was to include 33 County

1 *Report of the Proceeding of the Irish Convention* (*Cd.* 9019) p. 51.
2 Hansard, 21 May 1917, vol. lxxxiii, col. 1998.

John Redmond (1856-1918)

Earl of Midleton (1856-1942)

Lafayette, Dublin

Council Chairmen and 14 Mayors and other Urban representatives, most of whom had been elected six years earlier. There
were to be 5 representatives of the Irish Party, 5 of the Southern
Unionists and 5 of the Ulster Unionist Council. The Churches
were to have 7 representatives. The rest were to be Chairmen of
Chambers of Commerce, Peers, and 7 members representing
Labour interests. 15 nominated members completed the Convention. It was the *New York Times* which described it as "a
hand picked" body.

Sinn Fein among other stipulations made it a condition of
its own participation in the Convention that, in accordance with
the views of the majority of the Irish people, the Convention had
the right to decide for a wholly independent Ireland. This condition was refused, and Sinn Fein would not accept membership.

Almost immediately the same situation developed as over the
1916 proposals. The British Premier gave a private pledge to
Carson that the Ulster Tory delegation need not agree to any
decision the Convention might take, and on the grounds of that
disagreement Britain would refuse to implement the Convention's
findings.

These undertakings are fully set out in two accounts of the
particular proceedings both friendly to Carson.

The Ulster Unionist Council was reluctant to enter the Convention, and Carson visited Belfast to persuade them. Mr. Ronald
McNeill in his *Ulster's Stand for Union* [1] records:

> Carson accompanied Sir John Lonsdale to Belfast and explained
> the explicit pledges by Ministers that participation would not
> commit them to anything, that they would not be bound by any
> majority vote and that without their concurrence no legislation was
> to be founded on any agreement between the other groups in the
> Convention.

Describing the same meeting, which took place on 8 June 1917,
Mr. Ian Colvin in his *Life of Lord Carson* [2] summarises Carson's
speech:

> He was authorised by Mr. Lloyd George, whom he had seen the
> day before to say:
> 1. That unless the Ulster Unionists agree with the proposals at
> the Convention nothing could come of it,
> 2. That their position was not to be prejudiced by going into
> the Convention.
> 3. That he adhered to the statement that there should be no
> coercion of Ulster.

[1]   p. 257.
[2]   p. 293.

Here then again was the revival of the veto of the minority on the decisions of the majority. On the one hand the British Premier sets up a Constituent Assembly to draw up a Constitution for Ireland, publicly pledging his Government to pass into law whatever findings of that Assembly had "substantial agreement" behind them. At the same time, he gave "specific pledges" in the name of the same Government to a tiny Tory minority within the assembly that no legislation which had not their concurrence would be passed, even if all the other groups in the Convention agreed. To measure the extraordinary nature of the veto thus conferred, one has but to recall that the Ulster Unionist Council was to nominate only 5 delegates to a Convention of 100 members. To that 5 per cent of the whole body the real power of decision was handed over by the British Government, and there was the same secretiveness about doing this as about the Lloyd George letter to Carson which paralysed the proposals for settlement a year before.

The plan worked perfectly, from the British point of view. The five Ulster Unionist Council representatives drew to themselves a group from the nominated members and from fellow-party men among Chamber of Commerce representatives and the Mayors and County Council Chairmen of North Eastern Ulster. This bloc, which at its highest mustered 19 members, took no other part in the Convention than a wrecking one. Sir Horace Plunkett, the Convention Chairman, has left on record in his diaries the use the Ulster group made of the undertaking they had from the British Premier.

He records, in the words of his biographer, Miss Margaret Digby, how if left to themselves they might have aided the Convention, but "one and all were bound by the secret instructions of the Ulster Unionist Council from which they could not depart". It was not until the end of the year that Redmond discovered how again Lloyd George had deceived him:

> Redmond (writes Sir Horace in his diary) put a wholly new aspect of the Convention crisis before me. He had discovered that Carson obtained the consent of the Government to an understanding that the Ulster Unionist representatives should act as a delegation of the party organisation, thus placing them in a wholly different position from that occupied by the other members. This explains the extraordinary attitude of the Ulstermen in the sub-committee of Nine and the refusal of the Nationalists to place any trust in the Government's promise to legislate at once if there is *substantial agreement*. [1]

[1] Margaret Digby, *Horace Plunkett*, p. 229.

The Southern Unionists were anxious for a settlement but they had the same misgivings as the Nationalists as to Britain keeping her pledges. Lord Midleton, one of the Southern Unionists' representatives in the Convention, went to London in December 1917, and on the last day of the year received a written undertaking from Lord Curzon of Kedleston, Lord Privy Seal in the British Cabinet. Lord Curzon was, in one of the anomalies of the time, an Irish peer who had never seen Ireland, even on a visit. [1] But he was Chairman of the British Cabinet Committee dealing with Irish affairs. The undertaking he gave Lord Midleton was in these terms:

> If the Southern Unionist scheme is carried by the Convention with substantial agreement—i.e. with the Opposition of Ulster alone— the Prime Minister will use his personal influence with his colleagues, the sympathies of many of whom are well known, to accept the proposal and to give it legislative effect.
>
>   D.L.G. [2]

The initials are those of the British Prime Minister. For better security Lord Midleton had got Lloyd George to countersign this undertaking. It did, however, not satisfy Redmond, now getting used to Lloyd George's double-meaning phrases, for it was a watering-down of that gentleman's more definite pledge given on 21 May in the House of Commons. Its importance here is that it clearly defined what was meant by the words "substantial agreement" in the original public undertaking. Over the Premier's own initials it was now defined as anything which the Ulster group in the Convention alone opposed.

It was characteristic of Lloyd George that he had again given two pledges to two groups of Irishmen, both of which could not be honoured. The Ulster group no doubt received at the same time from the same source renewed assurances that their veto would stand, for of the concluding stages of the Convention the biographer of the Convention's Chairman writes:

> The Ulster Unionists were more dumb than ever and Plunkett likened them to an iceberg floating across the mouth of a harbour. [3]

Nevertheless, the condition Lloyd George had laid done was more than fulfilled. There was not only substantial agreement but, with the exception of the Unionist Council group, every

[1] Earl of Ronaldshay, *Life of Lord Curzon*, vol. iii, p. 178.
[2] Denis Gwynn, *Life of John Redmond*, p. 579.
[3] Margaret Digby, *Horace Plunkett*, p. 232.

other body in the Convention, while naturally they differed in detail, asked for a National Parliament for Ireland with wide powers. As Sir Horace stated in his letter as Chairman to the British Premier when transmitting the Report of the Convention:

> It (the Report) shows that in the Convention—whilst it was not found possible to overcome the objections of the Ulster Unionists— a majority of Nationalists, all the Southern Unionists, and five out of seven Labour representatives were agreed that the scheme of Irish self-government set out in Paragraph 42 of the Report should be immediately passed into law. A minority of Nationalists propose a scheme which differs in only one important particular from that of the majority. The Convention has, therefore, laid a foundation of Irish agreement unprecedented in history. [1]

The Convention which first met on 25 July 1917, in the Regent's House, Trinity College, Dublin, sat for eight months. In that period it surveyed the whole field of Irish self-government in its national, political, financial, judicial and general aspects. It came to its main conclusions by decisive majorities. The proposal for the establishment of an Irish Parliament was passed by 51 votes to 18, a majority of 74 per cent. The proposal that that Parliament have authority over all Ireland was passed by 51 votes to 19. An amendment to exclude the Province of Ulster from the jurisdiction of the National Parliament was rejected by 52 votes to 19, a majority of 73 per cent.

The remarkable fact was commented on by Sir Horace Plunkett in his letter to Lloyd George that the Unionists of 26 of the 32 Counties who, as their name implies, had opposed the national demand for self-government since the passing of the Union in 1800, now accepted the majority view and pressed Ireland's claim for a National Parliament, though within the Empire and subject to the Imperial Parliament in London. Their hatred of the partition of Ireland had brought them to this attitude. Rather than have their nation dismembered and they as a national minority sundered from their brothers in North-eastern Ireland, they abandoned their traditional policy and voted consistently in the Convention for the unity of Ireland under one Parliament.

The attitude of the Labour representatives was no less remarkable. Five of them signed a special report in which they declared self-government to be "in the best interests of the country" and urged that "a measure giving it effect should be passed promptly

---

[1] *Report of the Proceeding of the Irish Convention*, p. 3.

into law". They disagreed as democrats with the special concessions proposed by the Convention to meet the prejudices of the Ulster Tories. [1]

> But we feel so deeply the necessity of setting up a Parliament in Ireland in which Labour amongst other interests may be able to find a place, that we have been willing to subordinate our democratic beliefs to what we conceive to be the highest interests of Ireland.

The signatories to this Report included three leaders of Belfast Labour, R. Waugh, representing the Belfast and District Building Trades' Federation, C. McKay representing the Shipbuilding and Engineering Trades Federation, and H. T. Whitley representing Belfast and District Trades' Council.

It was, therefore, no exaggeration of the Convention's Chairman to report officially to the British Government of "Irish agreement unprecedented in history", particularly if the Convention is viewed in its relation to the proposals to partition Ireland. Against Partition were ranged such pro-British spokesmen as the Earl of Midleton, the Earl of Desart, Lord Dunraven, Lord Oranmore and Browne, the Earl of Mayo, His Grace Dr. Crozier, Archbishop of Armagh and Protestant Primate of All Ireland, His Grace Dr. Bernard, Protestant Archbishop of Dublin, Dr. Mahaffy, the Provost of Trinity College, Lord MacDonnell, the Earl of Granard, the President of University College, Cork. All these who belonged to the political minority in Ireland declared in the Convention either for a National Parliament or against the partition of their country. The Nationalists were, of course, unanimous on one Parliament for the nation and differed only on the extent of its powers. Of the 47 County Council Chairmen, Mayors, Lords Mayor and other Urban representatives, 38 asserted Ireland's essential unity. In all, 69 of the 88 active members (there had been deaths, illnesses and resignations) opposed over their names any proposal to divide Ireland, a majority of 78 per cent of a Convention whose members Britain herself had chosen.

In February, when difficulties arose over the obstructive attitude of the Ulster Unionists and also over the powers to be accorded to the Irish Parliament, Lloyd George invited a representative delegation of the members to visit him in London. He received them on 13 February and his address to them was capable of so many interpretations that

[1] They were to be given a far higher percentage of seats in both Commons and Senate than their number would justify.

afterwards, no two delegates were ever agreed on the actual words or even the meaning of the Prime Minister's utterances. [1]

The British Premier had learned from the delegation how substantial was the agreement reached by all but one section; he learned too that the Nationalists were divided on the single major point of whether the proposed Parliament should have control of the Irish Customs or not (all were agreed to the control of Excise). A Premier truly seeking a settlement could have at this stage made the Convention a complete success, for all the elements of agreement were present. Even individual Ulster Unionist delegates agreed with the ideal of an All-Ireland Parliament. In the *Life of John Redmond* Professor Denis Gwynn quotes a letter from the Earl of Midleton:

> You ask me what were the conditions under which the Southern Unionists entered the Convention and whether they had any reason to suppose the Ulster members would oppose an All-Ireland settlement. I can say with absolute certainty, and with the support of those of my colleagues who are still alive, that we were informed that the Ulster representatives entered the Convention without any limitations and certain of the most prominent Ulster members expressed themselves as determined to come to terms for an All-Ireland settlement. [2]

The obstructive tactics in the Convention, as this authoritative letter shows (for Lord Midleton had been the colleague of those men), had their clear origin outside that body. Now it was also from outside that there was delivered the blow which destroyed the Convention. It took the form of a letter from the Prime Minister which the Assembly had before it when they met on 26 February after the return of their delegates from London. Though worded with all the astuteness of which Lloyd George was capable and bearing on its face the aspect of the greatest friendliness and anxiety to help, the letter fatally changed the terms of reference of the Convention and made nugatory all the work already accomplished.

In this new letter Lloyd George exploited every division he had noticed among the delegates. He declared that a majority (of 73 per cent as we have seen), would not be enough: to prove substantial agreement there must be "mutual agreement among *all* parties". This was giving in public the veto to five Ulster Unionists which he had given secretly before the Convention sat.

1 Margaret Digby, *Horace Plunkett*, p. 233.
2 Denis Gwynn, *Life of John Redmond*, p. 568 footnote.

The Ulster Unionists now knew that they had only to continue their non-possumus attitude to bring all the efforts at settlement to nothing. Secondly Lloyd George's new terms of reference laid it down that it was not only to be within the British Empire that the settlement must be found, it must be found without disturbing "the fundamental unity of the United Kingdom" [1] which meant that Britain would only accept an Irish Parliament so restricted in its powers as to be acceptable to few of the members in the Convention. Further, Lloyd George now informed the Convention that there would be no immediate legislation on what the Convention had substantially agreed to, not even if the Convention were unanimous, should its proposals excite strong opposition in Great Britain. This important passage read:

> Questions on which there is an acute difference of opinion in Ireland or in Great Britain must be held over for determination after the war. [2]

Then so elemental a right of any National Parliament as controlling taxation within its area was debarred also, and in this Lloyd George adopted an attitude more conservative than even the Southern Unionists who had agreed to the transfer of Excise to the Parliament they proposed. The Premier's letter now said that that Parliament must not have transferred to it control of Customs or Excise because

> It would be practically impossible to make such a disturbance of the fiscal and financial relations of Great Britain and Ireland in the midst of a great war. It might also be incompatible with that federal reorganisation of the United Kingdom in favour of which there is a growing body of opinion. [3]

It was a wrecking letter and it achieved its purpose. The Convention faded away. Not wishing to let any chance of any agreement go it met to consider whether a settlement could be come to on the basis of this new and greatly constricted basis. But the life had gone out of it. Once more betrayed by British statesmen whom he had trusted, Redmond died on 8 March 1918. A month later, on 8 April, the Convention assembled for the last time to pass its Report.

In that Report agreement among the delegates was even still so strong that Sir Horace Plunkett felt that, despite everything,

[1] *Report of the Proceedings of the Irish Convention*, p. 20.
[2] Ibid.
[3] Ibid., p. 21.

the British Government could not ignore it in view of their pledge to legislate. [1] His biographer writes:

> On April 9th, 1918, Plunkett arrived in London dead tired, bringing with him the report of the Irish Convention. It was not an unanimous report but it put forward constructive proposals widely backed. There was good reason to hope that the government would use them as the basis of an immediate settlement. [2]

Instead, Lloyd George thrust the Report unread into his pocket and on that very day proposed to conscript Irishmen into the British Army by force. To lessen the bad propagandist effect this decision was certain to have in America now fully in the war, he promised that he would later bring in legislation on the basis of the convention report, but by coupling that promise with the imposition of compulsory service in the British army on a people who were seeking independence, he not only, as Plunkett said, "shocked the conscience of many high-minded Irishmen", but his action doomed any proposals he might make to instantaneous rejection.

While these things were happening in Ireland Lord Birkenhead (then Sir Frederick E. Smith) was on a British good-will mission to the United States to smooth away difficulties that were delaying United States help to Britain. An interview he gave to the *Boston Post* early in January 1918 caused much controversy. He himself declared it was an inaccurate account of what he said and repudiated the interview. The interviewer, Robert R. Morton, who later became the *Boston Post* correspondent in Washington, asserted that Lord Birkenhead had spoken what

[1] "Owing to the conciliatory and statesmanlike attitude of Mr. Redmond on the one side and of the Unionist leaders like Lord Midleton on the other, the Convention had advanced (as it appears from its Report in the Spring of 1918) though not the whole distance, yet a long way on the road to agreement." (Earl of Oxford and Asquith, K.C. *Memories and Reflections*, p. 189).

[2] Margaret Digby, *Horace Plunkett*, p. 238.
An idea of the extent of the wide backing referred to by Sir Horace Plunkett can be gathered also from Mr. Ronald McNeill's *Ulster's Stand for Union*. Mr. McNeill (afterwards Lord Cushendun and a member of the British Cabinet) said (pp. 259-60) that the Ulstermen had to listen to "proposals for giving the whole of Ireland, including their own Province, a constitution practically as independent of Great Britain as that of the Dominions. But", he goes on, "what astaonished the Ulstermen above everything was to find these extravagant demands supported by those who were supposed to be representatives of Southern Unionism". It is Mr. McNeill's way of stressing that the representatives of three of the four Irish Provinces and a large part of the fourth were agreed on Home Rule.

had been attributed to him. The importance of the interview was that it disclosed what must have been in the mind of the British Government from the beginning of this Convention idea.

The Convention came into being, as we have seen, following pressure from President Wilson. Britain found that its establishment quieted American concern over Ireland. The longer the Convention sat and talked, therefore, the better the effect in the United States. Lloyd George by his pledge to the Ulster Unionists ensured that, from the outset, it would talk to no purpose. In that setting what the interviewer attributed to Lord Birkenhead was entirely rational and to the point, and any American reporter would have to have a very detailed knowledge of Irish politics to invent anything so apt.

> It would be very inconvenient (Lord Birkenhead was reported in the *Boston Post* of Jan. 14, 1918, as saying) if anything should happen just now to overturn the attempt to bring about a settlement. In a few months, whatever happens, it won't amount to a damn.... The best thing that can happen in Ireland is to prolong the life of the Convention. Let them keep on talking. [1]

It was a month and a half later that Lloyd George wrote the letter which threw everything the Convention had achieved into confusion. American aid to Britain was flowing more steadily and, as Britain no longer felt the duress of self-interest in solving the Irish problem, Ireland had now come nearer the stage of "not mattering a damn". In these circumstances, it was typical of Lloyd George first to encourage them "to keep on talking" and then to offer not conciliation but conscription!

---

[1] Quoted from *Gaelic American*, New York, 17 Jan. 1918. Even less elegantly Mr. Ronald MacNeill M.P. in his book *Ulster's Stand for Union* (p. 259) expresses the same thought. Speaking of the Convention he says "It was a bone thrown to a snarling dog and the longer there was anything to gnaw the longer would the dog keep quiet. The Ulster delegates understood this perfectly and as their chief desire was to help the Government to get on with the war, they had no wish to curtail the proceedings of the Convention."

CHAPTER XI

"A MEASURE TO SECURE A UNITED IRELAND"
THE PARTITION ACT, 1920

ON 22 DECEMBER 1919 Lloyd George announced that his Government would introduce into the British Commons a measure which, with his facility for misnomers, he called "a Bill for the better Government of Ireland". It has been known ever since as the Partition Act.

This was the British Statute which split Ireland into two unequal parts, and it is important to study the circumstances under which it came into existence and into operation.

In the first place, there was no electoral mandate in Ireland for it. On the contrary the will of the people had been expressed only twelve months earlier, when they voted overwhelmingly for unity and independence. This was admitted by the authors of the Bill. In the principal debate on it, that on the Second Reading, the British Premier said on 31 March 1920:

> If you asked the people of Ireland what plan they would accept, by an emphatic majority, they would say "We want independence and an Irish Republic". There is absolutely no doubt about that. The elected representatives of Ireland, now by a clear majority, have declared in favour of independence. [1]

The leader of the House of Commons, Bonar Law, in the same debate enumerating the alternatives to the Bill, said on 30 March that one of them was

> to give self-determination to the representatives of the Irish people: that is to create an Irish Republic. [2]

Lloyd George and Bonar Law were referring to the General Election held in the whole of Ireland in December 1918. At that time, there was a strong British Army in Ireland and the demand for independence was regarded and punished as "sedition". The leaders of the independence movement had been deported to and imprisoned in England. A majority of the independence candidates were in jail with hundreds of their

1 Hansard, 31 Mar. 1920, vol. cxxvii, col. 1322.
2 Hansard, 30 Mar. 1920, vol. cxxvii, col. 1123.

election workers. Yet the independence party won 73 of the 105 seats and 6 others were won by candidates who stood for full self-determination for the Irish people.

It was in this general election that the Irish Parliamentary Party, which had represented Ireland for 40 years, was swept out of existence. On the eve of the poll it held 73 seats. In the contest with the independence movement it retained only 6. It is a result not easily paralleled in political history. The causes of this débâcle of a once powerful party were, as is usual in such matters, complex and numerous. But one of the principal charges laid against them in their opponents' speeches was that they had consented in 1914 and 1916 to the temporary partition of Ireland. Their defeat was the measure of the people's abhorrence of that proposal.

Subsequent to the 1918 General Election, local elections were held in January and June 1920 and in these also the independence parties, Republican and Labour, triumphed, winning 80 per cent of the seats in the whole country. They had a majority in 28 of the 32 counties and secured a far greater number of seats in Ulster than the Unionists, although the system of election was P.R., specially imposed by Britain to break up the Republican movement. [1]

If there was no demand for the Partition Act in Ireland as a whole, there was so little demand for it in the Unionist areas that Britain had to threaten and wheedle to get Unionist consent to it. Sir Edward Carson has left a description of the importunities of British statesmen when they were pressing him at least to acquiesce in the measure. Speaking in the House of Lords on 8 October 1924, Carson said:

> Mr. Lloyd George and Mr. Bonar Law over and over again said: "Don't you see how strong a position you are going to be in, because once a Parliament is elected the Imperial Government cannot interfere with it and its proceedings."

The prospect of Britain's forcing a Parliament on the North-east had no charm for Carson and, in the Partition Act debate, he said:

[1] "The Proportional Representation Act, as it is called, was introduced by Mr. Justice Samuels, when he was Attorney General for Ireland, the avowed object of the Government being to prevent Sinn Fein from capturing the machinery of Local Government in Ireland." *Belfast News-letter*, 6 Jan. 1920.

I know Ulster does not want this Parliament. [1]

Lord Long, British Cabinet Adviser on Irish affairs, has left on record the statement:

> I was very reluctantly induced to take charge of the 1920 Bill in the House of Commons. I took Worthington Evans to assist me. The measure found no support in any part of the House. The Liberals boycotted it and left the House. The bulk of the Conservative Party took no interest in it and only supported me because I made a personal appeal. But the Ulster people stood coldly aloof. They did not want the Bill. [2]

The former Liberal Premier, Asquith, said of the Bill on 21 May 1920 that it was "a paltering compromise unacceptable either to the majority or to the minority". [3] To compel the minority's acceptance of what they did not want the British Government of 1920 used another method. They pointed out that if the Ulster leaders would not accept this Bill then the original Home Rule Act, put on the Statute book before the war, must come into force. That was the measure against which Sir Edward raised his private army and against which the Covenant was sworn. The British proposal to allow it to operate was not aimed at giving an undivided Ireland even that much self-rule but at compelling Carson and his colleagues to support the new Bill they disliked less.

Austen Chamberlain, then Chancellor of the Exchequer, on 29 March 1920 said in reply to Lord Robert Cecil:

> My noble friend and other Unionists must remember that the Home Rule Act is on the Statute Book. The alternative to an Amending Bill is that that Act comes into force. [4]

Bonar Law on the next day, 30 March, said:

> The Home Rule Act is on the Statute Book. We are approaching the period when the last of the Peace Treaties, I hope, will soon be ratified and when that happens unless something is done this Act automatically comes into operation. [5]

Although their opposition to the Home Rule Act was, as we have seen, emotionally profound, this threat did no more than

[1] Hansard, 31 Mar. 1920, vol. cxxvii, col. 1298.
[2] London *Times,* 30 Sept. 1924.
[3] In his *Memories and Reflections* Asquith described the Bill as "giving to a section of Ulster a Parliament which it did not want and to the remaining three-quarters of Ireland a Parliament which it would not have." p. 190.
[4] Hansard, 29 Mar. 1920, vol. cxxvii, col. 980.
[5] Hansard, 30 Mar. 1920, vol. cxxvii, col. 1122.

neutralise the Six County Unionists. To them also the unity of Ireland was an underlying reality that could not be gainsaid, and though they did not vote against the Partition Act, they would not vote for it. They described it for what it was, a wholly British measure in which they had no part, but which they would accept to escape what they had campaigned so long and so violently against.

The Commons debate on the Partition Bill is remarkable for another reason. The British Ministers and others were fully conscious of the wrong they were doing in destroying the territorial integrity of Ireland and showed this sense of guilt in their speeches. They had no need to fear a defeat on the measure. The same election which had swept the independence movement in Ireland into power swept the Lloyd George Coalition to office with one of the biggest Parliamentary majorities ever known. Therefore, the sponsors of the Bill had no need to plead with the House to pass it.

There were only six Nationalist M.P.s from Ireland, and the Coalition held 477 seats. Lloyd George could have said to such a Parliament: the permanent division of Ireland into two States is justified and this Bill accomplishes that. Instead he and every other Government speaker stressed Ireland's fundamental unity and advocated their Bill as a temporary measure which would provide the speediest way of establishing that unity permanently.

Ian MacPherson, Chief Secretary for Ireland in Lloyd George's Cabinet, in opening the Second Reading Debate said that the division of Ireland was as distasteful to the Government as it was to Irishmen, and went on:

> All of us hope that the division may be temporary only and our objective has, therefore, been to frame the Bill in such a manner as may lead to a union between the two parts of Ireland.... In the very nature of things division must give rise to many inconveniences and ordinary men of commonsense will be anxious to remove them. [1]

He ended his speech by recommending the Bill as one

> which alone.... can secure what we all desire: a United Ireland within the Empire who shall flourish in prosperity and peace as mistress of her own destiny. [2]

Austen Chamberlain, Chancellor of the Exchequer, pressed the

[1] Hansard, 29 Mar. 1920, vol. cxxiv, col. 928-9.
[2] Ibid, col. 944.

Bill on the House on the same day (29 March) with the same
plea:

> For the first time in its history since the Act of Union, if this Bill
> passes it will be in the power of Ireland to create for itself un-
> hindered and uncriticised by us a Common Parliament for the
> whole of Ireland. [1]

Sir Laming Worthington-Evans, whom we shall meet again as a
signatory to the Anglo-Irish Treaty, was the Minister of Pensions
in the 1920 Government. In the same debate he denied repeatedly
that the Bill could possibly lead to the "permanent dismemberment of Ireland".

> Permanent dismemberment (he cried) in a Bill which provides
> every opportunity for the two Parliaments to come together if
> they choose!.... to say that the people who can join and fight
> shoulder to shoulder in the trenches (He was referring to the fact
> that Irishmen from all parts of the country had suffered heavily
> in the British Army in World War I) are to be permanently dis-
> membered when they were invited and almost compelled under
> this Bill to come together for the purposes of their common
> affairs!.... Whenever they like, without any reference back to us,
> they can form the one Parliament. [2]

All the Governmental speeches sooner or later struck this note:
that the Bill was actually a provisional one leading to the
restoration of Irish unity and to one Parliament for the whole
of Ireland.

That this should have been said so often in a House where
there was already an overwhelming majority for anything the
Government wished to put into law is of particular significance.
The British Parliament was told that the Bill would not really
partition or dismember Ireland: that the division it created was
temporary only: that the Bill was a unifying measure: that it was
indeed the quickest way to unity. On such recommendations from
its Governmental sponsors the British Parliament accepted and
passed the Bill. Even after the measure had passed through
Parliament, declarations that the intention of the Act was to re-
establish Irish unity came from the highest spokesmen in Britain.

His Majesty King George V in his speech proroguing the
British Parliament on 23 December 1920 said:

> I have given my assent to a Bill for the better Government of
> Ireland. This and the setting up of two Parliaments and a Council
> of Ireland gives self-government to the whole of Ireland and

[1] Hansard, 29 Mar. 1920, vol. cxxvii, col. 981.
[2] Ibid, cols. 1029-31.

provides the means whereby the people can of their own accord achieve unity. [1]

The British King's Viceroy, Lord French, speaking in Belfast on 2 March 1921, mentioned the speech of Carson himself on the closing stages of the Bill, and went on:

> I would recall to your minds the speech of that great statesman, Sir Edward Carson—whose retirement from Irish affairs all of us must so deeply regret—when he himself expressed the fervent hope that the time might shortly come when the ultimate object of this Bill would be achieved and the Northern and Southern Parliaments would become one. I am sure we all fervently re-echo this hope from the bottom of our hearts. [2]

In January 1921 an official "Summary of Main Provisions" was issued with the text of this Act. That summary stressed two points, both of which indicated how deep was the hostility of the Irish people towards its enactment. In its opening passages it reiterated that it was really a measure to undo Partition.

> Although at the beginning there are to be two Parliaments and two Governments in Ireland, the Act.... empowers the two Parliaments by mutual agreement and joint action to terminate partition and to set up one Parliament and one Government for the whole of Ireland. With a view to the eventual establishment of a single Parliament.... [3]

The concluding section of the Official Summary is headed "Refusal to 'Work the Act'"—and provision is made that if the Irish people will not accept this measure and put it into operation, then they will be completely deprived of all democratic government and placed under Crown Colony Government—i.e. the autocratic rule in which the people are permitted to have no real share. Crown Colony Government was at that time applied, especially on the African Continent, to countries regarded by Britain as not civilised. The last paragraph of the Summary reads:

> It will, therefore, be for Irishmen themselves to decide in the near future whether they will themselves take up the reins of Government in their own country or be ruled by the Government of the United Kingdom under a system analogous to Crown Colony Government. [4]

We have only to see the situation in Ireland as the Bill was

---

1 Hansard, 23 Dec. 1920, vol. cxxxvi, cols. 2253-4.
2 *Belfast Newsletter,* 3 Mar. 1921.
3 *Government of Ireland Act,* 1920. Summary of Main Provisions p. 2
4 Ibid., p. 8.

being discussed and passed to realise why it was necessary in the official documents and statements of the time to deceive the British Parliament and the people as to the effect of the Act of 1920 and officially to threaten the Irish people with the destruction of all self-government if they would not accept what the Act really offered—the dismemberment of Ireland. Had any considerable section, even, of the Irish people been in any degree favourable to the 1920 Act, neither the deception nor the threat would have been necessary.

The sequence of events was this: on 25 November 1918, the British Parliament was dissolved. A General Election was held on 14 December 1918, with the result already stated. The issue in Ireland was stated to the electors by the Sinn Fein movement without equivocation. It was set out as follows in the "Manifesto to the Irish People" issued by the Sinn Fein Standing Committee:

> Sinn Fein gives Ireland the opportunity of vindicating her honour and pursuing with renewed confidence the path of national salvation by rallying to the flag of the Irish Republic.
> Sinn Fein aims at securing the establishment of that Republic.

Among the methods to be adopted were the following:

> By withdrawing the Irish Representation from the British Parliament.... by the establishment of a constituent assembly comprising persons chosen by Irish constituencies as the supreme national authority to speak and act in the name of the Irish people.

The Manifesto, having condemned "the contemplated mutilation of our country by partition", asked the nation to elect

> the men who hold that Ireland must be as free as England or Holland or Switzerland or France and whose demand is that the only status befitting this ancient realm is the status of a free nation. [1]

This election manifesto was issued more than two months before polling day and was displayed in a thousand places throughout the nation.

The people overwhelmingly returned those pledged to independence. In pursuance of this mandate the first democratically elected Parliament ever to sit on Irish soil assembled in Dublin on 21 January 1919, and there proclaimed the full independence of Ireland. The Declaration of Independence contained those passages:

> Whereas the Irish people is by right a free people.... and whereas the Irish Republic was proclaimed in Dublin on Easter Monday

[1] Dorothy Macardle, *The Irish Republic*, p. 955.

1916 by the Irish Republican Army, acting on behalf of the Irish people,

And whereas the Irish people is resolved to secure and maintain its complete independence in order to promote the commonweal, to re-establish justice, to provide for future defence, to ensure peace at home and good will with all nations and to constitute a national policy based upon the people's will with equal opportunity for every citizen....

Now therefore we, the elected Representatives of the ancient Irish people in National Parliament assembled do, in the name of the Irish nation, ratify the establishment of the Irish Republic and pledge ourselves and our people to make this declaration effective by every means at our command.

We ordain that the elected Representatives of the Irish people alone have power to make laws binding on the people of Ireland and that the Irish Parliament is the only parliament to which that people will give its allegiance. [1]

The National Parliament, thus democratically established, elected a National Government and that Government was recognised by the Irish people as the only lawful authority in Ireland.

Lloyd George was not only aware of these facts, as his speeches when he announced the Partition Act in December, 1919, show. It is clear from the sequence of events that, in order to remove or diminish opposition to acceptance of the Act, he intensified military repression against the elected Irish government.

On 2 September 1919, Sir Edward Carson informed the Ulster Unionist Council that the Cabinet were "trying to make a settlement" of the Irish question. The decision had apparently been taken then to prepare a statute dismembering Ireland. On 10 September Dail Eireann, the elected Parliament of Ireland, was declared by a British military Proclamation to be an illegal body. On 20 September all Irish Republican papers were suppressed. In the first weeks of October a British Cabinet Committee of ten members presided over by the partitionist Lord Long was set up to prepare the details of the Irish "settlement". In the same two weeks 22 other Irish journals were suppressed.

On November 25, all Irish national organisations including Sinn Fein, the Gaelic League and the Gaelic Athletic Association were suppressed, and repression became so universal that Sir Herbert Samuel, M.P., a former British Cabinet Minister, was moved to say on 8 December 1919:

If what is now going on in Ireland had been going on in the

1 *Irish Historical Documents*, 1172—1922, Edited by Edmund Curtis and R.B. McDowell, pp. 318-9.

Austrian Empire all England would be ringing with denunciation of the tyranny of the Hapsburgs and of denying people the right to rule themselves.

On 17 December the *Westminster Gazette* said Ireland was "like a country invaded in time of war".

On 22 December Lloyd George announced in the House of Commons his intention to bring forward the Partition Act.

The Second Reading was not taken until 29 March 1920. Four days before that date there arrived in Ireland the first of the notorious terrorist corps known to history as the "Black and Tans" who put a new name for ferocity into the world's dictionaries. As the discussions went on in the Commons the glow of burning towns reddened the night skies of Ireland, and the prisons and the graves were filled with the people's national and local leaders, many of them killed outright after capture or executed by order of Courts martial. Their crime was participation in a resistance movement as noble, as self-sacrificial and as extensive as any in Europe during the Second World War. The final reading of the Bill was taken in November 1920. In that same month the former private army of Carson's—sectarian to a man and pledged to defeat the electoral demands of the majority —were, despite many excesses, officially enrolled and armed as part of the British Crown forces and turned loose upon the unhappy and unprotected Nationalist minority whom they regarded as an enemy in their midst.

The Act passed into law on 23 December 1920. It was brought into force during a period of sheer military terror on 19 April 1921. For a description of the state of Ireland between those dates we do not need to go to any Irishman or Irish source. Overwhelming testimony of it comes from spokesmen of the highest rank in Britain itself.

> In every part of Ireland that we visited we were impressed by the atmosphere of terrorism that prevailed.... We have no desire to overstate the facts; but the atmosphere of terrorism which has been created and the provocative behaviour of the armed servants of the Crown, quite apart from specific "reprisals" are sufficient in themselves to arouse in our hearts feelings of the deepest horror and shame. — Report of the British Labour Commission to Ireland. [1]
> We saw such a scene of wanton destruction of houses and shops that made me and members of the Commission ashamed of being

[1] Signed 28 Dec. 1920. Published Jan. 1921.

Englishmen. — Arthur Greenwood, British Labour Leader. [1]

Deeds have unquestionably been done by them (the Forces of the Crown) in Ireland which have lastingly disgraced the name of Britain in that country. British processes of justice which for centuries have commanded the admiration of the world have been supplanted by those of lynch law. — Editorial London *Times*. [2]

A system of vengeance had been established in Ireland and after what happened there he begged to hear no more talk about what the Germans did in Belgium. — Sir John Simon, British Liberal Leader. [3]

The British Government committed worse crimes in Ireland than Germany had ever committed in France. — General Sir Hubert Gough at Acton. [4]

Constitutional Government in Ireland has been suspended and a state of affairs prevails which is a disgrace to the British race. — Rt. Hon. A. Henderson M.P. (later Foreign Secretary). [5]

The treatment now being meted out to Irishmen was nothing more or less than indiscriminate vengeance. — Rt. Rev. Dr. Gore, Bishop of Oxford. [6]

There is a tendency to hesitate in regard to the impeachment of the Government.... Whatever may happen to the Government, it is the duty of Free Churchmen to protest against a policy which is at once illegal, unjust, ineffective and must be disastrous to Ireland and to this country. — Rev. Dr. Clifford, Non-Conformist Leader. [7]

I say deliberately that never in the lifetime of the oldest among us has Britain sunk so low in the moral scale of nations.... Things are being done in Ireland which would disgrace the blackest annals of the lowest despotism in Europe — Lord Oxford and Asquith. [8]

Proposing a Resolution at the National Council of Evangelical Free Churches at Manchester on 10 March 1921, condemning the indiscriminate use of force by British armed forces in Ireland, Rev. J. Scott Lidgett said:

> To give reign to lawlessness and indisciplined forces, to take matters into their own hands, to shoot at sight, to burn buildings, to reduce the whole system of the Government to chaos is the very worst application of force that can be imagined. The conscience of this country will not stand it and if it does, the conscience of the civilised world will rise up in judgement against us.

[1] At special British Labour Conference, 29 Dec. 1920, at Central Hall, Westminster.
[2] 29 Jan. 1921.
[3] At Sunderland, 29 Jan. 1921.
[4] Quoted in *Irish Independent*, 8 Feb. 1921.
[5] At Woolwich, 9 Feb. 1921.
[6] Reported in *Irish Independent*, 10 Feb. 1921.
[7] *Westminster Gazette*, 18 Feb. 1921.
[8] At Euston Theatre, 19 Feb. 1921.

Elections were held all over Ireland, in May 1921, to constitute the two Parliaments which had now by the means so graphically described by English leaders and English churchmen been imposed upon Ireland. Despite savage and universal repression of all who stood for a united and independent Ireland the people used the elections to reject the Partition Act with unanswerable emphasis. The "Southern Parliament" (whose area included Ireland's most northerly county, Donegal, and two other Ulster Counties together with most of the country) was to consist of 128 members. Of the 128 seats, the independence party won 124, leaving only the 4 Trinity College seats, secured on a limited register, to those ready to work the Act.

The "Northern Parliament" whose area omitted most of the Northern half of Ireland consisted of 52 seats. After a campaign of violence against the minority in that area in which Nationalist candidates, organisers, even election tally clerks were arrested, electoral literature seized and destroyed wholesale, and voters cruelly maltreated or prevented from entering the booths at all, the Unionists won 40 seats, leaving only 12 to the Nationalists.

Therefore, despite the "things that would disgrace the blackest annals of the lowest despotism in Europe" (Asquith's description), 136 seats were won out of a total of 180 in all Ireland by those who rejected Partition and who refused, in face of fearful penalties, to work the Act imposing it. That was a majority of 75.6 per cent, even greater than that which swept the independence party into power in 1918, and greater than any majority recorded in the history of the British Commons. The majority as a reflection of the people's will becomes greater if we omit the 12 University seats, for in these the electorate was limited to a few thousand graduates. On the popular vote 78.6 per cent of the deputies elected stood for the rejection of the Act which partitioned Ireland.

That Act never operated in the Twenty Six Counties, and it has operated in the Six Counties only by aid of a series of repressive measures continually restricting the freedom of the Nationalist minority. On 22 June 1951, the principal Tory newspaper in the partitioned area, the *Belfast Newsletter*, commemorated the thirty years of separate life of the Six County Parliament with an editorial. That editorial said:

> Thirty years ago to-day His Majesty King George the Fifth, accompanied by Queen Mary, formally opened the first Parliament of Northern Ireland.... Almost its first task was to deal with the

> state of grave disorder prevailing in 1921 and now thirty years afterwards it is pre-occupied with a Public Order Bill.

No statement by an Irish Nationalist could so succinctly record the failure of the Partition Act, even after a generation, to win the approval of the popular will.

This then is the Act which the Tory minority in Ireland now cite as its Charter. In the division accepting it not a single Irish vote was cast for it. It secured English votes on the pretence that it was a purely temporary measure dividing Ireland merely to ensure its speedy reunion.

> The late Government (said Austen Chamberlain at Birmingham on 1 November 1922) never affected to believe that the Act of 1920 could be permanent.

The Act was imposed by a powerful empire on the Irish people to the accompaniment of a ruthless use of the fire and sword, and in the first election held under it — and in every election since — it was emphatically rejected by almost 80 per cent of the Irish people. It is this British Act, condemned by every party in Ireland and inferentially condemned also and its permanence denied by its British sponsors, which is now solemnly put forward as validly constituting a State out of a fraction broken from the side of Ireland.

CHAPTER XII

THE TREATY SETTLEMENT

1. THE CORRESPONDENCE

AFTER THE IRISH people had rejected the Partition Act by an overwhelming majority, the struggle for independence went on. It was as part of the effort to defeat that struggle that the British Statute had divided Ireland. It enabled the British Government to deal with Ireland in two parts, and no limits were placed to the repression designed to force Ireland to accept this division.

Despite a ruthless military rule the Irish people held on to their determination to make the Irish nation an independent unit. In the end their resistance wore down British repression and, unable to break the people's will by force, the British Government proposed negotiations.

It is important to grasp the central point in these preliminaries to conference. In the Spring of 1921, Mr. Lloyd George through several channels made known to the Irish leaders his readiness to discuss peace. He indicated that he would be unable to confer on the basis of an independent Ireland, but if the Irish leaders would agree to accept British suzerainty, a settlement might be possible. The Irish reply was simply to declare that any conference should be held without any preliminary conditions whatever, adding that they were an elected Government and could not forego the independence their people had solemnly proclaimed.

Eventually on 24 June, the British Premier invited Mr. de Valera to a conference in London "as the chosen leader of the great majority in Southern Ireland". He also invited "Sir James Craig, Premier of Northern Ireland". Mr. de Valera replied saying he was consulting such "principal representatives of our nation as are available" — most of them were at that time in prison — but that while the Irish leaders most earnestly desired a lasting peace they "see no avenue by which it can be reached if you deny Ireland's essential unity". He informed the British Premier that he was seeking to confer with "certain representatives of the political minority in this country". Mr. de Valera as "spokesman of the Irish Nation" then invited leaders of the Unionists in the Six Counties and in the rest of Ireland to confer with him, saying to Sir James Craig, the Ulster leader:

> Irish political differences ought to be adjusted and can I believe be adjusted on Irish soil. But it is obvious that in negotiating peace with Great Britain the Irish delegation ought not to be divided but should act as a unit on some common principle. [1]

It was an appeal that in any nation free from outside interference would have been accepted. But the British had made the Six County leaders the agents of their own policy, and Sir James Craig, conscious of British backing in any intransigence he might wish to show, refused to meet the national leaders.

De Valera pursued his exchange of views with the representatives of the Unionists in the rest of Ireland, who readily conferred with him. He then informed the British Premier that, in response to the British Government's expressed desire "to end the centuries of conflict between the peoples of these two islands", he had "secured the views of the representatives of the minority of our nation" and now accepted the invitation to preliminary talks.

President de Valera with Arthur Griffith, Minister for Foreign Affairs, and other members of the Irish Government, went to London and met the British Premier on 14 July. On 19 July an interview given by Sir James Craig, whom the British Premier had also seen, was published. It implied that the Irish leader's negotiations were related solely "to that area outside which I am Prime Minister". De Valera wrote on the same day to Lloyd George making clear beyond any possible doubt on what basis the Irish were in consultation with him.

> You are aware (the letter said) that in meeting you in London I have been acting as the representative of Ireland in accordance with the mandate conferred upon me by the Irish people as a whole and that before accepting your invitation to come here I made perfectly clear that no conversations and conference were possible which would imply any denial of the essential right of the Irish people to full national self-determination.

He added that if the claim made by Sir James Craig were concurred in by the British Government, "there can be no purpose in pursuing our conversations", and before talks were resumed that he must ask the Premier if the British Government support-

[1] *Dáil Eireann; Official Correspondence relating to the Peace Negotiations,* June-Sept. 1921, p. 4.

ed Craig's view. Lloyd George replied that he was responsible neither for what Craig said nor for what was said by de Valera in reply.

On 20 July Lloyd George on behalf of the British Government presented to the Irish representatives the terms of a proposed settlement. Briefly they involved a form of self-government for Ireland subject to many limitations and to "full recognition of the existing powers and privileges of the Parliament of Northern Ireland which cannot be abrogated except by their own consent". De Valera declared the proposals to be wholly unacceptable. He consented, at the request of the British Premier, to give him a written reply. On 10 August the view of the Irish Cabinet, which had considered the proposals, was communicated officially to the British Premier. Having dealt with other short-comings in the proposals, the letter went on:

> As regards the question at issue between the political minority and the great majority of the Irish people, that must remain a question for the Irish people themselves to settle. We cannot admit the right of the British Government to mutilate our country either in its own interest or at the call of any section of our population. We do not contemplate the use of force. If your Government stands aside we can affect a complete reconciliation. [1]

Its members having been released from British prisons, Dáil Eireann, the Parliament of Ireland, assembled in Dublin on August 16 and approved the Cabinet's rejection of the British proposals. In the course of that session, the head of the Irish Government said of the minority that he wanted to tell them

> We have no enmity to them, because they are Irishmen living in Ireland, and that we were ready to make sacrifices (for them) we could never think of making for Britain. [2]

The efforts to find a basis for an Anglo-Irish Conference continued. The British strove to get the Irish to accept a prior recognition of British supremacy and of the division of Ireland. The Irish were determined to enter no conference in which they were not free to maintain the independence and unity of Ireland. At last, at the end of September, the British agreed to a conference on the simple non-conditional formula:

> with a view to ascertaining how the association of *Ireland* with the community of nations known as the British Empire may best be reconciled with Irish national aspirations. [3]

[1] Ibid., p. 11.
[2] Dáil Debates, 17 Aug. 1921, vol. 2, p. 14.
[3] *Dáil Eireann: Official Correspondence relating to the Peace Negotiations,* June-Sept., 1921, p. 22.

On 11 October 1921, the Anglo-Irish Conference began. The resistance of the mass of the Irish people to the partition of their country and their determination to undo it had by then been made clear to everybody concerned in the talks.

ii. THE NEGOTIATIONS

The negotiations in London between the two delegations lasted for seven weeks. The Irish delegates were led by Arthur Griffith, Minister for Foreign Affairs, and Michael Collins, Minister for Finance.

It was appreciated by the Irish Government that British statesmen were naturally concerned with the strategic position of Ireland in relation to Britain. It was realized also that as the British had in fact exploited the minority opposition to self-government for their own ends, they were concerned now with the fate of that minority. To meet these two difficulties the Irish Cabinet had decided

> 1. that in return for recognition by Britain of a united Ireland in full charge of its national affairs, the Irish Government would enter into a Treaty of "External Association" with the British Commonwealth in matters of common concern, including defence; and,
>
> 2. that the minority in Ireland located in North-east Ulster (where they formed a local majority) would receive local autonomy under the National Parliament and that that autonomy would be at least as substantial as that given them by Britain in the Act of 1920. The minority would also be fully represented in the National Parliament.

The discussions in London reached a point where the British undertook that, if the Irish delegation would accept a settlement in which Ireland would remain in the Commonwealth and acknowledge the suzerainty of the Imperial Parliament, Britain would recognise a united Ireland as a self-governing State. The British further undertook that if the minority did not accept that proposition, the Six Counties excluded by the 1920 Act would have their boundaries redrawn and suffer the loss of all those areas which in a plebiscite decided by majority to remain under the National Parliament in Dublin.

In the final instrument drawn up in the form of Heads of Agreement for a Treaty (afterwards known as the Treaty) between Ireland and Britain, and signed by the Irish and British delegations on 6 December 1921, this proposal is set out in Article XII. That Article declares that if within one month of the passing of the Act ratifying the Treaty the Six County Government decided to exclude themselves from the jurisdiction of the National Parliament,

> A Commission consisting of three persons, one to be appointed by the Government of the Irish Free State, one to be appointed by the Government of Northern Ireland, and one who shall be Chairman, to be appointed by the British Government, shall determine, in accordance with the wishes of the inhabitants, so far as may be compatible with economic and geographic conditions, the boundaries between Northern Ireland and the rest of Ireland, and for the purposes of the Government of Ireland Act, 1920, and of this instrument, the boundary of Northern Ireland shall be such as may be determined by such Commission.

The Irish delegation were slow to accept the fundamental change in the constitutional position of Ireland which inclusion of their country in the Commonwealth would involve. They were eventually persuaded by the British Premier to do so by two methods.

The first was a series of promises and assertions that if the Irishmen signed the Treaty the operation of Article XII would bring such large areas out of the partitioned North-east as must make the continued separate existence of that State impossible. Even on 5 December the Irish delegates still doubted that this would be the effect of Article XII. On that morning Michael Collins saw Lloyd George alone. The promises he then received decided Collins's action in signing the Treaty. Mr. Frank Pakenham (later Lord Pakenham, First Lord of the Admiralty in Mr. Attlee's Government) has the following passage in his book on the Anglo-Irish negotiations:

> If it had not been for expectations from the Boundary Commission held out to him on the last morning, Michael Collins would never have agreed to sign and there would have been no Treaty. Collins' memorandum written immediately after his interview with Lloyd George and some hours before signature of the Treaty records what after two months of discusssion centring perhaps around this clause more than any other the Irish believed they would get from it " . . . we would save Tyrone and Fermanagh, parts of Derry, Armagh and Down by the Boundary Commission . . . Lloyd George remarked that I myself pointed out on a previous occasion that the North would be forced economically to come in." [1]

[1] Frank Pakenham, *Peace by Ordeal*, p. 323.

By convincing the leaders of the Irish delegation that this was the correct and indeed the only possible interpretation of Article XII and must lead to the unity of Ireland, the British Premier had removed much of their hesitancy.

He then employed his second method to secure the signing of the Treaty by all the Irish delegates. This was to face them with an ultimatum: either all signed within two and a half hours or the British would resume "immediate and terrible War" against the Irish people. There have been many descriptions of the delivery of this ultimatum. The latest is by the Rt. Hon. Sir Geoffrey Shakespeare himself, at the time one of the secretaries of the British Cabinet, who in a book published in 1949, says,

> About seven thirty Lloyd George delivered his ultimatum. The Irish delegates, he said, were plenipotentiaries and must sign now. If they refused to sign war would follow immediately. [1]

The Irish delegates, Sir Geoffrey goes on, "bowed to it (the ultimatum) and signed."

Mr. George Gavan Duffy, one of the Irish signatories, later to be Foreign Minister and afterwards President of the High Court of Ireland, in the debates in Dáil Eirann described the position into which the Irish delegates were put by the ultimatum:

> the alternative to our signing that particular Treaty was immediate war ... we had to make this choice within three hours and to make it without reference to our Cabinet, to our Parliament or to our people ... We lost the Republic of Ireland in order to save the people of Ireland. [2]

III. ARTICLE XII

The events in Ireland which followed the signing of the Treaty are well known and need only the briefest reference.

[1] *Let Candles be Brought in,* p. 86.
Mr. Shakespeare, who was the companion and confidant of Lloyd George in these tense days and dined with him alone after the delivery of the Ultimatum on Monday evening, 5 Dec., records on pp. 85-6 of the same book: Through the persuasion of Tom Jones he (Lloyd George) secured an interview with Michael Collins alone early on Monday morning. Apparently he was able to satisfy him (Collins) on several points and in particular as to the probability of a Boundary Commission enlarging the territory of Southern Ireland by adding to it parts of Fermanagh and Tyrone. Lloyd George believed this would be the outcome of an impartial inquiry.... On December 16 during the debate he implied that both would be apportioned to the South.
[2] Dáil Debates, 21 Dec. 1921, vol. ii, p. 87.

A majority in Dáil Eireann, 64 to 57, voted to approve the Treaty. Many of the 64 had been told of the British Premier's interpretation of Article XII, and declared they so voted because they had become convinced that its implementation must lead to unity. The influence this single Article had on securing a majority for the Treaty was stated three years later by the then Governor General of Ireland, His Excellency, T. M. Healy. Mr. Healy, writing on 15 March 1924 on behalf of the Irish Government to the British Secretary of State for the Colonies, demanded the setting up of the Boundary Commission to implement Article XII. He referred to the gerrymandering of the local government constituencies which had just been carried out in the Six Counties in order to disfranchise large Nationalist areas and went on:

> My Ministers feel that the effect of a further postponement would be to deprive of the benefits of the Treaty those persons whose interest Clause XII, *without which the Treaty would never have been accepted,* was specially designed to protect. [1]

As will be seen when Article XII came to be implemented, Mr. Lloyd George and other British signatories of the Treaty pressed a wholly different interpretation of the Article on the public. But the contemporaneous statements of the Treaty signatories both British and Irish made clear what meaning they attached to it when it was being signed.

Michael Collins in an article to the *Hearst Press* in the United States of America (reprinted in the Irish newspapers on 13 March 1922) confirmed that what the Irish delegation was promised was the re-unification of Ireland through the operation of Article XII.

> Forces of persuasion and pressure are embodied in the Treaty of Peace which has been signed by the Irish and British plenipotentiaries to induce North East Ulster to join a United Ireland. If they join in, the Six Counties will certainly have a generous measure of local autonomy. If they stay out the decision of the Boundary Commission arranged for in Clause XII would be certain to deprive Ulster of Tyrone and Fermanagh. Shorn of these counties she would shrink into insignificance. The burdens and financial restrictions of the Partition Act will remain on North East Ulster if she decides to stay out. No lightening of these burdens or restrictions can be effected by the English Parliament without the consent of Ireland. [2]

---

[1] Cmd. 2155.
[2] Michael Collins, *The Path to Freedom,* p. 95.

On 6 December 1921, a few hours after the Treaty was signed, the Earl of Birkenhead, one of the British signatories, made a speech at Birmingham. He referred to an incident a few days before where the members of the Tyrone County Council were refused admission to the Council Offices, following an edict from the Belfast Government suppressing this chief representative body in a nationalist county. Lord Birkenhead said:

> We propose that a Boundary Commission shall examine into the boundary lines with the view of rendering impossible such an unhappy incident as that of a few days ago in which the popularly elected bodies of one or two of those districts were excluded from their habitations by representatives of the Central Government of Northern Ireland on the ground that they were not discharging their duties properly. [1]

A comment by a writer in the *Northern Whig*, one of the Unionist daily papers published in Belfast, referred to Birkenhead's speech and pointed the moral:

> What would any eager Sinn Feiner or any moderately vigilant Unionist imply from such a statement except that the effect of Clause 12 would be to transfer the County of Tyrone to the Free State.

The British delegation had during the negotiations led the Irish delegates to understand that one of the objects of the settlement was to restore the unity of Ireland. Less than a month before the Treaty was signed, Lloyd George had written to Sir James Craig, who had become Prime Minister of the Six County

---

[1] London *Times,* 7 Dec. 1921.
In a remarkable speech in the House of Lords on 9 Dec. 1925, the Earl of Birkenhead, one of the leaders of the British delegation, confessed in careful words that the Treaty was signed by the Irish delegation in the belief that Article XII would decisively alter the Boundary. He too confirmed that without that reading of Article XII the Treaty would not have been signed at all:
"Does any one think so lightly of the capacity of those who signed that Treaty (Lord Birkenhead asked) as to imagine that they were not alive to the dangers of Article XII? I state plainly to your Lordships that there was no signatory of that Treaty but knew that in Article XII here lurked the elements of dynamite. We knew it well. It was forced upon us in this sense, that whether it was for good or for bad that that Treaty should be signed, it never could have been signed, it never would have been signed, without Article XII.... Supposing that we had proposed to those who sat on the other side of the table at No. 10, Downing Street, to stereotype the existing boundary, what do you think the prospects would have been of a settlement?" (Hansard, House of Lords, 9 Dec. 1925, vol. lxii, cols. 1232-3).

Government under the 1920 Act. In a letter dated 10 November 1921, Lloyd George informed him that in the settlement for which His Majesty's Government was then working,

> The unity of Ireland would be recognised by the establishment of an all-Ireland Parliament upon which would be devolved the further powers necessary to form the self-governing Irish State. [1]

Referring to the area under the jurisdiction of the Six County Parliament he made it clear that unless an all-Ireland Parliament came into being that area must be delimited.

Sir James replied that "the possible unity of Ireland" was provided for in the clause of the 1920 Act setting up a Council of Ireland and, for the rest, the Six Counties stood on its rights under that Act and would not even discuss an all-Ireland Parliament. He claimed that the 1920 Act finally defined the Six County area as belonging to the State of which he was now head. On 14 November Lloyd George replied strongly, emphasising that the restoration of Ireland's unity was one of the very purposes for which the London talks were being held. He declared:

> All experience proves, moreover, that so complete a partition of Ireland as you propose must militate with increasing force against that ultimate unity which you yourself hope will one day be possible. The existing state of Central and South-Eastern Europe is a terrible example of the evils which spring from the creation of new frontiers, cutting the natural circuits of commercial activity; but when once such frontiers are established, they harden into permanence. Your proposal would stereotype a frontier based neither upon natural features nor broad geographical considerations by giving it the character of an international boundary. Partition on these lines the majority of the Irish people will never accept, nor could we conscientiously attempt to enforce it. It would be fatal to that purpose of a lasting settlement on which these negotiations from the very outset have been steadily directed. [2]

In view of Lloyd George's change of front when the terms of Article XII came to be implemented, it has been held that these letters to Sir James Craig, and his pledges to the heads of the Irish delegation in the same sense, were merely intended to deceive. What is important, however, is to establish the nature of the agreement to which the Irish signatories put their names and to discover what their country was bound to by their act.

When the Treaty and the consequential legislation arising

---

[1] *Handbook of the Ulster Question,* p. 31.
[2] Ibid., p. 33.

from it came before the British Parliament, the Premier and the other British signatories were faced with a strong Tory group, not all from North-east Ulster, who had been angered by Article XII. To placate them, Lloyd George, Churchill and others minimised the concessions made in regard to the final extent of the area to be cut off. It is clear, however, from even those guarded statements that they believed that the effect of the Boundary delimitation would be to restore at least two counties to Nationalist Ireland. Speaking on 14 December 1921, Lloyd George said:

> There is no doubt—certainly since the Act of 1920—that the majority of the people of the two counties (Tyrone and Fermanagh) prefer being with their southern neighbours to being in the Northern Parliament. Take it either by constituency or by Poor Law Unions or, if you like, by counting heads and you will find that the majority of these two counties prefer to be with their Southern neighbours. What does that mean? If Ulster is to remain a separate community you can, only by means of coercion, keep them there and although I am against the coercion of Ulster, I do not believe in Ulster coercing other units. [1]

In the same speech he instanced what was meant by the phrase in Article XII "geographical and economic considerations" by citing the case of the Glens of Antrim. There, he said, was a little Nationalist area completely cut off from the rest of Ireland by districts in majority Tory.

> Nobody proposes because the numbers there would be in favour of joining the South that they should be taken away from the North and put into the South. [2]

This first speech of the principal British negotiator after the signing of the Treaty confirmed what Collins recorded. It is true that in the course of this and other speeches both Lloyd George and Churchill denied they had given pledges or undertakings to the Irish signatories as to how Article XII would be operated. Clearly they were sheltering behind the technical meaning of the words they used. They had not given formal undertakings or put their pledges into writing, but it was obvious they had given them.

In addition to the direct statements of Birkenhead, Collins and Lloyd George which we have quoted, Churchill and Austen Chamberlain indicated in cautious language that the Boundary

---

1 Hansard, 14 Dec. 1921, vol. cxlix, col. 40.
2 Ibid., col. 41.

Commission was to operate to release areas in which Nationalists were in a majority.

Austen Chamberlain, speaking in the Commons two days after Lloyd George, emphasised that the areas which it was envisaged the Boundary Commission might deal with were those in which one or other of two parties had majorities.

> What we have proposed (he said) and what the Commission is required to do is to revise the boundary between North and South so as to include, where possible, having regard to economic and geographical considerations, men now excluded from the Government of Northern Ireland who would wish to come under it and to exclude from Northern Ireland men now included in it who would wish to come out of it. [1]

As there were spacious areas in the Six Counties with strong Nationalist majorities and only a few Tory pockets outside the Six County area, Chamberlain's description of the Boundary Commission's functions bore out Lloyd George's and Birkenhead's description.

The whole matter was debated again in the British House of Commons in February 1922, and in that debate other British signatories spoke. One was Winston Churchill, who spoke on 16 February. With his usual eloquence he told the House that in 1914 at the Buckingham Palace Conference there was no settlement because the inclusion of Tyrone and Fermanagh in the separated area would not be accepted by the Nationalist leaders. A great war had intervened and here again more than seven years later they were faced with the identical problem—the fate of Tyrone and Fermanagh and of parishes and districts inside those two counties. With obvious circumspection he went on:

> Certain of these districts in Fermanagh and Tyrone, even in the county boundary, may be districts in which—I am not prejudging— the majority of the inhabitants will prefer to join the Irish Free State. If that be true, and to the extent to which that is true, one

[1] Hansard, 16 Dec. 1921, vol. cxlix, cols. 357-8

In the same speech he indicated that a vital concession had been made to the Irish delegates which created an opportunity for agreement that had to be seized at once:

I understand how sensitive they (the Six County leaders) may fairly be on the subject, and how strong are their feelings. No one regrets it more than I do ... To have held up at that last moment ... the Articles of Agreement which were then ready for signature and which the Irish representatives were prepared to sign would have been to jeopardise, and in my opinion to destroy, all chance of an agreement (Hansard, 16 Dec. 1921, vol. cxlix, col 357).

Lafayette, Dublin

Eamon de Valera (b. 1882)

Arthur Griffith (1871-1922)

Keystone, Lo

Lord Craigavon arriving in Downing Street in 1938 to confer with Mr Neville Chamberlain. At that time he admitted privately that partition could not last. "In this island we cannot live always separated from one another. We are too small to be apart or for the border to be there for all time. The change will not come in my time but it will come!"

feels that the tremendous arguments which protect the freedom of Protestant Ulster have, in those districts, lost their applicaiton and have possibly an opposite application.... The Boundary Commission to be set up under Article XII affects the existing frontiers of the Ulster Government and may conceivably affect them prejudicially. It is far better to face facts and not to gloss them over. To that extent Ulster may have a ground of complaint against the Government. What is the answer the Government will make?.... We were bound, we considered ourselves bound, to try to reach a settlement. Had we waited to refer the details of that settlement at the last moment to the Northern Government, it is quite evident by what occurred in the Dail and by the violent opposition encountered there, that no settlement would have been achieved at all. Therefore, we agreed to the Boundary Commission. We agreed to it with, no doubt, a feeling that the argumentative position in this country in regard to some of those districts in Fermanagh and Tyrone was not as strong as in regard to what is characteristically the Protestant part.... There is no doubt whatever that we felt the difficulty in this matter. [1]

Churchill is here saying in words chosen with the greatest care that on the day the Treaty was signed the British negotiators agreed that Tyrone and Fermanagh should be liberated from the partitioned area. He indicates that a major concession had to be made on that date or the Treaty would never have been signed. And he draws a graphic picture for the House of what would have happened: Britain "sore-pressed with burdens, with threats, with menaces in every quarter of the world" if she had had to break off the conference, "destroy the negotations and embark on what was literally the reconquest of Ireland at enormous expense in money and men..." [2] It is obvious he is justifying a considerable surrender. He makes clear that the British had to yield because they had no arguments against the release of Tyrone and Fermanagh—for his use of the words "districts" is only to sugar the pill for the Ulster Tory M.P.s— and that they now expected the Boundary Commission to carry out what the signatories intended by the words of Article XII.

The gravity of Churchill's words, the admission that a matter of great consequence "prejudicial to Ulster" had been agreed between the British and Irish delegations and that that concession on the British side secured the signing of the Treaty—all that rules out the assertions made three years later that nothing was intended by Article XII but a mere minor alteration of the boundary line here and there.

[1] Hansard, 16 Feb. 1922, vol. cl, cols. 1271-2.
[2] Hansard, 16 Feb. 1922, vol. cl, col. 1272.

Another British signatory, Sir Worthington Evans, gave his view on the following day, 17 February. The main purpose of his speech was to placate the indignant Ulster Tories, and he minimised the Boundary Commission's area of operations to the border districts, but he stressed that the decision would be carried out by plebiscite.

> I propose to try and deal quite frankly with the House and show the House exactly what was in my mind when I, as one of the signatories to that Treaty, put my signature to it. I said at Liverpool that I would not be a party to coercion of Ulster. How can a Boundaries Commission be a coercion of Ulster? What have the commissioners got to do? They have got to consult the wishes of the inhabitants and to decide, after having consulted the inhabitants, and, subject to the economical and geographical limitations, whether this or that area is to be included in the North or the South. Is action in accordance with the wishes of the inhabitants coercion? Surely it is the very opposite of coercion! How can you get at an agreed settlement, how can you get at something which is agreeable to people without consulting them. If you consult them and follow their wishes how can that be said to be coercion? [1]

Sir Worthington Evans's speech did not placate the Ulster Tories.
They knew, as the signatories to the Treaty also knew (for the Irish delegates had supplied the British with a whole series of population and electoral maps), that, as Lloyd George had said, whatever electoral division was chosen the Nationalists had majorities not only along the Border, but deep into the partitioned area. Sir Worthington's speech establishes that the British signatories interpreted Article XII as providing for a regular consultation of the wishes of the people—i.e. a plebiscite by areas and a delimitation of the boundary in accordance with such plebiscite.

Yet another British signatory of the Treaty, Sir Gordon Hewart, Attorney General, speaking on 16 February, refused as a Law Officer of the Crown to give an interpretation of Article XII. He spoke, however, of the wishes of the inhabitants having to be determined "by suitable methods and with the help of appropriate machinery", which clearly indicated the plebiscite that the Irish delegation asserted they were promised. From the speeches of these six British signatories it can, therefore, be established that the facts were as stated in the Collins memorandum of 5 December after he had seen Lloyd George.

[1]   Hansard, 17 Febr. 1922, vol. cl, col. 1391.

Nor was the wording of Article XII (as was afterwards pretended) contrary to the transfer of considerable territories, such as two whole counties, if the Commission, having ascertained the wishes of the inhabitants, so decided. The Ulster Tory M.P.s fought the passage of the Agreement through Parliament persistently and bitterly on this particular point.

On 14 December 1921, their leader, Captain C. C. Craig, said in the Commons that the operation of Article XII

> may mean that our Northern areas will be so cut up and mutilated that we shall no longer be masters in our own house. The decision of that Commission may be a matter of life and death to us. [1]

Major O'Neill, another Ulster Tory M.P., speaking two days later, said the wording of Article XII made him wonder if the Prime Minister said to the Irish delegates:

> 'There are two counties in Northern Ireland where you have a majority. We will appoint a Boundary Commissioner and he is bound to give you those two Counties, for you have got a majority there and you may be quite sure that you will get them.' Did he put it to the delegates in such a way as to make them think that what he wished to do was to give them those two counties in respect to which they have had longings for some time past. [2]

On 8 February Captain Craig again emphasised the wide nature of the powers in relation to transfer of territory which Article XII gave to the Boundary Commission. The Article, he said,

> set up a Commission, of which an Englishman was to be the chairman and to have a casting vote, practically to play ducks and drakes with the territory which had been handed to Ulster a few months before by the Act of 1920. [3]

Mr. Ronald MacNeill, a leading Tory M.P. who was a strong opponent of Irish nationalism, spoke with anxiety of Article XII. He feared its strict legal interpretation, which he obviously believed must mean the transfer of large Nationalist areas to the National Parliament. Speaking in the Commons on 3 March 1922, he said:

> It is well known that when an Act of Parliament is cited before a court of law the judge will not take into consideration anything but the actual language of the Statute.... Is that rule to be followed by th 'Commission to be set up or not? If so, it makes the

1 Hansard, 14 Dec. 1921, vol. cxlix, cols. 56-7.
2 Hansard, 16 Dec. 1921, vol. cxlix, col. 314.
3 Hansard, 8 Feb. 1922, vol. cl, col. 192.

gravity of the case very much greater.... we shall have the bare
terms of Clause XII put before a judicial tribunal. [1]

On the same day, Captain C. C. Craig intervened again to stress
the powers of the Boundary Commission to which he and his
colleagues took such exception. He described it as "a Boundary
Commission which may hand over large portions of our territory
to Southern Ireland".

The quotations have been given with such fulness because
they put beyond doubt something that is of first importance to
the whole Partition controversy. The Treaty of 1921 has been
cited as one of the documents giving the Irish minority its title
deeds to the Six County area. The Treaty in fact was accepted
by the Irish signatories on the promise given by the British
Premier and his colleagues that it would so greatly reduce the
partitioned area as to make its continued separate existence
impossible, and so lead to unity. After the Irish acceptance of
the document had been secured by this British promise, it was
not unusual, in British practice, for the terms of the undertaking
to be altered in order to meet Tory prejudices. We have seen that
happen on several previous occasions, notably in regard to the
1916 proposals and the 1917 Convention. But the contemporary
evidence that such an undertaking was given is overwhelming.

There are Lloyd George's letters to Sir James Craig prior to
the signing. There is Collins's memorandum drawn up on 5
December, immediately after the interview with Lloyd George
which led to the signing of the Treaty. There is the embarrassed
British effort to steer this Article on to the Statute Book, now
evasive, now contradictory, but all the time evidently defending
a major concession to the Irish point of view, but unwilling in a
hostile House to admit how big that concession really was, and
indeed trying all the time to represent the changes of territory
envisaged as trifling. There is Churchill's fearful opening of
his first references to Article XII:

> I come to the difficult part of what I have to say to the House.
> I come to the question of the Boundary Commission. [2]

There is the same statesman's blunt admission that the concession contained in the Article was so important that it secured
the unwilling Irish delegations' signatures, and that there and
then the bargain had to be rushed through lest the chance that
was bought by this promise of the transfer of large territories

[1] Hansard, 3 Mar. 1922, vol. cli, cols. 733-4.
[2] Hansard, 16 Febr. 1922, vol. cl, col. 1269.

should never recur. And finally there is the clear interpretation of the meaning of Article XII by those most affected by it, the Ulster Tories. They themselves repeatedly described the Article as permitting, at a minimum, the two counties of Tyrone and Fermanagh to vote themselves under the National Parliament.

IV. THE BOUNDARY COMMISSION

It was not until three years after the Treaty was signed that the most important clause of all, from the point of view of the Irish signatories, was seriously taken up by the British. The causes of delay are more than usually interesting when studied in retrospect.

The British had admitted that the wording of Article XII made important concessions to those desiring Ireland's unity. They now appeared anxious to postpone the Boundary Commission that was to carry out the terms of that article. They knew the attitude of the minority in Ireland to the Commission almost immediately. As early as 14 December 1921, Sir James Craig indicated that he would have nothing to do with the Boundary Commission, and long before any attempt was made to establish that Commission, he had many times emphasised that this decision would be persisted in. He was encouraged, if not actually inspired, in this attitude by several of the British political leaders:

> James Craig came to see me in the (War) Office before lunch (writes Field Marshal Sir Henry Wilson in his diary on 8 February 1922). He and I discussed at length what his refusal to take part in the Boundary Commission would mean and we both agreed it would be the right course. [1]

Lord Derby, then Secretary for War in the British Cabinet, visited the Six Counties in April 1923 [2] and in a speech at Enniskillen made it clear that Sir James Craig would have the help of the British Army in any stand he might adopt. In the following September, Sir Montague Barlow, Minister for Labour in the British Cabinet, also spoke at Enniskillen and approved in only slightly veiled terms the attitude taken up by the Six County Unionists. A final example was the speech of Sir Laming Worthington-Evans, himself one of the British signatories of

[1] Caldwell, *Field Marshal Sir Henry Wilson*, p. 325.
[2] See *Irish Times*, 10 Apr. 1923.

the Treaty, who declared at Lexden, near Colchester, on 26 September 1924, without any ambiguity, that he approved Sir James Craig's refusal to appoint a Boundary Commissioner. This refusal, particularly as it had the support of one of the great British parties, is significant.

The Boundary Commission was an essential part of the Treaty. The Treaty had become British law. The Tory Party, through its leaders and its votes in the Commons, was instrumental in negotiating and ratifying it. Now they encouraged a breach of the law which threatened to negative the outstanding reason why the Treaty was signed by the Irish representatives. The Ulster leader and his supporters believed at this time (and were so advised by Counsel) that a simple refusal by them to nominate their member of the Commission would invalidate the whole clause and render it inoperative. They took this step, and in taking it they again disclosed their belief that if Article XII were fairly interpreted the partitioned area would be substantially reduced.

Soon a second step in this effort to put aside Article XII was taken. This time it was British signatories themselves who were the initiators. As Churchill disclosed in the Commons on 16 February 1922, [1] they pressed upon the Irish signatories that the month, at the end of which the Six County Government would have to decide whether to remain in or out of the Irish State, should run not from the date on which the British Parliament ratified the Treaty, i.e. December 1921, but from the date on which the consequential legislation arising from the Treaty should have been passed by that Parliament. The Irish demurred, but eventually, though recording their opposition, agreed in the interests of that unity which they expected from the operation of the Article. They had no reason to detect at that early stage that one of the grounds on which the Boundary Commission would eventually come to its decision was that the Six Counties had already been several years in existence as a State and it would now be wrong to disturb its administration by area changes.

Even when, in January 1923, the Six County Government formally opted out of the Irish State, the British showed no anxiety to go ahead with the implementation of Article XII. Pressure from the Irish side was met with evasion and recitals of difficulties. The correspondence which was published as a

[1] Hansard, 16 Feb. 1922, vol. cl, cols. 1274-5.

White Paper in June 1924 [1] begins with a letter from the Governor General of the Irish Free State dated 19 July 1923 saying that Dr. Eoin MacNeill had been appointed the Irish Government's member on the Commission. The British in reply proposed a conference which did not meet until February 1924 and after one session adjourned to April, when it ended without an agreement. The case was submitted by Britain to the Privy Council.

Meanwhile, a still more disturbing development than that of delay had manifested itself. It has been shown that the promises to the Irish delegation were that Nationalist areas would be restored to the jurisdiction of the National Government. The British Government soon afterwards were officially informed of the intention of the Belfast leaders not to conform to the law which had been passed giving legal force to the Treaty. Nevertheless, the British government began to arm and equip the Special Constabulary in the Six County area. That special constabulary was the old sectarian army raised by Sir Edward Carson from his following in the area. To arm it meant that there was placed at the disposal of Sir James Craig by the British Government a force by which he could prevent the fulfilment of a Treaty signed by members of the British Government.

The arming was carried out under the plea of "protecting the interests of Ulster". It happened that during all this period a pogrom was raging in Belfast. [2] As in the past, whenever Ireland looked like winning its way to freedom, a diversion was attemped wherever the Orangemen were strongest. The Nationalist minority was set upon. Nationalist workers were driven from their work-places. They were attacked in the streets and in their homes. Ghastly murders were carried out by Orange fanatics. In one case a whole Catholic family (the MacMahons of Belfast) unarmed, defenceless, were done to death on the night of 23 March 1922, by a raiding party, the youngest of six children, who hid himself, alone escaping. The Nationalists appealed for protection from the authorities, but the authorities were now their political enemies, and protection was denied. The *Manchester Guardian* commented that

> envenomed politicians in the Ulster Parliament are voting themselves power to use torture and capital punishment against citizens

[1] Cmd. 2155.
[2] For a full describtion and details of these Belfast pogroms see G. B. Kenna, *Facts and Figures of the Belfast Pogrom, 1920-22.*

whom they forbid to defend themselves while they scarcely attempt to protect them from massacre. [1]

The Nationalists' homes, unofficially raided with murderous intent by Orangemen now become Constables, were officially raided by British troops in search of the weapons by which alone they could defend their lives. The Ulster Nationalist leader Joseph Devlin M.P. protested fruitlessly in the British Commons. Citing many murders of his unprotected people, he said:

> If Catholics have no revolvers to protect themselves they are murdered. If they have revolvers they are flogged and sentenced to death. [2]

In the Commons on 21 March Churchill made it clear who were the aggressors and who the victims of this progrom. There were, of course, Nationalists who would not submit to murder and who struck back and caused the deaths of those who came to take their lives. But, although the Catholic population in Belfast was outnumbered by four to one, Churchill told the Commons:

> Considerably more Catholics have been killed and wounded than Protestants.[3]

It was the day of his father Lord Randolph Churchill all over again; and now, as then, any impartial report of the excesses was "not pleasant reading and proved when finally published damaging to the Orange party". Yet now, as in 1848, it was the Orange party that Britain set out to strengthen and actually to enrol in the armed forces of the Crown, even against the Irish majority with whom so recently a Treaty had been signed promising peace and the restoration of Irish unity.

Lord Birkenhead, Lord Chancellor of England, announced in the House of Lords on 22 March 1922 that in addition to thirteen battalions of British troops in the Six Counties:

> There are some 15,000 men in the various police forces who have been equipped with rifles by the British Government. [4]

[1] *Manchester Guardian,* 25 Mar. 1922.
[2] Hansard, 28 Mar. 1922, vol. clii, col. 1286.
[3] Hansard, 21 Mar. 1922, vol. clii, col. 212.
[4] The full passage is: "Certainly we as a Government have not been lacking in proper exertions to protect the interests of Ulster. There are at this moment in Ulster thirteen battalions, not indeed at full strength, of British troops who are there for that purpose and there are some 15,000 men in the various police forces in Ulster who have been equipped with rifles by the British Government in order that they may be effective for protective purposes should intervention become necessary and we are constantly giving pecuniary subventions and assistance to Ulster." Hansard, House of Lords, 22 Mar. 1922, vol. xlix, cols, 728-9.

Churchill on 21 March 1922 in the Commons put the number to be equipped at 25,000. Later he announced the number as 35,000. [1]

Every one of these Special Constables was anti-Nationalist. Worse still, they were in vast majority fanatically anti-Catholic. Members of the force were at the moment of Churchill's speech engaged in assaulting and harassing the Catholic minority. Yet the British Government was arming and organising them at the British taxpayers' cost to the tune of millions of pounds, although the intentions of their leaders had been made plain— they would resist the operation of a British Statute.

v. OVERAWING THE COMMISSION

On 5 June 1924, it was announced in the Commons that the British Government had appointed Mr. Justice Feetham of the South African Supreme Court to be Chairman of the Boundary Commission. Mr. Feetham began his career as "one of the brilliant band of young Oxford Tories whom Lord Milner induced to go to South Africa". [2] Before a week had passed a campaign was opened in the British Press to influence this newly appointed Commissioner.

A party of British M.P.s toured the border areas in the Six Counties from 8 June to 10 June being received everywhere by representatives of the Partitionist minority. They visited several Tory and Orange Halls; and in the towns they passed through, a lavish display of Union Jacks had been arranged. The Nationalist city of Derry was the starting point of the tour, and, says the *Irish Independent,*

> good care was taken that they did not come in touch with anyone holding Nationalist opinions. They were shepherded by the chiefs of the Special Constabulary and the heads of the local Unionist Party. [3]

In 1922, as explained in detail elsewhere in this book, the Belfast Government had altered the electoral divisions in practically every local-government constituency throughout the Six County area. The purpose of the alteration was to take from the Nationalist majorities, especially in the border counties, their control of the local councils. At the same time and for the same

---

[1] Hansard, 21 Mar. 1922, vol. clii, col. 211.
[2] Political correspondent, London *Daily Herald,* 10 June 1924.
[3] *Irish Independent,* 11 June 1924.

purpose the electoral system was altered; and in the elections of 1923, fifteen public bodies, including Derry Corporation, Enniskillen Borough Council, Armagh and Omagh Urban Councils, two County Councils and nine Rural Councils which had Nationalist majorities were either abolished altogether or turned into Councils under Unionist control.

These Councils were in areas in which the Nationalists still had a majority on the voters' lists or of voting age. It was those deliberately fabricated Unionist Councils which entertained the visiting M.P.s and represented to them that the Border areas were for Partition too! Although they travelled through Fermanagh and Tyrone, where no less than ten Nationalist Councils had just been gerrymandered out of existence, they were not introduced to a single representative there of the Nationalist majority. The ruse was successful. The British M.P.s made a series of speeches declaring that the Border areas were "loyalist" and that the boundary must remain as it was. These speeches were given wide publicity in Britain.

The refusal of Sir James Craig to appoint a Boundary Commissioner had, as we have seen, caused a legal impasse, as it prevented completely the operation of Article XII. The British Privy Council, to whom Britain had submitted the case, decided that amending legislation would now be necessary if a third Commissioner were to be appointed and Article XII to come into operation. This was followed by a meeting of the British signatories to the Treaty in London, and a Bill empowering the British Government to nominate the third Commissioner was introduced on 6 August 1924.

Whether the minimising of the importance of Article XII was decided upon at this meeting of the British signatories is not clear, but almost immediately the signers of the Treaty who had previously asserted the vital nature of Article XII began a chorus of new public "interpretations". These were obviously directed at Mr. Justice Feetham.

Mr. Feetham had asked that while he was consulting with the parties to the dispute and studying the economic and geographic facts for himself "members of the public and the Press both in Ireland and Great Britain" would assist him "by abstaining as far as possible from controversial comment on the questions involved in Article XII of the Treaty". On the Irish side, that request was generally responded to. In Britain it was generally ignored, and particularly by those who hoped by their position to influence the Boundary Chairman most.

On 10 August Mr. Austen Chamberlain, the first of the British signatories to speak, said at Norwich:

> What they had agreed to was, in the opinion of the great lawyers who had advised them, the rectification of the existing boundary, it was not the creation of a new boundary. [1]

On 6 September Lord Balfour published a "secret" letter addressed to him on 3 March 1922 by Lord Birkenhead, another signatory, which begins with the words:

> I understand that you wish to be reasured as to the meaning of the clause in the Articles of Agreement which relates to the determination of the Boundary between Northern Ireland and the rest of Ireland.

It then says:

> The Article contemplates the maintenance of Northern Ireland as an entity already existing—not a new state to be brought into existence upon the ratification of the Articles of Agreement. It is regarded as a creature already constituted having its own Parliament and its own defined boundaries. [2]

This secret letter then ridicules (though not for publication) Collins's interpretation about Tyrone and Fermanagh, which interpretation Lord Birkenhead himself had clearly supported by his speech of 6 December 1921, at Liverpool. The concluding passage of the Birkenhead letter was pointed straight at Mr. Justice Feetham by Lord Balfour's publication of it at that moment:

> I have no doubt that the tribunal, not being presided over by a lunatic, will take a rational view of the limits of its own jurisdiction and will reach a rational conclusion. [3]

Four days later Lloyd George at Penmaenmawr brought all his influence to bear on the Boundary chairman, actually naming him. In the concluding passages of a speech in which, haunted by his former pledges to the Irish signatories, he still echoed his 1921 promises about Article XII, he now approved Birkenhead's letter and said:

> That letter seems to me to contain the only responsible interpretation of that important clause. I am not accepting the gloss or the perversion of that letter by either friends or critics but I stand by

[1] *Irish Times*, 11 Aug. 1924.
[2] London *Times*, 26 Sept. 1924.
[3] London *Times*, 8 Sept. 1924.

> the letter itself and all that is contains. The eminent Judge who was called in from South Africa to assist the present Government to interpret that Treaty is a man whose ability, integrity and impartiality is above challenge. I cannot imagine he will come to wild and unreasonable decisions which would tear up the territory of Ulster and leave it as a province with nothing but an unconsidered remnant of its land and population. [1]

This gross partiality and use of undue influence did, as is known, succeed. But here it is important to interpolate that Lloyd George in his speech indicated that what he had promised the Irish signatories was in fact possible under Article XII. He would have had no reason to warn Mr. Justice Feetham against taking the large Nationalist territories out of the partitioned area, if the Article the Commission was to implement did not, in fact, by its wording enable that to be done.

Lord Birkenhead voiced his current view on the same day. On 10 September a statement by him was circulated by the Press Association. He referred to his secret letter of 3 March 1922, and said:

> The letter represented the view I held then: it represents the view which I hold now. Reflection indeed on this point has only strengthened and deepened my conviction. [2]

As we know, his secret letter did *not* represent what he said or believed when he used words on the day the Treaty was signed. On that day his words had only one meaning, that by Article XII Tyrone would be liberated.

Winston Churchill, whose pledges to the Irish in 1921 had been particularly definite, as is obvious from his speeches already quoted, spoke at Edinburgh on 25 September 1924. Although the recollection of the Treaty negotiations and their aim made him even now refer to

> the hope which all those who signed the Treaty had in view—an Ireland free, united—the friend of Britain. [3]

he went on to echo the advice being pressed on the Chairman of the Boundary Commission that nothing was intended by Article XII but "minor readjustments of boundary".

The next British signatory to take a hand in impressing on Mr. Justice Feetham how he should act was Sir Laming Worthington-Evans. He, speaking near Colchester, the day after

---

[1] Ibid., 11 Sept. 1924.
[2] Ibid., 11 Sept. 1924.
[3] London *Times*, 26 Sept. 1924.

Churchill, also approved the Birkenhead letter, but he added something that could not have failed to influence Mr. Justice Feetham. Approving of Sir James Craig's attempted veto on the operation of Article XII, Sir Laming Worthington-Evans said:

> I cannot say that this attitude is anything but reasonable. He (Sir James Craig) cannot afford to take risks. If by any chance the Commissioners felt themselves at liberty to order the transfer of one of these (Nationalist) counties, nothing would induce the Ulster people to accept such a decision and no British Government would be guilty of the supreme folly of trying to enforce such a decision upon them. [1]

These words betray Worthington-Evans's own belief that under the terms of Article XII such a transfer was possible, but he warned the Chairman that if he dare take that interpretation, the British Government would refuse to implement it.

The Earl of Selborne, the same who by his resignation from the British Cabinet eight years earlier had begun the betrayal of Redmond over the 1916 proposals, now took a hand. On 28 September 1924 he gave the Press Association a memorandum by Lord Long, who had just died. Lord Long was the Walter Long of Carson's rebel days. He had later become the British Cabinet's adviser on Irish affairs. This memorandum [2] said that when the Partition Act was going through the Commons, "the measure found no support in any quarter." Lord Long, who had charge of it, saw Carson and Craig and learned from them that they would tolerate the Bill and work it, if they received a definite pledge from the Cabinet that thereafter the boundaries of the Six Counties would be inviolable.

> I brought this before the Cabinet and recommended them to authorise me to give this definite promise which, on their agreeing unanimously, I did.

That pledge, [3] secretly given in 1920, was now produced by Lord Selborne to defeat undertakings given by the same Government in 1921 in exactly the opposite sense. It was apparently the right time to make public secret pledges, for Lord Carson on 29 September stated in the *Morning Post* that

[1] Ibid., 27 Sept. 1924.
[2] Ibid., 30 Sept. 1924.
[3] In the House of Commons, Lloyd George on 1 Oct. denied that the Cabinet gave that pledge or that he had pledged himself to Carson in 1916. Hansard, 1 Oct. 1924, vol. clxxvii, cols. 183-191. Carson published Lloyd George's letter on 3 Oct.

he had received a pledge of permanent partition from Lloyd George in 1916. When Lloyd George denied he ever gave such a pledge, Carson promptly issued to the press the letter of 29 May 1916, which had remained secret for eight and a half years.

The British newspapers published these documents, statements and letters in full at a time when the Boundary Commission had not even been fully constituted and the whole question was *sub judice*. Their publication had one aim: to prevent the Chairman of the Boundary Commission from finding in accordance with the ordinary meaning of the words of Article XII.

Already in addition to innumerable minor Lords and M.P.s, the following signatories of the Treaty had instructed Mr. Feetham how to read the Article: Austen Chamberlain, Winston Churchill, Lord Birkenhead, Lloyd George and Sir Laming Worthington-Evans. Cabinet pledges to Carson and Craig had been cited, Lloyd George's and Lord Birkenhead's secret letters made public, and such august political figures in Britain as Earl Balfour, the Earl of Selborne, Lord Long of Wraxham, all three members of the highest Tory hierarchy and colleagues of Lord Milner to whom Mr. Feetham owed his first preferment, had had their say. The Chairman of the Boundary Commission would have had to be made of refined steel if he were not impressed.

Sir James Craig in the Belfast Parliament on 7 October 1924 announced the organisation of a new Civil War, if any other reading were given to the clause:

> I would then resign and place myself at the disposal of the people no longer as Prime Minister but as their chosen leader to defend any territory which we may consider has been unfairly transferred. [1]

Everybody who heard or read that passage, knew that Britain had legalised and armed the Orange Army and that Sir James would use that army now against the Treaty, as ten years earlier he used it against the Home Rule Bill. On the next day, in a final overwhelming instruction to Justice Feetham how to act, the whole British House of Lords summarised all that had already been said in a special declaration. In passing the Bill enabling the British Government to appoint the third Commissioner, a resolution was adopted by the Lords in which it was declared:

> That this House, having taken note of the opinions expressed in

[1] Northern Ireland Debates, 7 Oct. 1924, vol. iv, col. 1207.

Parliament and elsewhere.... by members of his Majesty's Government who were signatories of the Irish Treaty that Article XII of that instrument contemplated nothing more than a readjustment of boundaries between Northern Ireland and the Free State believes that no other interpretation is acceptable or could be enforced. [1]

No wonder that this resolution called forth sharp protests from the successors of Arthur Griffith and Michael Collins.

Mr. Kevin O'Higgins, Vice President of the Irish Executive Council, said of the Lords' Resolution in an interview with the London *Evening News* that it was

> a very deliberate attempt to influence the Commission on an international question such as they would not attempt on the lowliest petty session Court in their own country. [2]

Mr. William Cosgrave, President of the Executive Council, made as sharp a protest on 15 October 1924 in Dail Eireann when he said:

> I have observed references by British politicians and British signatories to the Treaty, and opinions which were carefully concealed when the negotiations which resulted in the Treaty were being undertaken. Had these pronouncements been made at the time, there would not have been Irish signatories to the Treaty. [3]

As soon as the Lords had passed the Bill, the British Government appointed the third member of the Commission. He was one of Sir James Craig's own colleagues, Mr. J. B. Fisher.

The net effect of the action of Britain's political leaders in prejudging the issue was that on the day the Boundary Commission was at last constituted, its findings had been determined. With Mr. Fisher's appointment there was now a majority against the interpretation of Article XII which induced Irishmen to sign the Treaty. Mr. Justice Feetham acted throughout the year of the Commission's life as he had been told to act by the most influential British statesmen, many of them of the party which had given him his first chance in life.

Lest he enter into danger of having to decide according to the wishes of the inhabitants, he refused to permit any kind of plebiscite or direct consultation with the electorate. He based his views on the plea that, as the Six Counties was now four years in existence as a separate political entity, it should not be disturbed. He was well aware that three of those four years of

---

1 Hansard, House of Lords, 8 Oct. 1924, vol. lix, col. 664.
2 London *Evening News*, 12 Oct. 1924.
3 Dail Debates, 15 Oct. 1924, vol. viii, col. 2502.

existence had resulted from the British and Belfast refusal to allow Article XII to operate. He rejected the claim of the Nationalist areas that the Article gave them the right to place themselves under the Government of their choice. When the Report of the Commission was drafted in November 1925 it became known through an inspired forecast in the *Morning Post* that not only did it break all the pledges the British Premier and his co-signatories had made to get the Treaty signed and accepted, but it proposed to take populous and prosperous territory from free Ireland and add it to the partitioned area in exchange for rough unpeopled land.

The Report was never published. A crisis developed, and under pressure of it a Boundary Agreement was signed on 3 December 1925 by representatives of Britain, the Twenty-Six Counties and the Six Counties. By that Agreement the Boundary stood as Mr. Lloyd George had drawn it in 1920. The British had achieved their aim of as permanent a partition of Ireland as such methods as they had used could accomplish. But from the beginning, they were methods which forever robbed the Partition of Ireland of any moral sanction.

CHAPTER XIII

THE SPECIAL CONSTABULARY

THERE IS IN the Six Counties of North-eastern Ireland an armed force which goes by the name of the "B" Specials. It is a Special Constabulary now over thirty-five years in existence. It is not an ordinary police force. Indeed, though recruited and operating in a mixed community, it has one characteristic not usual in a police force. It is a sectarian body. This is not an accusation by its opponents or its critics. It is a boast which comes from those who founded the organisation and have since directed it.

Sir Henry Wilson, formerly Chief of the British Imperial General Staff, and later employed by the Belfast Government to co-ordinate its police forces, wrote in his diary on 26 May 1922:

> "The Specials are now all Protestants". [1]

Sir James Craig, first Premier of the Six County Government, spoke at an Orange Demonstration on 12 July 1922, and is reported in the Tory *Belfast Newsletter* as saying:

> It is also from the ranks of the Loyal Orange Institution that our splendid 'Specials' have come. [2]

The Loyal Orange Institution is an exclusively Protestant organisation.

On 11 August 1922, a minute from the Minister of Home Affairs in Belfast was circulated allowing members of the Royal Ulster Constabulary to join the Orange Order. A Constabulary Lodge was formed known as the Sir Robert Peel Loyal Orange Lodge, and the Minister, Sir Dawson Bates, attended the first annual meeting on 13 April 1923. He made a purely partisan speech in which he denounced the British Government for making with Ireland's leaders a Treaty affecting the Six Counties, and declared that he and his Government would not permit

---

[1] Maj.-Gen. Sir. C. E. Callwell, *Field Marshal Sir Henry Wilson*, vol. ii, p. 340.
[2] *Belfast Newsletter*, 13 July 1922.

an acre of the area to be taken from them. His Constabulary audience applauded him loudly when he said:

> He was not an Orangeman of yesterday. He came of a family of Orangemen. His father had been an Orangeman and he hoped in time his own son might also be privileged to become a member of the Orange Institution. [1]

On 29 January 1924 the Worshipful Master of the Sir Robert Peel Loyal Orange Lodge presided at the installation of officers of the Belfast No. 7 District Lodge and, proposing the toast of "the Royal Ulster Constabulary", he referred to the mass of the Irish people as "the enemy" and went on:

> The opinion in the Free State was that they were to have a slice of Ulster but he assured them that if the loyal men of Ulster stood together and did what they said they would do they need have no fear of the fulfilment of the promises of their Protestant and Orange leaders that not an inch of Ulster soil would be yielded. [2]

The Worshipful Master who used these words was a District Inspector of the Royal Ulster Constabulary. There were present as he spoke a member of the Six County Government and two members of Parliament, none of whom dissented from the speech. But on this occasion a storm of criticism arose outside the ranks of the Orange Order that any police officer should interfere so blatantly in politics. The Belfast Government, compelled to bow to this outcry, suspended the District Inspector nine days later, and eventually he was dismissed. [3]

The suspension led to a procession and protest meeting in Belfast "of enormous dimensions", in which many members of the Special Constabulary took part.

Commenting on these events the *Manchester Guardian* of 21 February 1924 said:

> The British Government pays a subsidy of something like a million and a half towards the maintenance of the Ulster Special Constabulary. They also, no doubt belong to Orange Lodges. But in that event we ought not to pay for them. If Ulster insists on having a partisan police we cannot prevent her but let her pay for it herself.

The sectarian character of the Constabulary was, as we have seen, admitted by all those associated with it in its early years. It has retained that character.

---

[1] *Belfast Telegraph*, 13 Apr. 1923.
[2] *Belfast Newsletter*, 30 Jan. 1924.
[3] *Belfast Newsletter*, 29 Feb. 1924.

It would like to point out (Mr. Wm. Grant, M. P., said in February 1936) that the Special Constabulary are composed entirely of loyal Protestant workingmen... There are no Roman Catholics among the Special Constabulary.

In the same year the Report of a Commission of the British National Council for Civil Liberties, which had visited the Six Counties, contained the following reference:

In practice membership of the 'B' Specials is confined to members professing the Protestant faith who are also members of the Orange Order — that is supporters of the Unionist Party.

In 1947 Mr. Edmond Warnock K. C., Attorney General in the Six County Government, visited London. He held a Press Conference there on 30 May 1947 and was reported in the *Irish Press* of 31 May as follows:

The "B" Specials were exclusively Protestant but he denied they were recruited from Orange Lodges although, he added, they all "belonged to his side of the House".

That has been the character of the Special Constabulary, a force which, since it was established, has fluctuated between a strength of 10,000 and 35,000. The members of it are armed as soldiers and are posted in every village and town in the cut-off part of Ireland.

The Special Constabulary were founded in 1920 in consonance with the British policy of arming one section of the Irish people against the other. The year of their foundation was a bitter one in Ireland.

A great movement had arisen bent on winning back Ireland's independence. This movement, known as Sinn Fein, was at first a purely civil movement seeking the achievement of its aim by peaceful action. It succeeded, as we have seen, in establishing a Parliament and a Government, and was in the course of setting up Departments of State, when the British Government decided to use all available force to suppress this creation of a self-governing Ireland.

To carry out its policy Britain established two new forces for operations in the greater part of Ireland — the Black and Tans, a semi-military "police" recruited in Britain from the tougher veterans of the First World War; and the Auxiliaries, an officer corps of the same kind. These two forces were given *carte blan-*

---

1 Northern Ireland Debates, 19 Feb. 1936, vol. xvii, cols. 208-9.
2 *Irish Press*, 31 May 1947.

che in their treatment of the Irish people, and their excesses brought great odium not only on themselves but on the Government they served.

Britain felt she needed a different kind of corps in the Six County area, and the use of the partisan army created by Sir Edward Carson to defeat Irish self-government was decided upon.

By arrangement the demand was made on 12 July 1920 from many Orange platforms that for the "protection of the community" the Ulster Volunteer Force should be raised to the dignity of a Constabulary. The mere idea of creating a police out of this fiercely partisan force shocked not only the Irish public but the British. The London *Times* commented anxiously next day:

> If indeed that organisation were revived as a defensive police force for Ulster the most serious consequence would almost certainly ensue. Upon Sir Edward Carson lies largely the blame for having sown the dragon's teeth in Ireland. We cannot but warn him that, whatever provocation Sinn Fein may have offered to Ulster Unionism, the British people are not prepared to endorse any counter provocation from the Ulster Volunteers. [1]

In between happened the one thing that should have made such a development impossible. Mobs belonging to the dominant Orange group in the city of Belfast set upon the Nationalist minority in a series of ferocious pogroms. These attacks had, before the middle of September, when the Government decided officially to recognise and establish the Orange forces as a fully armed police, cost 53 lives, the wounding of many hundreds, the driving of 10,000 Catholic workers from their places of employment in the shipyards, the burning of whole Nationalist streets, the wholesale looting of Nationalist business houses and shops. [2]

During the end of August and the beginning of September, the matter was before the British Cabinet, and the decision was taken.

> Moderate men (said the Belfast Correspondent of the London *Times,* on 1 September) could hardly believe that the Government could take such a dangerous step. [3]

To cover the madness of this decision, it was necessary to secure a demand from Belfast for it and to base it on the need for

[1] London *Times,* 13 July 1920.
[2] See G. B. Kenna, *Facts and Figures of the Belfast Pogrom,* 1920-22.
[3] London *Times,* 1 Sept. 1920.

restoring order to that distracted and smouldering city. This was arranged by sending Sir James Craig, who was then a member of the British Ministry (Financial Secretary to the Treasury), to Belfast, where a deputation of the best-organised section of the Orange Order, the shipyard workers, met him on 3 September 1920. They had passed the requisite resolution and handed it to Sir James, who then discussed it with the Ulster Unionist Council. With their approval of it he returned to London.

The first intimation that the scheme was being operated was made by the London *Morning Post,* which all through this time was the mouthpiece of the Tory section of the Cabinet. In the second week of September the *Morning Post* published the news that, though there was no official information on the question

> of creating and arming a force of Special Constables in Ulster ...
> the fact, however, that there has just been landed at the Port of
> Belfast from a government vessel a large number of service rifles
> and revolvers of the latest pattern is accepted in well informed
> circles as a sign that the Cabinet have agreed to establish and arm
> the force. [1]

Two days later the same paper announced in another news item from Belfast:

> It can now be said that during the weekend the decision of the
> Cabinet was known. Notices were sent out to the members of the
> Ulster Volunteer Force warning them to be ready to mobilise. [2]

It was reported that only "well-disposed" persons would be recruited. In the next few days influential sections of the English Press reflected the horror with which the decision was received. The London *Daily News* said:

> It seems to us to be the most outrageous thing which even they (the
> British Government), have ever done in Ireland ... A citizen of
> Belfast who is "well disposed" to the British Government is almost
> from the nature of the case an Orangeman ... These are the very
> people who have been looting Catholic shops and driving Catholic
> women and children from their homes. [3]

Commenting on the qualifications required of a recruit to the new force the *Westminster Gazette* said:

> It will be enough that he belongs to the dominant faction in Ulster.
> All the eager spirits who have driven Nationalist workmen from the
> docks or have demonstrated their loyalty by looting Catholic shops

1 *Morning Post,* 13 Sept. 1920.
2 *Morning Post,* 15 Sept. 1920.
3 London *Daily News,* 15 Sept. 1920.

will be eligible. This is quite the most inhuman expedient that
the Government could have devised. [1]

Even the staid London *Times* protested firmly:

> The Government should have taken the public fully into their
> confidence before deciding to establish as an embodied force men
> who only six years ago defied and cowed their predecessors ...
> If ... the Ulster Volunteers are to be armed for the repression of
> Sinn Fein ... the Government must incur the suspicions of having
> yielded to the counsels of despair. [2]

The British Press did not know their Irish history, or they
would have perceived that what was being done was fully in
line with the precedents of the past. The British Government
was arming the minority against the majority and arming them
at a time when their passions were at the highest, and when they
could be relied upon to create the greatest bitterness among
their fellow-countrymen.

The first official announcement of the establishment of the
new force was made by Sir Hamar Greenwood in Belfast on
13 October 1920, after seeing a deputation from the Ulster
Unionist Council. It was a suitable occasion, and Sir Hamar
a suitable mouthpiece for the Government, for he had just
established the Black and Tans and loosed them upon Ireland.
At Belfast he said:

> We have decided to set up a system of Special Constabulary ... a
> force of selected and patriotic men. [3]

During November 1920, the Six County newspapers carried
a series of proclamations signed by His Majesty's Lieutenants
for the various counties and countersigned by officials of the
British Government in Ireland inviting

> all law-abiding citizens between the ages of 21 and 45

to apply for enrolment in a new force to be formed under the
Special Constables (Ireland) Act of 1832.

In the terminology of 1920 (when 80 per cent of the Irish
people were striving to establish national independence against
Britain's armed opposition) "law-abiding" simply meant those
opposed to the national ideal. But it was soon clear that the
term was to be pushed to an even more exclusive use.

A meeting of the Special sub-committee of the Ulster Unionist

---

1 *Westminster Gazette,* 16 Sept. 1920.
2 London *Times,* 20 Sept. 1920.
3 *Northern Whig,* 14 Oct. 1920.

Council held in the old Town Hall, Belfast, on 1 November 1920 passed a resolution

> strongly recommending all Loyalists to join and give the new force their support in every way possible. [1]

It will be seen that the word "law-abiding" had already given place to "Loyalist", which is purely a party designation in the Six County area coterminous with Tory, Unionist, Orangeman.

Former members of the "Ulster Volunteer Force" were then summoned to meetings in their districts. At one meeting in Belfast reported in the *Northern Whig* on 6 November the principal speaker, Mr. R. J. Calwell, said:

> Those who belonged to the Ulster Volunteer Force would like to see the force principally a Protestant force ... Every man who could give a hand should join up. He hoped they would take advantage of the opportunities that were offered in the scheme and that every man would come forward and do his share in the work.

Lt. Col. W. B. Spender at the Duncairn Unionist Club, having first paid a tribute to the Ulster Volunteers, was reported in the *Northern Whig of* 12 November as saying, in relation to this Special Constabulary:

> The Government were now prepared to recognise the loyalists as a distinct element ...

As the Carsonite leaders had by their defiance of British law won places in the British Cabinet so now their more extreme followers were to be included in Britain's Crown Forces in reward for their earlier sedition.

The Orangemen flocked into the Special Constabulary, of which there were to be two main classes: Class "A" a small whole-time body based on barracks, Class "B" a large body of part-time members based on their own homes. Class "B", which was to be the important political section of this Constabulary, were to be fully armed with rifle, bayonet and side arms and to have all the rights of servants of the Crown.

The Specials played the part generally assigned to the Black and Tans and other British forces at that time. Repression had become intense throughout Ireland and included the burning and partial wrecking of many towns, the systematic destruction of the property of insurgent spokesmen and the frequent murder

---

[1] *Belfast Newsletter*, 2 Nov. 1920.

of leaders in their own homes. The same fate engulfed many Northern towns and many local Nationalists at the hands of the Special Constabulary.

No oppression was more terrible than that which raged in Belfast and in many neighbouring areas from November 1920 onwards in which the Special Constabulary were openly engaged: "Orange mobs, led by Specials", as the *Manchester Guardian*'s correspondent said. [1] There is no need here to dilate on these grim events. It is well, however, to emphasise that the ultimate responsibility for them rests on the British Government. Many another minority, if armed, paid and incited against the majority by a powerful outside Government would in a crisis similar to that which then existed in Ireland have behaved in the same way.

The Specials were, after the signing of the Treaty, given another task by the British Government. It is, in this connection, of quite extraordinary interest. It will be recalled that the British and Irish Governments were in negotiation from October to December 1921 in an endeavour to find a settlement of the age-old conflict between the two nations. A Truce had been declared in the previous July by which each side bound itself not to increase its military or police strength.

The Divisional Commissioner of the Royal Irish Constabulary, Lt. Col. Sir Charles Wickham, on 9 November 1921, issued from Belfast an instruction to all County Inspectors of the R.I.C. and County Commandants of the Special Constabulary. It was marked "secret" and announced "that the Government have under consideration" the establishment of yet another class to the Special Constabulary in Ireland, this time on completely military basis.

> They (the Government) (said the Divisional Commissioner's circular) have decided that the scheme most likely to meet the situa-

1 "The Unionists have an important ally—they have a coercive police force of their own.... By one of the most disastrous acts of political folly the Government last autumn gave way to Sir Edward Carson and embodied the Ulster Volunteers he raised to fight England in 1914 and turned them into a part of the regularly armed defenders of law and order in Ireland. They have become what everybody who knew Ulster prophesied they would become—the instruments of a religious tyranny... Some of them, the A Class become regular R.I.C., the rest the B and C classes parade their districts at night with arms harassing, threatening, beating and occasionally killing their Catholic neighbours and burning their homes." (Special Correspondent of *Manchester Guardian*, 19 May 1921.) These articles in the *Manchester Guardian* of the last half of May 1921 should be read in full.

tion would be to enrol all who volunteer and are considered suitable into Class "C" and to form them into regular military units ... The force is intended as a military one only, to be called out in grave emergency, to act in a military capacity. They will not of necessity be utilised for local defence, but may be drafted to any theatres of operations within the Six Counties ... The most suitable class for this force are ex-soldiers who possess already the necessary military training and knowledge of arms ...

As the matter is URGENT replies should be sent at the earliest possible date.

The final sentence of this Secret circular is remarkable for the scarcely-veiled instruction it gives that this new military body must be exclusively Tory:

There is no necessity to endeavour to produce the maximum possible number of units, what is required is to ensure that every unit recommended for formation can be constituted from a *reliable section of the population.*

What was the purpose of this new military force?

That soon became apparent. The British negotiators were in November 1921 impressing upon the Irish plenipotentiaries that if they accepted the terms Britain offered, Irish unity must follow. The Boundary Commission was already envisaged. Lloyd George on 3 November told Lord Riddell [1] that the Irish delegates might be got to agree to other British proposals if the Nationalist Counties of Tyrone and Fermanagh were included in the self-governing part of Ireland.

On 5 November, and again on the 7th, Sir James Craig visited Lloyd George in London: the Ulster Tory leader had once more an army at his back, thanks to the formation of the Specials. He refused to budge on Tyrone and Fermanagh, and it was apparently then that the British Cabinet decided on its double policy — to persuade the Irish delegates that they were getting unity in whatever settlement was to be made, but to be prepared at the same time to make that unity impossible if Tory resistance to concessions became so strong as to endanger the life of the Coalition Government over which Lloyd George presided.

There has been no official link established between the Wickham circular of the 9th and the Ulster Tory Leader's visits to the British premier of the 5th and 7th, but subsequent developments suggest that the British knew of the circular and that only its publication and denunciation by Dáil Eireann as a breach of the truce caused its operation to be temporarily

[1] Lord Riddell, *Intimate Diary of the Peace Conference and After*, pp. 330-2.

postponed by Sir James Craig. In Lord Riddell's diaries it is recorded that Bonar Law at this time was pressing Lloyd George hard on behalf of the Six Counties, and the visit of Sir James Craig appears to have clinched the matter. Years afterwards, on 21 April 1924, Captain Herbert Dixon M.P., speaking at an Orange demonstration at Portadown, said:

> No man living could have persuaded the Cabinet to accept the Special Constabulary except Sir James Craig.

The purpose to which the Specials were later openly put certainly must have satisfied Sir James.

As we have seen, when the Irish delegates signed the Treaty of 6 December 1921, they had been convinced by the British that Clause XII must bring about Ireland's unity. We have, as already recorded, the statements and suggestions of other British signatories that this would have been the automatic effect of the operation of Clause XII, fairly interpreted.

Only positive intervention in the other direction could have prevented such an outcome. That intervention took place almost immediately after the Treaty was signed, and the main instrument of it was the Specials.

Within a few months of the issue of the Wickham circular the Six Counties were being provided with the army envisaged on 9 November 1921. Britain not only paid for this army but armed it, although its very existence was a breach of the Act of 1920 by which the Six County State was brought into being. For that Act denies the Belfast Government the right to raise or maintain armed forces.

On 22 March 1922, Birkenhead told the House of Lords that the Six Counties had been turned into an armed camp "to protect the interests of Ulster", with thirteen battalions of British troops and 15,000 men "in various police forces" equipped by the British Government. [1]

Churchill told the Commons a week later that the British Government was supplying the money to maintain 25,000 Special Constables, some of whom were already fully armed and others "in the process of being armed", all at Britain's expense.

Both Churchill and Birkenhead had pledged themselves only three months before to the Irish delegates to restore the Nationalist areas of the Six Counties. Now they were arming those who made no secret as to how the arms would be used—to resist by

[1] Hansard (House of Lords) 22 Mar. 1922, vol. xlix, cols. 728-9.

force the restoration Birkenhead and Churchill had undertaken to make.

> I say quite plainly (Captain Craig, Ulster Tory Leader had said on 16 February to the Commons) that if that (Boundary) Commission were to sit and if it were to make anything more than the very minutest change in our boundary, the inevitable result of that would be bloodshed and chaos of the worst description. [1]

It was after that statement that the British Government announced that additional arms were being supplied to the Specials. Three months later Captain Charles Craig again referred to the unfulfilled clause of the Treaty.

> If that Clause is enforced and it is still sought to take any considerable portion of Northern territory from the Government of Northern Ireland without its consent it can only be done at the expense of Civil War. [2]

On 27 February 1923, Sir James Craig, Premier, spoke in the Belfast Parliament:

> The British Government have treated us so generously and fairly with regard to the coming financial year that there will be no necessity whatever to change the general scheme of our Special Constabulary, to reduce in any way their numbers or to alter their pay... the general scheme which was outlined by us two years ago and approved by Field Marshal Sir Henry Wilson, still holds the ground... There is nothing so precious to us as the safety of the Border and... no alteration in the number of (British) troops in a locality or even their withdrawal from the Ulster area is done without... consultation and advice being given. [3]

In April 1923, Lord Derby, British Secretary of State for War, visited the Six Counties. He inspected the "A" and "B" Specials of Co. Fermanagh, and said:

> I felt it was a great opportunity to come over here to see the state of affairs for myself and above all to see the constabulary which, on the good principle of standing on your own legs, had been set up here to take the place of His Majesty's forces. [4]

And he promised Sir James Craig help and "not only from the military point of view", if it were ever required. Sir James on the same occasion made quite clear what the British War Minister's visit was intended to do:

[1] Hansard, 16 Feb. 1922, vol. cl, col. 1289.
[2] Ibid., 31 May 1922, vol. clix, col. 2149.
[3] Northern Ireland Debates, 27 Feb. 1922, vol. iii, cols. 22-3.
[4] See *Fermanagh Times*, 12 Apr. 1923.

> It means that ... any call that we make upon the British Govern-
> ment in a time of trial will be honoured without any more hesit-
> ation in the Imperial Parliament. It means too that the great ques-
> tion of the border is thrown practically altogether into the back-
> ground and probably will never arise again. [1]

Lord Derby was a member of the British Government pledged to
carry out the Border clause in accordance with the wishes of the
inhabitants. In the county Fermanagh in which he promised
military aid to Sir James Craig, the people were in majority
Nationalist, ready in a plebiscite to vote themselves out of the
partitioned area.

In the following October, Sir James Craig was again in County
Fermanagh and on the 13th spoke in the village of Garrison,
the majority of whose inhabitants were Nationalist. Having addressed his audience as "We Protestanats and loyalists", he spoke
of the Special Constabulary not now as a police, but as an army:

> In Garrison they had their platoons and their system of defence
> and he could assure them that if necessary, they would have twelve
> platoons of Specials and further, if necessory, the British Army...
> the British troops were at his disposal.

The *Westminster Gazette* asked had Sir James "any authority
from the Government to make this statement" [2] as he was pledging himself to resist with British Troops the Irish Treaty by
which the British Government was bound. As we have seen Sir
James had the best authority of all, that of the British Minister
for War.

The Chairman of the Boundary Commission was appointed
in August 1924 and almost immediately there were mobilisations,
parades and meetings of Specials along the Border. There were
reports such as this:

> There was a big mobilisation of "B" Class Special Constabulary in
> Fermanagh in the eastern end of the County yesterday, says our
> Enniskillen Correspondent. The Great Northern Railway supplied
> special trains.... Close upon 1000 men were mobilised. [3]

The *Belfast Newsletter* in September [4] described a mobilisation
in full kit and uniform of close on 1,000 Specials in the Southern
part of another disputed area, County Tyrone, and they were

1 See *Fermanagh Times*, 12 Apr. 1923.
2 *Westminster Gazette*, 15 Oct. 1923.
3 *Irish Times*, 3 Sept. 1924.
4 *Belfast Newsletter*, 5 Sept. 1924.

there inspected by the Parliamentary Secretary of the Belfast Ministry of Home Affairs and by high officials.

The purpose of these military manoeuvres was evident from the first: to impress on the newly-appointed Boundary Commission Chairman that there would be "Civil War" if he dared to carry out the terms of Clause XII in regard to Tyrone, Fermanagh and other majority Nationalist areas.

On 19 February 1925, while the Boundary Commission was in session, Churchill as British Chancellor of the Exchequer moved a vote of £1,250,000 for the "upkeep of 35,000 Special Constabulary of various classes distributed in various towns" of the Six Counties. He told the House that this grant-in-aid which had been given "every year since the Irish Treaty"

> was a matter not of right but of concession freely made by the House of Commons in aid of the Government of Northern Ireland for high reasons of State policy. [1]

Mr. Justice Feetham was left in no doubt that armed resistance to any Report of the Boundary Commission unsatisfactory to Belfast would have British support "for high reason of State policy".

The plan succeeded. Mr. Feetham showed in a letter of 7 December 1925 [2] to the then British Premier, Stanley Baldwin, how every phrase in Clause XII was strained to refuse liberation to Tyrone, Fermanagh and other Nationalist areas and to justify leaving the boundary more or less undisturbed.

Mr. Feetham in this letter recorded that the two British nominees on the Commission of three had not taken the unit of Ireland (never broken until 1921) as their norm but regarded the recently imposed boundary as the unchangeable thing

> and must treat that boundary as holding good where no sufficient reason, based on considerations of which the Commission can properly take account, is shown for altering it.

They further held that though the "wishes of the inhabitants" had been laid down as "a determining factor" a mere majority would not do. It must, they recorded, be "a substantial majoriy representing a high proportion of the total number of persons entitled to rank as inhabitants". Finally Mr. Feetham reported that the British Commissioners rejected all existing electoral

---

1 Hansard, 23 Feb. 1925, vol. clxxx, cols. 1663-5.
2 Published in the daily press of 18 Dec. 1925, and herein quoted from the *Belfast Newsletter* of that date.

units as areas for testing the wishes of the inhabitants. They rejected the county and the Poor Law union as being too large and, though they decided that the smallest area would be best, they rejected that too for unexplained reasons. The county unit would have enabled the inhabitants of Tyrone and Fermanagh to decide in favour of the National Parliament. As to the Poor Law Union, there were 28 Poor Law Unions used for normal electoral purposes in the Six Counties. 14 of these had Nationalist majorities and 14 had Tory majorities. Had these been taken as the area of decision the result would have brought under the Dublin Parliament half the Six County area—i.e. all Tyrone and Fermanagh, South Down, South Armagh, Derry City and a considerable portion of Derry County. The British Commissioners also rejected the Parliamentary constituencies which would have brought in the greater part of Tyrone, the greater part of Fermanagh, all South Armagh, East Down, South Down and Derry City.

The Commission, Mr. Feetham told Mr. Baldwin,

> not being required to adopt any particular type of local division as the unit of area in reference to which the wishes of the inhabitants is to be ascertained is free to mark out for the purpose of its work, as occasion requires, convenient units of area in the light of the three factors which it is required to take into account— wishes of the inhabitants, economic and geographical conditions.

In fact no unit of area was adopted and the wishes of the inhabitants, whether modified or unmodified, were never ascertained. Thus, as Mr. Feetham's letter made clear to Mr. Baldwin, the Boundary Clause was used not to abolish but to keep the existing Border. If the people of any area were in a majority against separation from their fellow countrymen the Commission could decide the majority was not substantial enough. (Newry with a 79 per cent Nationalist majority, Strabane with 75 per cent, Derry with 61 per cent were refused union with the rest of Ireland). Or if they had a substantial parliamentary majority or local governmental majority, or a majority in the Poor Law Unions or in the local electoral divisions, the Commission could decide that on economic grounds or geographic grounds they had no right of majority decision at all. By these means the Boundary Commission, which had been accepted with such high hope for the reunification of Ireland, was used to complete the sundering.

In Britain's view the work of the Specials was done when the

Border was left to stand on the line which Lloyd George declared on 11 November 1921 he could not justify and which Austen Chamberlain on 1 November 1922 condemned as illogical and as "no more than an expedient". The Six Counties were now to be permanently created into a State, the very area of which Sir Laming Worthington-Evans, one of the Treaty signatories, said on 17 February 1922:

> it is no use denying the fact—for it has been current knowledge for very many years—that the Six County area was not an ideal division.

It was Churchill who in December 1925, immediately after the Boundary Agreement, announced the disbandment of the Special Constabulary. Speaking in the British Commons on 8 December 1925, Churchill did not hide the connection between the Specials and the maintenance of the Border. He said:

> While the Boundary question was in suspense, Sir James Craig and his Government felt it necessary to maintain between 30,000 and 40,000 armed special constables in various degrees of mobilisation. Every year to every (British) Government they were bound to make their request for financial assistance. On the basis of there being no settlement they were proposing to me.... that we should provide for the maintenance of all the Special Constables in their present state of efficiency up to at least September 1926, and they were pressing for a sum of £2,250,000 on that account. But so soon as this settlement was reached Sir James Craig informed me that he would be able to proceed immediately with the winding up of the Special Constabulary and in consequence we were able to agree upon a final and terminating payment of no more than £1,200,000. [1]

Churchill like Frankenstein soon found he could not control the monster he had created. Sir James Craig did disband the least numerous section of the Special, "Class A", who numbered less than 1,000 men. There was an immediate munity on the announcement of their disbandment. The "A" Specials refused to be dissolved, arrested their officers and seized their barracks, challenging the Government to endeavour to retake them. After a week of revolt they surrendered, probably because they realised British support had been withdrawn from them.

The main force, the "B" Specials, despite the undertaking which Sir James Craig gave to Churchill, were not dissolved. Speaking in the Belfast Parliament the day after Churchill's announcement in the Commons that the force was being wound up, Sir James Craig said:

[1] Hansard, 8 Dec. 1925, vol. clxxxix, cols. 361-2.

> For several years the British Government have recognised the special claims of Ulster and have generously given us grants each year to assist us in defraying the cost of our Special Constabulary.. When I explain that the cost of the Specials for the past five years has amounted to a total sum of £7,426,000 and that towards this the British Government have contributed £6,780,000, the House will realise the magnitude of the problem we have had to face ... No one would be foolish enough to disband the whole of the Special Constabulary in one day.... but of course we must make a beginning at once.

Sir James Craig then announced the disbandment of the "A" force and went on to speak of the "B" Specials:

> While we have not yet perfected our plans, a scheme will be speedily devised for the retention of this branch of the Constabulary in a modified form and at a cost which will be within our own resources. [1]

The "B" Specials have ever since remained a part of the machinery of State. Over the years their numbers have been reduced but the authorised strength of the force as shown in the officials estimates for 1955-6 is 11,250. [2] Though, as the quotations at the opening of this chapter show, they are purely a sectarian organisation from which anybody who is not an Orangeman is excluded, they are maintained out of public funds through taxation taken equally from those who can and those who, because of their religious and political views, cannot become members.

The purpose of the continuance of this force is purely political. There is little ordinary crime in the great part of the Six Counties. What there is of it, it is within the competence of the Royal Ulster Constabulary to deal with. That Constabulary numbers 3,000, and at that strength the Six Counties are more heavily policed than the rest of Ireland. The Royal Ulster Constabulary are, as well, an armed police force.

Were the Special Constabulary to be regarded as police, it would mean that in the partitioned area there is one policeman to every forty-eight adults, a rate not known in any other country with democratic institutions.

The Special Constabulary is, however, not a police force in any sense understood west of the Iron Curtain. It is a paramilitary force and carries much of the equipment of an army.

[1] Northern Ireland Debates, 9 Dec. 1925, vol. vi, cols. 1858-60.
[2] *Estimates for services under the Government of Northern Ireland.* Class III. Ministry of Home Affairs (Belfast, 1955).

The major difference between it and any regular army is that its members are carefully chosen so that they will have but one political outlook.

The fabrication of a State, in defiance of the majority of the people, out of an area which never in geography, history, economics or tradition had a separate existence has led from the beginning to an unnatural form of government. A third of the people in the cut-off area have never really been regarded as citizens. They have been looked upon as enemies and indeed have been spoken of by Ministers and other State executives as "enemies". Special restrictive legislation has been put on the Statute Book which in practice applies only to them. This legislation is made up of the Special Powers Acts passed in the period 1922 to 1933. Those, with occasional modifications, additions, omissions and re-impositions are still the law in the Six County area. They are draconian laws described in 1935 by a British Civil Liberties Commission as

> contrary to the fundamental principles of democratic government.

They empower the police to arrest without proferring any charge, to enter and search homes without warrant and if necessary by force, at any hour of day or night. They empower the Executive to prohibit meetings, to imprison without trial, to order the seizure and forfeiture of property without compensation, to examine banking accounts and confiscate monies, to prohibit the possession of films and gramophone records, to remove and destroy monuments and memorials, to prohibit the display of emblems, flags or colours. These Special Laws also permit the suspension of Coroners' inquests (a power taken over from the days of the Black and Tans, when inquests on civilians shot in Ireland by the Crown forces became so numerous as to embarrass the Government). The Special Powers Acts revive punishment by flogging and deny to all accused under the Acts any claim to trial by jury. Under this extraordinary code those whom the Government wish to examine as witnesses can be arrested, forcibly detained and compelled under penalties to answer questions. One regulation under the Acts (22B-3) says:

> A person examined under this Regulation shall not be excused from answering any question on the ground that the answer thereto may criminate or tend to criminate himself.

A citizen without any charge being laid against him can by an exclusion Order against which there is no appeal be compelled to live in an area designated by the Executive and not leave it without severe punishment. Under these Acts a Minister may order the internment of any citizen for any period, and there is no court of law in which this decree can be reviewed. A person held in prison without trial can be deprived, under these Special Laws, of his right to see or even to communicate with his legal adviser. An arrested person is left practically defenceless in the hands of the police, and the British Commission, already referred to, has recorded these instances of their treatment when in custody:

> Persons arrested and detained whether under charge or not have been subjected to interrogation frequently of many hours duration, by large numbers of police. The prisoner having been questioned as to his name, address and movements by one squad of police, is passed on again and again to other squads by whom the process is repeated. During the interrogation the prisoner is surrounded by his questioners and unsatisfactory replies may produce blows. These interrogations are often held late at night and are carried on until the prisoner's strength is well-nigh exhausted.

These Special Powers Acts are not designed, as such Acts are in other nations, solely to meet some great emergency. They have become part of the ordinary law and were added to in the second half of 1951 when an Act called the Public Order Act was passed. Its effect is to give the police power to ban the flying of any flag which they *think* might lead to disorder and to use their own absolute discretion whether to permit any procession organised by no matter how peaceful or constitutional an organisation. The aim in both cases is, as it has always been under the Special Powers Acts, to prevent the Nationalist minority ("the enemy") from manifesting its ideals or demonstrating even by the most non-violent means, its desire for the reunion of Ireland.

For over thirty years none but Nationalists have been systematically arrested, imprisoned, tried, raided, interned and compelled to live wherever the State dictated. None but Nationalist organisations, meetings, processions, demonstrations have been systematically banned, proclaimed or broken up. The pretence that these Special Powers Acts are applied impartially all round is merely for international consumption. Everybody in Ireland knows the truth—that it is only these organisations and individuals who remain devoted to Irish unity that are the victims of these permanent "emergency laws".

For the first and only time on record these Special Powers

were used against an Orange organisation in June 1952. The
following are the circumstances. In Annalong, Co. Down, on 15
June, an Orange Procession was prevented by the police from
using a route through a Nationalist District. As a protest the
procession was called off and the Government bitterly criticis-
ed. [1] Twelve of the twenty-five Special Constabulary in the area
handed in their uniforms and their rifles in protest.[2] The matter
was reconsidered by the Government, and the Orangemen were
allowed to march through the Nationalist area in 3 July, and a
clash was narrowly averted. [3] This was the only reported occasion
in which the Special Powers were impartially used. This impartial
use lasted from 14 June to 3 July 1952.

And perfectly to round off this description of a partisan police
force it has only to be recorded that the "agents of the law"
who carry out such unfair legal penalties on the minority
include the Special Constabulary. They have all the rights of
interference with the individual or his home or his property that
the Acts give to the regular police. Not only therefore is the
former private army of Sir Edward Carson armed and paid for
by the Six County State out of general taxation, but they are
given powers almost of life and death over the section of the
community which they have always regarded with the most
profound hostility. How can the British Government which
originally created, established, armed and paid for this force
escape responsibility for its existence to this day?

---

[1] *Belfast Newsletter,* 16 June 1952, page 4, col. 4.
[2] *Irish Press,* 18 June 1952, page 5, col. 2.
[3] *Irish Times,* 5 July 1952, page 1, col. 3.

CHAPTER XIV

DISCRIMINATION

THE FATE OF A MINORITY

THE PROTECTION OF minority rights is essential to the survival of a democratic system in any State. The treatment of minorities is in fact regarded as a test of a community's claim to have governed well.

In almost every country there are groups who differ from the majority in political outlook, religion or economic status. There is such a national minority in Ireland.

In the whole island it numbers just over a million, of whom two-thirds are concentrated in two counties in the North-east of Ireland. Its main divergence from the rest of the island's population is in political outlook: while the majority seeks full national independence, the North-eastern minority desires to be a subordinate part of the British system.

The Irish people, well-informed as to the causes of this difference in political outlook, aware that it is historically of recent origin, nevertheless respect it. By this minority, as we have seen, the majority was for long denied the exercise of its own rights, yet the mass of the people, on recovering the right to rule, have treated the section of the minority in their midst with scrupulous fairness.

That is not a claim made by the majority for itself. It is a grateful assertion from the minority made on innumerable occasions. Its members volunteer such tributes in every national crisis. When to defeat Gladstone's Home Rule Bill in 1886 British propaganda sought to rouse the sectarian passions of the Tory minority against the Nationalist majority, scores of Protestant spokesmen expressed views of the following kind:

> I have now lived in Ireland, as you know, for a long period, for more than thirty years, and have had control of a large and very increasing business, with branches all over Ireland (wrote Charles Eason, 80 Abbey Street, Dublin on 11 May 1886). I have never known an instance of Catholic intolerance towards me personally, nor towards the business I have governed, nor does memory recall any case of intolerance from Catholics coming under my own knowledge at any time. I shall not have the slightest fear to entrust

my own liberties and those of my family to the control of an
Irish Home Rule Parliament....

The Protestant Chancellor of Cork, Very Rev. George Webster,
D.D., wrote on 13 May 1886:

> I have been twenty nine years in Cork and I have met my Roman
> Catholic fellow subjects here in all the public and in many of the
> private relations in life. I have never experienced anything from
> them other than the treatment of tolerant Christian gentlemen.

From Borris, Co. Carlow came this comment from Mr. John
George Little, L.R.C.S.I.:

> Catholic intolerance! I have often heard of it but I have never
> seen a case of it. I have been living for the past fifteen years amidst
> my Catholic fellow countrymen and never during that time have
> I observed any one instance of illiberality amongst them. I am
> of opinion that my liberty, together with the free exercise of my
> religion, could stand intact under a native Government. [1]

It would be easy to go on quoting. It is unnecessary. Seventy
years have passed since these letters were written. From every
year of that period similar tributes could be cited. It is enough
to quote the experience of the minority spokesmen after thirty
years of native Government.

Senator W. B. Stanford, speaking in the Methodist Church,
Sligo, on 9 January 1952, [2] said:

> The question was often asked: Did Protestants get a fair chance
> in Ireland today. As far as his experience went he could affirm
> that they were given a fair chance. The successive Governments
> had been true to the principles of liberal nationalism to which
> Tone, Emmet, Mitchel, Davis and other Protestants had so greatly
> contributed.

Very Rev. George Seaver, D.D., Dean of Ossory, preaching at
the Citizenship Sunday Service in Christ Church Cathedral,
Dublin, on 18 November 1951, [3] said:

> From them (the Catholics) we enjoy a toleration, a consideration
> and I will add, a respect, such as our forefathers were very far
> from according to their forefathers. In this respect, thank God,
> the sins of the fathers have not been visited on their children. Our
> fellow-countrymen of the Roman Communion have shown them-
> selves to be charitable and forgiving when they might have been
> vindictive. Gone are the days of religious persecution and ostracism;

[1] See among other sources *The Opinions of Some Protestants* (Dublin 1886).
[2] *Irish Times*, 11 Jan. 1952.
[3] *Irish Times*, 19 Nov. 1951.

we are free to conduct our worship in our own Churches and in our own way. Let us never forget that, let us never cease to be grateful for that toleration and let us strive to prove ourselves more and more worthy of that regard.

Mr. David A. Webb, Fellow of Trinity College, Dublin, wrote in the *Irish Times* in August 1950:

> I maintain that the Protestant minority here is protected by excellent guarantees that are honourably kept. [1]

Another Trinity College man, Professor Joseph Biggar, speaking in the Irish Senate on 9 December 1948 paid this tribute:

> There is complete liberty here. The Protestant minority if there was a united Ireland with a majority of Catholics in power would be just as well treated as they are in the Six Counties at present, in Great Britain or in any other part of the world. The fear of persecution or lack of freedom is entirely unfounded. I will go further than that and say that in worldly affairs the Protestant minority here are not merely well treated, but they are too well treated. The various Governments of this country have been so anxious to be fair that they have awarded far more preferment to them than the numerical strength of the Protestant minoriy would warrant. [2]

On 16 May 1953 Lord Templemore, Privy Councillor, formerly British Under-Secretary for War, said of the Twenty-Six Counties at a review in Dublin of the Protestant Boy's Brigade:

> We have to be very thankful that we are living in this wonderful country in which there is complete religious toleration. [3]

Although it would have been in the interest of these British statesmen to say otherwise, we have Lloyd George and others paying the same tributes. The British Chancellor of the Exchequer was later one of the authors of Partition, but he said in the British Commons in June 1912:

> We have every testimony that where the Catholics are predominant in Ireland, the Protestants receive absolute fair play. [4]

Mr. Edward Shortt, later to be in the British Cabinet as Chief Secretary for Ireland, said in the same debate on 1 May 1912:

> With regard to the position of the minority in Ireland and their treatment under any majority that might exist there, I believe a

1 *Irish Times*, 11 Aug. 1950.
2 Seanad Eireann Debates, vol. xxxvi, col. 109.
3 *Irish Times*, 18 May, 1953.
4 Hansard, 13 June 1912, vol. xxxix, cols. 1127-8.

study of the history of Ireland during the last 100 or 150 years will make it perfectly clear that there has never been any indication on the part of the Roman Catholics of Ireland in any way to persecute, oppress, or treat unjustly their Protestant fellow countrymen. Indeed, I say so far as outward indications go, any signs of persecution and oppression have been on the part of Protestants. [1]

Nine years later, in 1921, we have Sir Hamar Greenwood, the last and the most bitterly anti-Irish of all the British Chief Secretaries, saying more succinctly exactly the same thing:

I am bound to say that the only part of Ireland where I see religious intolerance is in the North. [2]

No fact has been so well established as that the national minority in Ireland has been, and is being, treated with a tolerance as broad as it has been long-continued. The proof is available even statistically. An analysis of the religious volumes of the various State Censuses disclosed that in higher State appointments, in the professions, in lucrative employment everywhere in the free part of Ireland, the minority has twice, three times, up to six times the share that its percentage of the population would entitle it to [3] bearing out Professor Biggar's words already quoted: They (the various Governments) have awarded far more preferment to them than the numerical strength of the Protestant minority could warrant.

But there is not only one minority in Ireland. Partition produced a second. That second minority, the Nationalists within the partitioned area, taste to-day all the bitterness endured by the helot. They are deprived of their rights in a manner that has no parallel in Western Europe.

Little over fifty years ago Ireland was ruled through what was known as an Ascendancy. It was a small group of overlords opposed politically to the national ideals of the majority, rejecting Ireland's distinctive culture despising, the symbols of her separate nationality and usually differing in religious persuasion from the mass of the people. The group stood for British supremacy and against the nation though from it there had come individuals to participate in and to lead the great movements for freedom. Tone, Emmet, Davis, Mitchel, Butt,

[1] Ibid, 1 May 1912, vol. xxxvii, col. 1879.
[2] Ibid, 28 Apr. 1921, vol. cxli, col. 441.
[3] *Study on Catholic Ecclesiastical and Religious Statistics* by T. J. Kiernan, M. A., Ph. D. read at the Statistical and Social Inquiry Society of Ireland on 6 Oct. 1950.

Parnell spanned a century of such leadership. From that group have also come journalists, poets, archaeologists, philologists, experts in Celtic lore and literature, who, drawn by their studies into closer contact with Gaelic civilisation, understood the people's ideals and lived to make them their own. But these were the exceptions. The group as a whole gave themselves the name of "the British garrison" and put first the British interest. All major official appointments were given to them: the franchise was for long restricted to them and when it had to be widened was designed still to preserve their domination.

In the passage of time the refusal of Ireland's democracy to accept an inferior position broke down this feudal organisation in the greater part of Ireland. Now all sections of the people share in the governance, organisation and administration of the Twenty Six Counties, where those who formerly were the sole holders of power now pay tribute to their fair treatment.

The Ascendancy still remains in the Six County area. There, as we shall soon see, the national minority has been able to continue the system by which a group ruled, excluding from all true participation in Government the members of the national majority. It is all done by an elaborate system of discrimination.

We have the highest international political authority for a definition of discrimination in its various forms. At its Sixth Session the Economic and Social Council of the United Nations requested the Secretary-General to

> organise studies and prepare analyses designed to assist the Sub-Commission on Prevention of Discrimination and Protection of Minorities in determining the main types of discrimination which impede the equal enjoyment by all of human rights and fundamental freedoms and the causes of such discrimination....

In December 1949 the United Nations published a Memorandum from its Secretary-General entitled "The Main Types and Causes of Discrimination".

This Memorandum thus defines discrimination:

> Discrimination might be described as unequal and unfavourable treatment, either by denying rights or social advantages to members of a particular social category; or by imposing special burdens on them; or by granting favours exclusively to the members of another category, creating in this way inequality between those who belong to the privileged category and the others.

The Secretary-General's Memorandum takes up the classification of discrimination and sets out in detail the many forms in which it appears.

1. Speeches or writings encouraging discrimination.
2. Discrimination by official authority—inequality of personal security, denial of freedom of movement or residence, or of peaceful association.
3. Denial to a minority of its just share of publicly-built housing.
4. Restrictions on a minority's right to vote.
5. Division of electoral areas to nullify the voting strength of particular groups.
6. Denial of employment or promotion in the public service.
7. Denial of employment by private persons.
8. Restrictions on the right to buy property.

Every one of these forms of discrimination is used against the minority in the six partitioned counties of North-east Ireland set up by Britain as a separate state. Under every heading illustrations can be given of the injustices visited with full official approval on the half-a-million Nationalists in this severed part of Ireland, more than one-third of the population of the area.

The United Nations Memorandum referred to the deliberate creation of

> prejudice which leads not only to discriminatory behaviour but goes further and gives rise to propaganda for further discrimination. This propaganda.... may develop into public manifestations, such as speeches or written incitements to acts of discrimination.

When the Secretary-General used these words he might well have had in mind the utterances and the actions of Sir Basil Brooke (now Viscount Brookeborough), Prime Minister of the Belfast Government, and of his predecessors in the same office.

The Six County area has had three Prime Ministers in its thirty-five years of separate existence. All have advocated discrimination, both in their capacity as heads of a Government and in their private capacity, and the methods used by these Governmental leaders and spokesmen and practised by them are exactly as condemned by the United Nations.

Discrimination of any kind does not come easily or naturally to a neighbourly people. They have to be incited and mentally browbeaten into acquiescing in it. This is usually done by representing to the majority that the minority seeks to destroy them, to enslave and despoil them and to overthrow and desecrate what they hold dear. That is what has been done in the partitioned area of Ireland.

The Nationalist minority in the Six Counties has over a long period been described in such a manner by Tory spokesmen and press as to make it the object of angry hatred. In order that this hatred should affect all the members of the minority the campaign against them had to be linked with something more permanent than their political opinions. Official publications by The Tory party (see for example *Ulster is British* [1]) declares that a useful guide in the partitioned area is to regard Protestants as usually Tories and Catholics as usually Nationalists.

This is no exact rule, for many Protestants support the ending of Partition. But it indicates how difference in religious beliefs can be employed to mark clearly all who are to be discriminated against, since the altar a man worships at is generally known to his neighbours.

If political opinions having first been linked with religious practice can then be represented as "loyalty" [2] and "disloyalty", it follows in the untutored mind that because a man is of such a faith he is thereby "disloyal". Those who are behind the campaign of discrimination believe that if a man's neighbours can be convinced that he is "disloyal", they will permit his penalisation, not, they are assured, because of his politics or his religion, but simply for security reasons — his "disloyalty" endangers the State.

The work of equating the terms "loyalty" and "disloyalty" with the religious beliefs of the population was undertaken many years ago by no less a person than the present Prime Minister of the partitioned area. In 1933 he marked out who were to be regarded as "loyal" and who as "disloyal" and has ever since driven that distinction into the minds of his followers, either himself personally or through other members and the Press of his party organisation.

In 1933 Sir Basil Brooke was a Minister in the Government he now controls, Minister for Agriculture, and he had already made several declarations of which the Secretary-General of the United Nations would hardly have approved. On 12 July of that year he spoke at Newtownbutler in the County of Fermanagh where those against whom he advocated discrimination formed a majority of the population.

Reported in the *Fermanagh Times* (his own organ) his words were:

> There were a great number of Protestants and Orangemen who

[1] Published by the Ulster Unionist Council, March 1949.
[2] The misuse of the word "loyalist" to describe opponents of national freedom has a long history: those who opposed the independence of the United States were called "loyalists" by the British.

employed Roman Catholics. He felt he could speak freely on this
subject as he had not a Roman Catholic about his own place.
He appreciated the great difficulty experienced by some of them
in procuring suitable Protestant labour but he would point out
that Roman Catholics were endeavouring to get in everywhere. He
would appeal to Loyalists, therefore, wherever possible to employ
good Protestant lads and lassies. [1]

He went on to refer to a criticism by Mr. Cahir Healy, Nationalist M.P., who had said that in public appointments the minority got less than their share. Rousing the hatred of his audience
against the penalised group he replied:

> He [Mr. Healy] was quite wrong, as in his opinion they had got
> too many appointments for men who were really out to cut their
> throats if the opportunity arose. It would be sheer madness to keep
> on giving such men appointments under existing conditions." [2]

This speech aroused criticism to which Sir Basil replied a
month later:

> He made certain remarks regarding the employment of Roman
> Catholics which created a certain amount of controversy. He now
> wished to say he did not intend to withdraw a single word of
> what he then said . . . When dealing with this subject of employ-
> ment he was not speaking from the religious point of view but
> because he knew the vast majority of Roman Catholics in Ireland
> were disloyal. [3]

This second speech created still greater controversy, and Sir
Basil Brooke as a member of the Government of the area was
accused of organising the disemployment and dismissal of workers solely because they belonged to a minority group. His reply
did not lack clarity.

Speaking at the Annual Meeting of the Londonderry Unionist
Association on 19 March 1934 he is reported as follows:

> The amount of talk and print produced by my statement on the
> question of disloyal Roman Catholics is phenomenal. I would assure
> you, however, I have not lost one night's sleep over it . . . At the
> last twelfth of July I said what I did after thinking out the whole
> question carefully . . . I recommended those people who are loyalists
> not to employ Roman Catholics, ninety-nine per cent of whom are
> disloyal. It is not as though I raked this out of the back of my
> mind without giving full consideration to it. . . . I want you to
> remember one point in regard to the employment of people who are
> disloyal. There are often difficulties in the way, but usually there

[1] *Fermanagh Times*, 13 July 1933.
[2] Ibid.
[3] *Fermanagh Times*, 17 Aug. 1933.

are plenty of good men and women available, and the employers
don't bother to employ them. You are disfranchising yourselves in
that way. You people who are employers have the ball at your
feet. If you don't act properly now before we know where we are
we shall find ourselves in the minority instead of the majority. I
want you to realise that, having done your bit, you have got your
Prime Minister behind you. [1]

The speech, with its declaration that the Prime Minister himself stood over this incitement to refuse jobs to the minority lest
they remain in the area and use the franchise, was raised by
Nationalist M.P.s in the Six County Parliament the day after
its publication. [2] The Prime Minister (then Lord Craigavon) did
not leave the House in doubt. He refused to disassociate himself
from the speech. In his reply to the debate, having denied the
interpretation the Nationalists put upon Sir Basil Brooke's words,
he nevertheless went on:

> My right hon Friend (Sir Basil Brooke) spoke as a member of His
> Majesty's Government. He spoke entirely on his own when he made
> the speech to which the hon. Member refers, but there is not one
> of my colleagues who does not entirely agree with him, and I
> would not ask him to withdraw one word he said. [3]

On 12 August 1935, at Ballinamallard, Sir Basil Brooke crys-
tallised into one phrase the ideas which he had expressed two
years before — that everyone of the inhabitants who were of a
different religion to his made up one disloyal mass not fit for
public or private employment:

> I repeat once more (the *Fermanagh Times* reports him as saying)
> as I have said before that I deeply regret that the division of loyal
> and disloyal should follow so closely the line of religion as to be
> almost indistinguishable.

1 *Londonderry Sentinel,* 20 Mar., 1934.
2 Northern Ireland Debates, 20 Mar. 1934, vol. xvi, cols. 612-22. Many
years later, on 29 Mar., 1950, Sir Basil Brooke was on his way to the United
States where his welcome was in doubt. He had become Prime Minister
and at a Press Conference in London was taxed with this advocacy of discrimination. He replied that at the time there was a plot to kidnap his
son and for that reason he could not "have a Catholic about my place".
But as we have seen the speech of 1933 was not an isolated one. It was
first spoken and subsequently adhered to as a policy and that policy is in
vogue to this day. In the many forms in which the advice not to employ
Catholics was given in 1933, 1934, 1935 or 1936 there was no reference to
kidnapping. The speeches of 1933 and 1934 were debated in the Belfast
Parliament in March 1934. Sir Basil Brooke spoke. He did not mention the
kidnapping plot.
3 Northern Ireland Debates, 20 March 1934, vol. xvi, col. 618.

What these tags "loyal" and "disloyal" meant in practice had, on 21 November 1934, been stated with as brutal frankness by the then Prime Minister, Lord Craigavon. In a debate in which the refusal of public appointments to the minority was being discussed, Lord Craigavon said from his place on the Treasury Bench:

> The appointments made by the Government are made as far as we can possibly manage it of loyal men and women ...
> *Mr. O'Neill:* How do you test their loyalty?
> *The Prime Minister:* There are ways of finding that out. [1]

The Prime Minister went on to state that one of the requisites for appointment was that "a man is heart and soul" for the Act of 1920 (the Partition Act) and against the re-unification of Ireland. He added to his definition of loyalty that his was a "Protestant Government for a Protestant people". He could not have made it more clear that, if he could help it, Nationalists would not receive any appointments that could be filled by Tories. To-day that is still the rule in this State set up by Britain in a pocket of Irish land.

During the World War there was a cessation from the advocacy of this discrimination. It would not sound well to the accompaniment of the Four Freedoms. Since the war ended Sir Basil Brooke, now Prime Minister, apparently has felt himself debarred from personally advocating discrimination, but he has given the support of his presence to those who carried on where he left off.

The United Nations Memorandum specifies as discrimination

> Establishment of property ... or other qualification having no necessary connexion with the process of selecting candidates or casting votes ... Accordance, by law, of a lesser weight to the votes of members of particular social groups. Establishment or enforcement of specific legal barriers to, or restrictions upon, the right of individuals to vote ...

A special chapter has been devoted to the variety of ways in which the minority under Lord Brookeborough's Government are deprived of their electoral rights.[2]

The United Nations Memorandum sets out another form of discrimination:

> the denial or restriction of the right to buy property, the sale of which has been publicly offered to the highest bidder.

[1] Northern Ireland Debates, 21 Nov. 1934, vol. xvii, cols. 72-73.
[2] See Chapter 14.

On 13 February 1947 the Prime Minister of the severed territory was one of the speakers at a meeting in Derry to raise a fund to prevent members of the Nationalist minority from buying land at public auctions. Lord Brookeborough expressed his pleasure that a similar scheme had been successfully in operation in his own constituency, in Fermanagh, for a decade. When taxed by the Nationalists in the Belfast Parliament on 11 March 1947 with his presence, and his statements, at the meeting the Prime Minister repeated his wholehearted support for the project. [1]

In 1948 a leading member of the Prime Minister's party advocated the liquidation of the Nationalist majority in Fermanagh. [2] He has since been promoted by Lord Brookeborough to a lucrative post. In 1949 the official organ of the Tory executive of which Lord Brookeborough is a member urged the Tories so to vote in the local elections that they retain control of making appointments, letting of houses etc. [3]

Finally, Lord Brookeborough was present and spoke at a meeting at Omagh on 14 February 1950, and heard a member of his party (Mr. Thomas Lyons, M.P.) say:

> There were, and it grieved him so say it, people enjoying large salaries and influential positions who refused to subscribe to the Unionist funds and were rude to the collectors. He wondered if these people realised that they were in their positions by virtue of the fact that the bodies they worked for were administered by loyalists. [4]

So completely are the ordinary rules of public appointments departed from in favour of "loyalists" that the recipients of the jobs can be called upon publicly in the presence of the Prime Minister to give a "quid pro quo" to the party funds.

What has been quoted puts beyond dispute that discrimination has been condoned and advocated by those holding the highest executive offices in the Six Counties. What was openly said before the war — in 1933, 1934 and 1935 — was repeated as

---

[1] Northern Ireland Debates, vol. xxx, cols 4719-20.
[2] Speech of Mr. E. C. Ferguson, 9 Apr. 1948 (see Page 245).
[3] *Voice of Ulster*, November 1949
[4] *Tyrone Constitution*, 17 Feb. 1950.

[5] How much discrimination is taken for granted as part of the ordinary life of the Six Counties is indicated by a passage in T. Wilson's *Ulster under Home Rule* (1955). He writes (p. 208) "From any objective point of view it cannot be said that the grievances of the Catholics are always very real. They have less to complain about than the U.S. negroes, and their lot is a very pleasant one as compared with that of the nationalists in, say, the Ukraine."

soon as the war was ended — in 1946, 1947, 1948, 1949 and 1950 as our quotations show.

The United Nations Memorandum recognised that the denial of employment was one of the grossest forms of discrimination. It cited as "discriminatory conduct by an official authority" any action

> denying or restricting the right of individuals to be appointed to a non-political, non-confidential public office, (or achieving the same end by) any arbitrary administrative action or omission.

As well as this, the Memorandum cites "discrimination by private persons" by which

> opportunities for employment may be denied to individuals belonging to a particular social group, or members of such a group are given employment only in menial tasks; or, if they obtain better jobs, these jobs are restricted to a very small number; or they have to meet insurmountable difficulties in obtaining promotions; or the salaries paid to them are lower...

This use of employment, or the limitation or denial of it, as a political weapon against a minority, is general in the Six County area. It can be illustrated by many instances, though it is, as the United Nations Memorandum warns,

> usually disguised in such a way that it is very difficult to prove the existence of any unfair motive.

Two cases (both in April 1950) illustrate this. A painter was refused a post by the Enniskillen Borough Council because, though otherwise well-qualified and a World War veteran, he had no experience in sign-writing. A few days later a Welfare Visitor was appointed by the Tyrone Health Committee "subject to getting examination". On the face of things, these two actions may have been perfectly impartial and just. When, however, it is seen that each decision was come to by a party vote, suspicions are aroused. Then it is found that the rejected painter is a Nationalist, and the Welfare Visitor, to whom consideration has been shown, is a Tory, and we realise that something else may have been at work.

On this difficult question of proof of motive, there is one over-all way of examining the problem, and of providing evidence of discrimination which the common sense of ordinary observers will recognise and accept. In this Six County area there are some 500,000 Nationalists and some 900,000 Tories. Both sections are stratified in similar ways. Generally speaking, there are proportionally the same number in the professions, in the trades, in clerical groups, and so on.[1] Generally speaking, too, they are of the same educational level, since the same curriculum is taught to both and the same examinations must be passed by both. Consequently it can be said that there are as well-qualified doctors, chemists, lawyers, accountants, clerks, artisans in one group as in the other. There is no reason, therefore, why a third of any given section of public appointments should not be held by the minority.

A full analysis has been made of all grades of officials, craftsmen and manual workers employed by the seventy-three local government bodies of the partitioned area (Corporations, Borough Councils, County, Urban and Rural District Councils). The results are illuminating and are confirmed by a more recent survey, also specially carried out.

There were at the time of the analysis (1951) 3,476 officials and workers of all kinds in the employment of these bodies. Of that number 1,096 were Nationalist, or 31.5 per cent of the whole. The Nationalists' percentage in population is 34.4, therefore Nationalists appeared to get from these local councils something like the share to which their percentage in the population entitled them.

It would be a happy result if further analysis did not show something very different. It has been possible to break down these total figures into two main classes of employees:
1. Executive, Administrative and clerical workers: and
2. Manual labourers.

As soon as the figures are examined under these heads we begin to see another picture. Of the manual workers the Nationalists have just over 40 per cent. These are workers, some of

[1] This is borne out by the last Census in which the occupations of the people in the Six Counties were shown by religions. That was in 1911. Then the percentage of Catholics in the whole professional group was 28.8. The secondary schools of the North-east now have 26.4 per cent Catholics students, and in addition many Catholics families in the Six Counties send their children to secondary schools in the Twenty-Six Counties. The percentage of Catholic children in the primary schools of the Six Counties is 39.8. Though the figures are not officially available it is known that a large percentage of the young people at technical schools in the Six Counties are Catholic. In Belfast University it is estimated that about 20 per cent of the students are Catholic, and large numbers of Catholic students come from the North-east to the Dublin College of the National University.

whom are permanent, some temporary. Their grade of pay is the lowest in the service. Most of them are either road workers or street cleaners. The Nationalists are coralled into the menial jobs. Once the scale starts to ascend, however, the Nationalist percentage begins to fall. The Nationalist is, for instance, completely excluded from every Higher Division post under the Belfast Corporation. Of the next grade of 65 principal officers of the same Corporation all but one are Tory. Not even one of the twenty-nine principal employees of Derry Corporation is a Nationalist, though Nationalists form 63 per cent of Derry's population. In the other main towns the disproportion is similar. In Armagh City, which has a Nationalist majority, only two of nine principal officials are Nationalist, but nineteen of the twenty-five scavengers are Nationalist. Enniskillen Urban Council has two Nationalist officials out of 13; in Omagh there are three out of fourteen, but all the scavengers are Nationalist. The following is an analysis of the Executive Administrative and Clerical staffs of all the Councils in each of the six counties:

Antrim	257 Officials of whom 19 are Nationalist
Armagh	129 Officials of whom 16 are Nationalist
Derry	206 Officials of whom 16 are Nationalist
Down	294 Officials of whom 56 are Nationalist
Fermanagh	53 Officials of whom 5 are Nationalist
Tyrone	156 Officials of whom 18 are Nationalist

Of 1,095 of these posts the Nationalist, who form 34 per cent of the population, have 130, or 11.8 per cent of the appointments. Four of the six counties—Armagh, Derry, Fermanagh and Tyrone—have together a population of 232,604 Nationalists to 222,538 Tories. Yet in that bloc, Nationalist in majority, of the 541 officials only 55 belong to the majority. The minority get 90 per cent of the appointments.

The same spirit is shown in staffing the least as well as the most important local-government body in the separated area. Of the 32 Rural Councils 18 employ not one Nationalist official and 5 others employ only one. The 28 Rural Councils which are Tory-controlled employ 11 Nationalists out of a total of 218 Officials, or 5 per cent. As regards the County Councils, which are the principal rural bodies, the clerical and higher appointments work out as follows:

Antrim with 22 per cent of its population Nationalist has 4 Nationalists out of 97 Officials.

Armagh with 46.5 per cent of its population Nationalist has 3 Nationalists out of 50 Officials.

Derry with 43.1 per cent of its population Nationalist has 4 Nationalists out of 52 Officials.

Down with 30.1 per cent of its population Nationalist has 7 Nationalists out of 78 Officials.

Fermanagh with 55.4 per cent of its population Nationalist has 3 Nationalists out of 34 Officials.

Tyrone with 55.3 per cent of its population Nationalist has 6 Nationalists out of 66 Officials.

This discrimination is exercised most completely and most persistently in Nationalist areas where the Tory minority has seized control by gerrymandering or other means. There are 18 of those areas, and in them only 23 out of 278 officials are Nationalist, or 8.3 per cent, the minority giving themselves 91.7 per cent of the appointments to all salaried posts.

How does it work, this system of keeping Nationalists, even in Nationalist areas, out of jobs, especially out of salaried posts? When the Tory minority secures for itself a majority on the local council it proceeds to appoint Committees. With those Committees rests the making of appointments, the letting of houses, the giving of contracts, etc. In a word these are the key bodies.

The Tyrone County Council provides all the examples needed to understand the system. By the manipulation of the electoral districts the Nationalist majority in the County is prevented from electing more than 12 of the 35 Councillors. The Council then elects its Committees. These are packed with an unshakeable majority of Tories. Here is the membership of these bodies in this Nationalist county at the time of writing:

General Purposes Committee: 7 Members, 1 Nationalist
Finance and Tenders Sub-Committee: 8 Members, 2 Nationalists
Roads' Committee: 9 Members, 1 Nationalist
Education Committee: 22 Members, 3 Nationalists
Health Committee: 21 Members, 4 Nationalists
Welfare Committee: 17 Members, 5 Nationalists
Agricultural Committee: 9 Members, 1 Nationalist
Combined Hospitals' Committee: 25 Members, 5 Nationalists.

The minority in every case is overwhelmingly represented, and, as an added safeguard, not a single chairmanship is allowed to the Nationalists, who represent the majority of the people. It is not surprising then that not one principal officer of these

Committees is a Nationalist. For example, of the Public Health organisation of the County, the Secretary, County Medical Officer, County Nursing Officer, County Sanitary Officer, County Dental Officer are Tories; under the Education Committee, although the children from Nationalist homes form a considerable majority over all others (11,064 to 8,845), the Chief Education Officer, the Deputy Chief Education Officer, the Accountant and the Schools Architect are all Tories, and the whole clerical staff is Tory.

The same story can be told of the Committees and staffs of other Councils. In the employment of the Derry County Council there are 13 principal officers (Secretary, County Surveyor, County Medical Officer of Health, etc.). Not one of these 13 key posts is held by a member of the minority. There are 32 other substantial posts (Assistant Surveyors, various Inspectors, Rate Collectors, etc.). One of these, an Assistant Surveyorship, is held by a Nationalist. The 42 per cent minority holds 2 per cent of the higher positions.

In Derry City, with its Nationalist majority of 63 per cent, not one of the headships of any Department of the Corporation or even an assistant headship is held by a Nationalist. The Town Clerk, City Accountant, City Surveyor, Town Planning Consultant, City Electrical Engineer, Medical Officer, Director of Education, City Solicitor and twenty other key posts are occupied exclusively by members of the 36 per cent Tory minority.

This wholesale discrimination is not something that happens now and again: it is applied as a set policy and is often carried on openly. If a Tory cannot be found for a lucrative post there is no appointment made. There have been cases in which, when an advertisement drew but one applicant and it was discovered he was one of the minority, it was decided not to fill the post.

In January 1950, the Derry Rural Council advertised in six journals for an engineer, the Council declaring that a great deal of urgent work necessitated a permanent appointment at once. Seventen schemes were held up for want of one. The salary offered was £650.

Captain William Joseph Guckian, a citizen of Derry, a bachelor in Civil Engineering of Belfast University, applied for the position. He had had several years war service as an officer of the British Royal Electrical and Mechanical Engineering Corps. He was fully qualified in every way and was the only candidate. He did not get the post. When the Council met to make the appointment, it decided, on discovering that Captain Guckian was a Catholic, that the appointment of a permanent engineer was not really necessary, and postponed the appointment indefinitely. [1]

It is of course never stated that a particular applicant cannot be accepted because of being a member of the political or religious minority. But when a Nationalist or a Catholic appears as an applicant, an excuse is found in a score of contrary ways for debarring him.

The excuses used to debar Nationalists from appointment are infinite in variety. From a wide selection noted in the Six County Press the following are typical. A Nationalist doctor was refused a post in a Derry hospital because he came from the neighbouring county of Donegal and was therefore a "foreigner". [2] but a Tory nurse was soon after appointed to another Six County hospital although she also came from Donegal. [3] The only applicant, a Nationalist, for the job of foreman under a rural council was rejected because he came from an urban area, [4] but a Tory who came from a rural area was soon after appointed by an urban council over an urban applicant who was a Nationalist.

A Tory lorry-driver was appointed who had no war service, which the advertisement for the job stipulated; [5] but some time later a Nationalist applicant was rejected as a van-driver on a war-service clause. [6] A Nationalist nurse fully qualified, the only applicant to fulfil all the conditions, was rejected for appointment as Health Visitor, [7] but no such exactitude has been insisted on for other more important Health posts when the applicants were Tories.

Sometimes the penalisation practised so generally on Catholics affects an otherwise eminently suitable candidate, not because of himself but because a near relation is a Catholic. The plum of the local-government service in the partitioned area is the Town Clerkship of the City of Belfast. In January 1942 from among several applicants Mr. W. Lawrence Allen, Town Clerk of Barrow-in-Furness in Britain, was unanimously chosen by the Selection Committee of the Belfast Corporation for his high

[1] See *Derry Journal*, 17 Mar. 1950 and 3 Apr. 1950 for full report of this case.
[2] *Irish Echo*, 11 Oct. 1947.
[3] *Fermanagh Herald*, 15 Nov. 1947.
[4] *Tyrone Constitution*, 24 Oct. 1949.
[5] *Irish News*, 3 Dec. 1947.
[6] *Strabane Chronicle*, 15 Oct. 1949.
[7] *Irish News*, 26 July 1950.

qualifications (the Committee having first asked him his religion: he was a Protestant). The decision of the Selection Committee was then unanimously confirmed by the Corporation itself, who formally appointed him Town Clerk of the City. But the Belfast Ministry of Home Affairs refused to sanction the appointment. They had discovered that Mr. Allen's wife was a Catholic! The post had to be readvertised! [1]

Discrimination takes no account of who may suffer because of it. In August 1950 the implementation of the General Health Scheme caused a grave shortage of officers for the School Dental Services everywhere, and the Service under the Tyrone Health Committee was crippled by it. The Medical Officer of Health, Dr. G. A. W. Neill, asked that the post of dental assistant be advertised as a matter of urgency. The only applicant was Miss Elizabeth Counihan of Co. Clare. The M.O.H. pleaded for Miss Counihan's appointment, as two-thirds of the school children were in urgent need of attention. He said dental officers were impossible to get in England or Scotland and "were worth their weight in gold". But Miss Counihan, like the majority of the children she would have to treat, was a Catholic, and the Health Committee, rejecting their M.O.'s appeal, refused to appoint her and decided to readvertise in England and Scotland. [2]

What is done by the local bodies, often with the Ministry's express approval, is done also by the Ministry itself. As the Tory-controlled councils act through Committees, the Ministry acts through Boards. Either the Nationalists are not represented on those Boards at all, or they are given ineffectual representation. The Civil Service Commission, which is composed of three members, has no representative of the minority; again the Promotion Board for the Postal Service has no member of the minority; the Unemployment Assistance Board has no member of the minority; the Hospitals Authority [3] is overwhelmingly Tory. There is no member of the minority on the Appeal Tribunals dealing with Unemployment Insurance. There is no representative of the minority on the senior staff of the Belfast Parliament, on the Government Secretariat, or the Land Com-

[1] *Northern Whig*, Belfast, 5 Jan. 1942 and subsequent dates.
[2] *Belfast Telegraph*, 28 Aug. 1950.
[3] "Apart from nurses and domestic servants, of whom there is a great shortage, Catholics employed by the Hospital Authority that controls the Hospital Services do not number 5 per cent". Editor's note to news item re hospital in *Irish News*, Belfast, 21 Jan. 1950.

mission. As this chapter is being prepared for the Press the Belfast government announces the appointment of twelve members of a Fire Authority. Not one of the twelve is from the minority.

In control of the various Departments of State there is a total of forty principal officers. Not one is a member of the minority. There are forty judges, registrars and senior officials in the Higher Courts. Not one is drawn from the minority. In 1941, of over 120 key posts in this artificial State, not one in the first grade was held by a Nationalist or a Catholic. Of the second grade two posts were so held, a percentage of 1.6 for a 34 per cent minority. 1

This has continued for thirty years. It means the exclusion of more than a third of the population from any real share in the governmental administration of the area. How deliberate this policy is of debarring so large a section of the people from the senior positions in the public service has shown itself in the professional field.

On 11 February 1951 Dame Dehra Parker gave a list of 139 medical, surgical and other consultants appointed by the Northern Ireland Hospitals Authority under the Health Act. In that list there were but 9 drawn from the minority!

Speaking in the Belfast Parliament in May 1950, on this subject, Mrs. Irene Calvert, M.P. for Belfast University, and herself not a member of the minority, described how even the staff of Belfast's most famous hospital, the Catholic Mater Infirmorium, was penalised because, as it was entitled by law to do, the Governing Body opted out from state control.

> Since that decision was made (she said) no member of the Mater Hospital staff has been able to obtain an appointment under the Hospitals Authority. In other words these people who have the highest qualifications recognised by the University for teaching purposes are not able to be graded; they are not able to receive any of these distinction awards (which, Mrs Calvert had said earlier, reach £2,500 a year in some cases).... These distinction awards are given for a life-time of service to medicine, not for two years service to the Hospital Authority. It seems to me quite wrong that it should be impossible for any consultant of standing to be eligible for awards which are given from public funds.... It would appear to be the will of the Authority to deny these people's services to the Community. That is what it would appear to any impartial person. 2

1 The figures quoted in this and the former paragraph appeared in *Discrimination* (published by the All-Party Anti-Partition Conference) in 1950.
2 Northern Ireland Debates, 3 May 1950, vol. xxxiv, cols. 748-9.

What is done so universally by the central and local Government is a guide to other institutions and to private employers. In Queens University, Belfast, a fifth of the students come from the minority. It has as its principal officers the Chancellor, Pro-Chancellor, Vice-Chancellor, Registrar, Secretary, Librarian. Not one of these officer was in 1951 a member of the minority. Only two of the 36 Professorships, none of the 6 Readerships, and only 17 of the 203 lesser academic posts were so held. The minority held 2 of the 76 administrative posts in the University!

The Transport Authority staffs in Derry City total 666. Were there no discrimination the Nationalists, who are 64 per cent, would have around 400 of these. In fact they have 123, or 18 per cent, and of the higher-paid posts they have only 10 per cent. Of the same Transport Authority's services in Belfast, Councillor T. O'Sullivan said at a meeting of the Belfast Corporation of 3 March 1952:

> Out of 105 transport inspectors in the employment of the Corporation only ten belong to the minority, the other 95 being supporters of the Unionist (Tory) Party.

Accusing the Corporation of "vicious discrimination" against the Nationalist minority (which is more than a quarter of the city's population) Councillor O'Sullivan went on:

> How could the Corporation hope to have efficiency in the working of the transport department when appointments were made purely on political grounds.

He could have said "on politico-sectarian grounds".

The discrimination extends to Government-aided industry as well, and in this sphere its weight falls heavily on the Nationalists in the border counties. Fermanagh is such a border county and is typical.

When, in recent years, a factory was established in that county with Government aid, not one of the six key posts went to a Nationalist and only 76 of the 242 ordinary jobs. In this Nationalist county only 3 of the 27 Public Assistance Board Officials are Nationalists, and of the 9 principal judicial, legal and police officials not one is a Nationalist. And, as we have seen, although children from Nationalist homes far outnumber those from all other homes, every official of the 13 in the Education Office of County Fermanagh is a Tory!

This closing of every door to Nationalists or Catholics seeking higher employment, especially to young people, is regarded by serious social workers as extremely grave.

In 1940 a Committee of the Y.M.C.A. issued a report based
on a study of a group of boys of various religious beliefs who
had been at Ballymoyer Camp, Co. Armagh, during June and
July of that year. The report recognised the frustration caused
by the refusal of work to young people among one religious
group. It urged that

> with the instruments of propaganda now in the hands of the
> Government it is of the utmost importance that the refusal by many
> to employ Catholic boys should be discouraged.... The evidence of
> quite good boys who have been constantly looking for jobs and
> who have failed to get them in works where at least the majority
> of workers are Protestant and where Protestant boys are constantly
> taken on is—to say the least of it—suggestive. We neglect this
> problem at our peril. [1]

That was written more than a decade and a half ago. Its
warning note has had no effect. In 1955 as well as in 1940 the
young people of one religious group see door after door shut
in their faces.

In the *Ulster Herald* for January 1952 appears the report of
the rejection by a Party vote at the Omagh Urban Council of a
Nationalist candidate for a clerkship at the Omagh gas works.
Mr. R. O'Connor M.P. said: "Every appointment of the Council's
commanding a good salary had been filled by the Unionists.
Was that to continue for all time or would there come a time
when the Nationalist people would realise that their boys and girls
had some chance of getting even junior appointments." [2] Time
passes but the spirit does not change. One of the Tory candidates in
the Six County local elections after World War II was Mr. H.
McLaughlin of Derry. The *Derry People* reported his views in
the following paragraph:

> At a meeting in Derry to select candidates for the Corporation
> Mr. H. McLaughlin said that for the past forty-eight years since
> the foundation of his firm there had been only one Roman Catholic
> employed—and that was a case of mistaken identity. He would do
> everything in his power to further the cause of Unionism and to
> fight for it at all times. [3]

There has been set out in the foregoing figures and quotations
a fixed, long-term policy of denying employment, promotion or
high appointment to members of a minority simply because they
have political or religious views differing from the majority.

---

[1] Cahir Healy, M.P., *The Mutilation of a Nation*, pp. 21-2.
[2] *Ulster Herald*, 19 Jan. 1952.
[3] *Derry People*, 26 Sept. 1946.

That this has been permitted is Britain's clear responsibility. What has been done is completely contrary to the British Act from which the Six County Tories derive their governmental powers. The danger that just this might happen was known to the authors of that Act.

Mr. Winston Churchill speaking at Bradford on 14 March 1914 said:

> What treatment do you suppose these Orangemen would mete out to their fellow countrymen in their midst... We know well how the Conservative Party governed Ireland in the 'eighties and in the 'nineties. We know the treatment that they would consider quite appropriate to mete out the Nationalists to-morrow if they obtained a majority. [1]

The Act of 1920 itself laid it down:

> In the exercise of their power to make laws under this Act neither the Parliament of Southern Ireland nor the Parliament of Northern Ireland shall make a law so as either directly or indirectly to... give a preference, privilege or advantage or impose any disability or disadvantage on account of religious belief... Any law made in contravention of the restrictions imposed by this subsection shall, so far as it contravenes those restrictions, be void.

Despite this legal prohibition Britain has permitted the wholesale penalisation of one religious group in the matter of employment, appointment, and promotion. Power rested with the British Government to prevent this discrimination. It has never been used.

Next to the denial of employment, no penalty can be more severe on a minority than to discriminate against them as regards housing. Yet the Nationalists of the Six County area have been so long and so persistently penalised in this way that, like the deprivation of employment, it shows itself statistically in the public records.

In 1944 a survey of *Housing in Northern Ireland* was issued officially by the Belfast Government. It remains the most up-to-date all-over survey of its kind. From it a remarkable fact emerges: that though at that date the housing situation in the whole area was deplorable, the minority was far worse housed than the majority. The method adopted by the Survey is to set out the need for new houses in any particular area as a percentage of existing housing. By that method the deficiency is measured for the Six Counties as a whole at 30.2 per cent. But in the Nation-

[1] *Irish Times*, 16 Mar. 1914

alist areas both urban and rural it is much higher. For instance, in the rural districts of Antrim and Down, where the Tories are strongest, the deficiency shown in the Report is only 28 per cent, but in Tyrone and Fermanagh, where the Nationalists are strongest, it is almost twice that, 53 per cent. In the urban areas as a whole the deficiency is 27.3 per cent, but in Nationalist towns, where the local governing body (responsible for re-housing the people) is in the hands of the Tory minority, the deficiency is 41.8 per cent. Four towns have even a greater deficiency than this high figure. Three of the four are Nationalist towns all under Tory rule: Enniskillen, 43.7 per cent; Derry, 44.8 per cent; and Dungannon, 48.3 per cent.

In Belfast City the housing situation as regards overcrowding is particularly bad. The Survey records that the overcrowded and unfit houses as a percentage of the whole are 37.2 per cent. But in the three wards of the city which are most strongly Nationalist, the percentage of unfit and overcrowded houses is much higher. Dock (45 per cent Nationalist) is 54 per cent overcrowded; Falls (91 per cent Nationalist) is 62 per cent overcrowded and Smithfield (91 per cent Nationalist) is 76 per cent overcrowded. In the category of houses "wholly unfit for human habitation" the percentage is lowest at 19.8 per cent in Tory rural areas, but highest in the Nationalist Counties of Tyrone, 40 per cent, and Fermanagh, 41 per cent.

The inescapable conclusion from these official figures is that in Nationalist districts, and especially in Nationalist districts under Tory control, housing conditions are so bad as to be explained only by studied neglect of people's elementary needs where these people are Nationalists.

There was no slum clearance in urban areas, a neglect inexplicable unless it is remembered that an escape from overcrowded tenements into separate dwellings might mean increased Nationalist votes. The need to re-house the overcrowded Nationalists in the Dock, Falls and Smithfield wards of Belfast would have been regarded as an urgent duty by any normal Corporation. Mrs. Irene Calvert, M.P., referred to this in the Belfast Parliament in June 1952:

> There is the question of slum clearance. The fact that the Belfast Corporation has never to my knowledge done anything in the way of slum clearance is a rather remarkable thing because I think that practically every other city of a size comparable with Belfast in the

United Kingdom has over the past number of years carried out a
slum clearance programme. [1]

This preoccupation with votes rather than houses governs the
allocation of what public housing is built. If the new dwellings
are sited in an electoral district where the numerical difference
between the Nationalists and Tory voters is small, no Nationalist
will get a house until every Tory applicant has been accommo-
dated.

On 11 March 1950, the Omagh Rural Council came to allocate
40 houses at Coneywarren, Co. Tyrone, the first built in the area
for many years. The Nationalist members of the Council submitted the names of 22 desperately badly-housed families in the
hope of moving the Council's majority to a just allocation. By
a party vote, every Nationalist applicant was rejected and the
houses were given to 40 Tories, a majority of whom were either
not married at all or were married and without children, or had
but one child! Some who were allocated houses were already so
comfortably housed elsewhere that they refused to move in.

This 100 per cent Tory allocation was made because in the
Parliamentary constituency (North Tyrone) where Coneywarren
is situated, the Tories have a slender majority and wish to increase it. They will house there only those who vote for them.
Questions of need, or family distress, or just dealing vanish in
such circumstances. [2]

This allocation of houses on partisan grounds is constantly reported in the Six County Press. On 12 July 1950 the Derry papers
reported the allocation by the Strabane Rural Council of twelve
cottages in a strongly Nationalist area. [3] All but one were given
to Tories. Enniskillen Rural Council decided in March 1950
by a party vote to eject Joseph Owens from a Council house
built for his father in 1906. The Owens family had given much
war service in the British forces. The house was given to a
Tory. [4] The Omagh Rural Council attempted a similar ejection
of Miss Mary McGuigan, a Nationalist, from what had been her

---

[1] Northern Ireland Debates, 24 June 1952, vol. xxxvi, col. 1209. See also the
speech of Mr. Harry Midgley (afterwards Minister for Education) on 20 Mar.
1946 in Northern Ireland Debates, vol. xxx, col. 294.

[2] On the same day twelve houses were allocated in the Carrickmore district of the same area. There the Nationalists got half the houses. Carrickmore is 93 per cent Nationalist, and the Tory need to maintain a majority
does not exist; nevertheless, they took half the new houses.

[3] *Derry Journal*, 12 July 1950.

[4] *Strabane Chronicle*, 11 Mar. 1950.

home for 37 years. She was saved by a round robin from her neighbours, Nationalist and Tory, an illustration of the point already made that discrimination is imposed from the top and left to themselves neighbours will be neighbours the whole world over. [1] But Miss Margaret Nolan was less lucky and lost her home to a Tory after 40 years. [2] In May 1952 Mr. Cahir Healy, M.P., raised in the Belfast Parliament many cases of blatantly partisan allocation of houses. [3] There were fourteen separate protests in 1951 over cases in which Nationalists with large families living in condemned houses were turned down for already well-housed Tories many of them unmarried. Nationalists having war service with the British armies were entitled to an absolute preference. They were again and again refused shelter in favour of Tories with no war service. [4] In April 1954 Mr. Healy was moved to protest: "To-day they had housing estates in Enniskillen, Omagh and Derry where a man's Christian faith debars him from getting a house." [5]

Speaking in the Six County Senate on 17 June 1952 Senator P. J. O'Hare said: [6]

> Last week the press conveyed the information that Magherafelt Rural Council having 52 houses to let gave 47 of them to Unionists and 5 to the Nationalists.

Magherafelt Rural area is Nationalist in majority. The Senator then cited other recent allocations and went on:

> That represents a total of 122 houses given to the Unionist minority and a grand total of 19 given to the Nationalist majority.

He added other examples recently, and went on:

> That is the sort of performance of which the Unionist gerrymandered public bodies are guilty every day of the week and it simply cannot be outside the knowledge of this House.

Not only was it not outside the knowledge of the House but it had been raised there again and again, always to meet with the same insensibility.

Even scrupulous fairness in the past by a Nationalist Council in the allocation of housing does not secure like treatment for

[1] *Irish News,* 12 Dec. 1949.
[2] *Irish Press,* 11 June 1949.
[3] Northern Ireland Debates, 27 May 1952, vol. xxxvi, col. 941.
[4] See *Ulster Herald,* 16 May 1951, *Irish News,* 25 May 1951 and *Ulster Herald,* 10 Nov. 1951.
[5] *Irish News,* 21 Apr. 1954.
[6] Northern Ireland Debates (Senate), vol. xxxvi, cols. 385-6.

Nationalists once that Council has been taken from them by gerrymandering. An outstanding example is the record of the Omagh Urban Council which since 1935 has been under the control of the 38 per cent Tory minority. When the Council had a Nationalist majority it allocated 164 houses: to the 38 per cent minority it gave 56 houses (or 34 per cent) and to the 62 per cent. Nationalists it gave 108 (or 66 per cent). From 1935, when it was given a Tory majority, to 1952 the Council allocated 172 houses. Of these it gave 130 (or 75 per cent) to the Tory minority and only 42 (25 per cent) to the Nationalist majority, an even more unjust allocation than the figures show, for the Tories all over the partitioned area are the better housed. In this case the Tory need for houses was so small that tenants had to be brought in from other areas as far away as Belfast, while Nationalists living locally in shacks applied for shelter in vain.

In many other allocations the Tory Council had to go outside the district for tenants. In the Nationalist area of Killyclogher, Omagh, Co, Tyrone, of 20 new houses 17 went to Tories, "Only two of the 17", said the *Ulster Herald* [1], "had any residential connection with the locality".

After the June 1949 local elections an editorial in the *Strabane Weekly News* openly warned the local Tory Councillors, who in this predominantly Nationalist area had secured all but 8 of the 28 seats on the Strabane Rural Council, that any Tory

> who sells a farm or lets a house to an Anti-Partitionist is assisting the Anti-Partitionists to win the Local Government representation in that area at the next election and their action can only be regarded as treachery to their party. [2]

The Memorandum of the United Nations condemned the

> establishment or enforcement of ... restrictions upon the access of individuals belonging to a particular social group to ... public housing programmes.

That discrimination has been suffered by Nationalists in the Six Counties ever since that area was separated from the rest of Ireland.

The meanest form of discrimination to which minority voters are subjected is the siting of polling booths in such a way as to discourage the recording of their votes. This form of penalisation dates back to the early years of partition and has often been

---

1 *Ulster Herald*, 8 Dec. 1951.
2 *Strabane Weekly News*, 11 June 1949.

discussed in Parliament. Notably in March 1929, [1] there was a debate in which Labour speakers described the arrangement of the booths as designed rather to prevent the minority from voting at all. It was raised in the British Parliament in March 1948, [2] when M.P.s gave examples of how the system worked: voters living west of Omagh in Nationalist Tyrone must walk through the town and three miles east before they could vote; those living south-west must go five miles south-east beyond the town. In Down electors must cross a mountain and go five miles further on to vote. Others have to walk eight miles, others again must pass ten polling places before they come to that alone in which they could vote. The British said it was a matter for the Belfast Parliament, the Belfast Parliament said it was entirely the concern of the County Councils. When in November 1949 the Nationalists pleaded with the gerrymandered County Councils of Tyrone and Fermanagh for a fairer placing of the polling booths, each Council, on a party vote, refused to make any change. [3]

Three other forms of discrimination, as described by the United Nations, flourish in the partitioned area.

> "Inequality in personal security", including that of privacy, family, home and correspondence,
> "Inequality in freedom of movement and residence", including compulsion as to place of residence, etc., and
> "Inequality in the enjoyment of the right of freedom of peaceful association."

These inequalities are visited upon the Nationalist minority in the Six Counties through what are known as the Special Powers Acts, described in the chapter dealing with the Special constabulary.

These Special Powers have in recent years been used to prevent wholly peaceful demonstrations by the Nationalists. A procession at Moneymore, Co. Derry, in honour of St. Patrick, organised by a Nationalist organisation of long standing, was banned on 17 March 1950. Twelve months later, on St. Patrick's Day 1951, when members of the Derry Corporation were carrying the National Flag through this strongly Nationalist city, the flag was seized by the police and the Corporators were arrested. On 15 August 1951 (15 August is a day which, by tradition, is devoted to Nationalist processions in the Six Counties) the carrying of the

1 Northern Ireland Debates, vol. 10, cols. 1132 et seq.
2 Hansard, 24 Mar. 1948, vol. 448, cols. 3202 et seq.
3 See *Belfast Newsletter,* 13 Dec. 1949, 18 Feb. 1950.

National flag in a parade through the Nationalist town of Enniskillen was banned by the police, and when the flag was flown from an upper window of the house of Mr. Cahir Healy, then a member both of the British Parliament and of the Belfast Parliament, the police used long sticks with spikes to tear the flag to ribbons. In neither Enniskillen nor Derry was there on these occasions other than an entirely peaceful effort by the majority of the citizens to assert their right to carry the national flag which is the symbol of their movement. Flags and emblems of the Tory movement, on the other hand, have never been interfered with.

The effect on the rights of the minority of giving to the police such powers as are contained in the Special Powers Acts is obvious. The very existence of these powers has been, and must always be, a curb on normal political opposition. The Nationalists know that under them they may, without warning, have their homes raided and that they themselves may be taken away to imprisonment without any charge or trial. This implied threat to them is all the more real because, as we have seen, one of the governmental organisations charged with implementing the Special Powers is the body knows as the "B" Special Constabulary. Sections of the minority have shown bitter and violent resentment at the discrimination used so incessantly against them. But that, too, is provided for. As the United Nations Memorandum says:

> A group suffering from discrimination frequently becomes disaffected or rebellious and the evidence of its disaffection in turn is used as a new ground for discrimination.

The more the minority struggles, the more the noose tightens around its neck.

When the Council of Europe was discussing Human Rights in August 1949 and the pernicious nature of these Special Powers was exposed at Strasbourg, the operation of some of them was suspended. But since then many of the suspended powers have been reimposed. The police have again been authorised to make forcible entry to any house; to search houses without warrant; to seize and dispose of property without compensation. They are empowered to hold up citizens in the streets and search them without producing any authority. They can arrest without charge and imprison any "suspect" without trial. They are empowered to remove those arrested to any district they themselves decide on, and to take, forcibly if need be, the fingerprints of all whom they arrest.

The members of the Belfast Government and the leaders of the Tory party in North-east Ireland must share with Britain the responsibility for the wholesale penalisation of the minority which has been outlined in this chapter. The rank and file of the supporters of that Government and party are not charged with these injustices. These ordinary men and women, who normally desire to be just and kind to their neighbours, are the victims of constant incitement and propaganda.

In 1935 the Orange mob in Belfast had been roused to acts of savage violence against the unprotected minority by speeches such as have been quoted in the foregoing pages. Later an inquest on the dead was held. The Coroner of Belfast, Mr. T. Alexander, himself a member of the majority, spoke words over those dead bodies with which this chapter might most suitably come to an end:

> The poor people who commit these riots are easily led and influenced. They are influenced almost entirely by the public speech of men in high and responsible positions. There would be less bigotry if there were less public speech-making by so-called leaders of public opinion.

CHAPTER XV

GERRYMANDERING

1. AN ELABORATE PROCESS

ONE OF THE greatest wrongs that can be done to a minority in a democratic State is to deprive it of its political rights, particularly of its electoral rights; for these are so often a shield for the rest. That wrong has been done to the minority in the Six Counties and it has been done stealthily. A casual observer would find no proof of it. In Parliamentary elections the minority have adult suffrage: in both Parliamentary and local elections they have the secret ballot, they are as free as any other group to put candidates into the field, they have almost the same rights to publicity. Yet despite all this the essence of operative democracy is denied them.

That denial is achieved by an arrangement of the electoral boundaries. By this simple device the vote of a member of the minority within the partitioned area is given only half, and often less than half, the value of the vote of a member of the majority. Everything else that belongs to democracy remains — adult suffrage, secret ballot, equal candidature, freedom of speech — yet democracy itself has been extinguished. This does not occur only where the Nationalists are in a minority. It occurs particularly in those areas where the Nationalists are in the majority.

Nothing illustrates this so dramatically as the outstanding Nationalist areas such as Derry City and Fermanagh County, both of which have nevertheless a majority of Tory representatives. In local elections, where voting qualifications more restrictive to the minority than to the majority are used to buttress boundary manipulation, there are seventeen areas with Nationalist majorities which without exception are made to elect strong Tory majorities in the local councils.

How is it done — this getting majority Tory Councils from majority Nationalist areas? And what is its purpose? This chapter answers both questions.

Gerrymandering, as the manipulation of electoral boundaries is called, presents no real difficulty if those in power are partial to one political group and if they know the sympathies of the

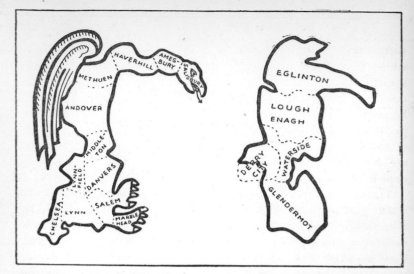

The electoral areas in Essex County, Massachusetts, U.S.A., were re-arranged when Governor Gerry was in office, giving an outline to which the artist, Gilbert Stuart, finding it in the office of Benjamin Russel, the Boston editor, added wings, beak and claws, and said it was like a salamander "Better say a Gerrymander," growled Russel; and a new word entered the world's dictionaries.

A modern example of boundary manipulation in the partitioned area of North-East Ireland. In order to Gerrymander the Nationalist majority in Derry out of representing that city in Parliament, a new City Division was designed by the Belfast Government. Part of the city is omitted altogether, and rural areas up to eight miles away have been brought in to outvote the Nationalists in the city proper.

Partition cuts across some of the oldest geographical and economic units of Ireland. Amongst the oldest administrative divisions are the dioceses. This map shows how the Six-County boundary cuts across the diocesan boundaries of Armagh, Clogher, Kilmore and Derry.

voters in particuler areas. Electoral districts can then be set up whose boundaries are so drawn that a majority can win only a minority of the seats. In almost every country there are certain areas where the political views of the people are known to be traditionally in favour of one party — Liberal or Tory, Republican or Democratic, Socialist or Conservative. In the part of Ireland with which this book deals the fundamental divisions are Nationalist and Tory. As in other countries the areas occupied by each party are generally known.

Thus, it is known to everybody in Ireland that the majority in Derry City, South Armagh, South Down, and in the countries of Tyrone and Fermanagh are Nationalist, and that the majority in most of Antrim, in North Down, in Derry County and in Belfast City are Tory. Those who live in these actual localities can get a still more detailed picture.

With this knowledge a line can be drawn around one set of townlands or streets which will encircle the main strength of the Nationalists and leave the rest of the district to be divided up into safe Tory constituencies.

Derry City is a typical instance. In Derry City there are 31,620 Nationalists and 18,479 Tories. It would seem from these figures to be beyond the wit of man to give Derry a Tory City Council. Not at all. The city, with the active assistance of the régime, is divided into three unequal wards as follows:

North Ward: 13,896 inhabitants who elect 8 representatives
South Ward: 24,768   „   „   „   8   „
Waterside Ward: 11,435   „   „   „   4   „

On the surface there is nothing unusual in that division. Many cities, owing to their configuration, have to have wards with populations numerically unequal. The difference is that in those other cities an honest effort is made to maintain a just ratio between the number of voters and the number of seats. Let us break down those Derry figures into electors with their party affiliations and we shall see the political significance of this arrangement of wards:

PARLIAMENTARY ELECTORS: 1954-55

	Nationalists	Tories
North Ward	3,153	4,903
South Ward	12,139	2,114
Waterside	2,570	4,119
	17,862	11,136

It will be seen that the wards have been so arranged that more

Nationalists have been crowded into the South Ward than there are Tories voters in the whole city.

There is the same picture when we consider the wards in relation to local electors, except that the Tory total of 11,136 Parliamentary voters have been reduced by only 2,309 to 8,827, whereas the Nationalist total of 17,862 has been reduced by 7,191 to 10,671:

LOCAL ELECTORS

North Ward	2,006	4,223
South Ward	7,167	1,667
Waterside	1,498	2,937
	10,671	8,827

The Tories win the eight seats of the North Ward and the four seats of the Waterside Ward, and thus for 8,827 electors have 12 seats on the Derry Corporation, while the Nationalists win but one ward, the South, and have but eight seats, although they have 10,671 electors. The Tory minority are thereby given control of the Derry City Government.

Though this arrangement of the wards of Derry City is remarkable, it is, as will be shown, not exceptional. Wherever a Nationalist majority could be disfranchised by the manipulation of electoral boundaries, this was done. It was an elaborate process, a description of which will interest all students of politics.

In October 1922 the Belfast Parliament passed an Act called the Local Government (Northern Ireland) Act. The first section of that Act abolished Proportional Representation, which was made part of the Partition Act for the protection of the Nationalist minority in the Six Counties. The second section gave the Ministry of Home Affairs complete power to alter boundaries of electoral divisions or to alter the number of such divisions in any urban or County Council area. Rural council electoral areas were not mentioned in the Act.

Section 2, subsection (1) of the Act says:

> The Ministry may from time to time make orders
> (a) dividing a borough urban district or town into wards and fixing the boundaries of such wards, altering the number and boundaries of the wards, or altering the boundaries of the wards without altering their number....
> (b) dividing a county into county electoral divisions, altering the boundary of a county electoral division, or the number of county councillors and county electoral divisions for a county....

Though the Section binds the Minister to "consult with" the

existing local body, he is free to ignore their advice and is free also to put through his alterations of boundaries with or without holding a local inquiry. As soon as the Act was passed, the Minister for Home Affairs, who was Sir Dawson Bates, a Tory and a leading member of the Orange Order, appointed as a Commissioner, Mr. John Leech, K.C., a fellow Tory.

Mr. Leech was appointed with the powers of a Judge to visit areas in which objections to the alteration in the number and the boundaries of local electoral districts might be anticipated. These were naturally the areas in which the Nationalists were in majority and in which they might resist the changes designed to deprive them of representation. To the surprise of everybody he devoted himself to altering the Rural Councils both in electoral areas and membership.

Until 1922 there was an accepted procedure before any such alterations were made. It was that the demand for changes must come from ratepayers or electors of the area. This was then remitted to the local authority concerned for its agreement. The Department of Local Government then prepared and published a scheme for the particular area and invited local consideration of it. Voters and ratepayers were given access to all documentation concerning the proposed change and were allowed ample time to discuss it. At a subsequent inquiry they submitted their criticisms, which were seriously discussed.

Under the 1922 Act, however, the procedure was different. No details were published for local examination and criticism. The first announcement that a change was intended took the form of an advertisement which said that Judge Leech would be in such and such a district on a specified date to consider the "alteration of district electoral divisions". Electors were invited to forward any representations they wished to make with any relevant maps and statistics to reach Judge Leech at the Ministry of Home Affairs, Belfast, "at least one week" prior to the date of the inquiry. The advertisement usually appeared from 17 to 21 days before the inquiry was held, thus leaving 10 to 14 days for the preparation of a scheme. For instance on 20 January 1923 appeared the notification of the inquiry into the Clogher Rural District area to be held on 6 February, [1] on 25 January the announcement of an inquiry on 13 February into the Dungannon Rural District area, [2] on 3 February the notification

[1] *Ulster Herald,* 20 Jan. 1923.
[2] *Tyrone Courier and News,* 25 Jan. 1923.

of the Castlederg inquiry on the 20 February and the Omagh inquiry on the 21st. [1]

As will be realised the detailed preparation of any such scheme would be quite beyond the capacity or resources of an individual. The electoral areas for Rural Councils cover sometimes many hundreds of townlands and many scores of electoral divisions. [2] The working-out of new electoral divisions for such areas required much technical documentation: official records covering a long period of time, statistics of valuation as well as of populations, the preparation of elaborate maps etc.

Before Mr. Leech was appointed and probably before the Act was passed, it seems that the local Tory party leaders were informed what was afoot, and the work of preparing the new electoral areas was carried on with great discretion. When at last a notice appeared, a fortnight in advance, that Commissioner Leech would visit the area, the Tory party had ready fully detailed schemes accompanied by maps, diagrams, schedules and statistics which had obviously taken months to prepare. The Nationalists, convinced that the operation of Clause XII of the Treaty, would undo all this, nevertheless expected the ordinary procedure: proposals would first be propounded and published and criticisms sought. They were taken by surprise.

Reports of the sitting of the Inquiry in the various districts usually opened with such words as appeared in the *Ulster Herald* with regard to Strabane Rural Council on 24 February 1923:

> The Judge announced that only one scheme accompanied by schedules giving information and a map had been sent in on behalf of Mr. Wm. T. Millar M.P. and no other person had made any representation.

Mr. Millar was the local Tory M.P. If Judge Leech, who knew who Mr. Millar was, had been an impartial judge he would of course have asked how was it that in so important a matter involving the representation of all parties he had received but one scheme and that from the minority party. Nowhere did he ask that question or express any surprise! Rather, in reply to Nationalist protests, he pretended that they had had an equal opportunity of submitting a detailed scheme and in fact he made

[1]   *Ulster Herald,* 3 Feb. 1923.
[2]   The Clogher Rural area, one of the smallest in Tyrone, embraces 304 townlands, grouped in sixteen electoral divisions. Omagh Rural area on the other hand embraces 569 townlands in thirty-nine electoral divisions.

their failure to do so a reason why he must accept the only scheme before him.

The scheme in question in the *Ulster Herald's* report was for the Strabane Rural district in which the Nationalists had a majority in population and had won 10 of the 19 seats on the Council in the last election. Judge Leech accepted Mr. Millar M.P.'s scheme which expanded the Strabane Council from 19 to 28 seats of which the Nationalist majority could now secure only 8!

Judge Leech also accepted the only scheme submitted to him at Dungannon. It too, had been drawn up by the forewarned Tory Party and was described by the Judge as "very elaborately prepared". The Nationalists' strength on the Downpatrick Rural Council, where they held 9 seats to the Tories' 8, coincided with their majority among the population viz. 52.4 per cent to 47.6 per cent. The scheme accepted by Judge Leech increased the seats on the Council to 19 and so arranged the boundaries that the Nationalist majority now get 6 seats and the Tories 13.

Around all the Border areas in which the Nationalists were in majority, this elaborately staged "judicial tribunal" operated. In Clogher the only scheme submitted was by Mr. Wm. Coote, Tory M.P. for the area. [1] The Judge accepted it without question, with the effect as shown by the quotation below. In Cookstown also only the Tories got long enough notice to put forward a scheme. The Nationalist majority in the rural district was 53 per cent. The Tory scheme which Judge Leech approved increased to sixteen the fourteen electoral areas. Of the fourteen, Nationalists had held a majority of 8, but of the new sixteen divisions, carefully chosen borders ensured that the Nationalist majority could win only 7. The comment of the *Ulster Herald* of 7 July 1923 explained the process. Townlands where the Nationalists were in majority were detached from their present electoral division and attached to a nearby division in which the Nationalists already had a majority. Thus of two adjoining areas

1 "I have received only one representation submitted on behalf of Mr. Coote, M.P. It looks a business-like one and it has been very carefully prepared and contains a great deal of useful information", Judge Leech at Clogher Inquiry. *Tyrone Courier and News* 15 Feb. 1923.

The *Ulster Herald* reports Mr. Pringle, K.C. who presented Mr. Coote's scheme at the Inquiry as saying, "He was greatly struck with the map and schedules prepared by Mr. Coote, the latter of which showed the different divisions, with populations and valuations, on the old scheme and that now submitted to his Honour". *Ulster Herald,* 17 Feb. 1923.

each with a comfortable Nationalist majority there were made two others, one with an overwhelming Nationalist majority and an area beside it in which the removal of the Nationalists left a small but useful Tory majority.

> For instance (said the *Ulster Herald*) they have made the Clogher division secure by placing the townlands of Shanco, Ballyscally, Cloghin, Corleachan and Grange Mountain Bar (which have only a few Unionist residents) in the Cullamore Division that had already a Nationalist majority of about 200. In a similar manner Augher has been lost to the Nationalists by the inclusion of the Unionist districts of Glenhoy, Longridge and Mullands. By the same method Aughethine Division and Aughnacloy Urban Division have been made Unionist. So far as it is possible to anticipate the results of the elections in May next under the new arrangement, those best qualified to judge believe that the Council will consist of 5 Nationalists and 11 Unionists.

The care that went into this scheme of depriving a majority of its majority voting power is illustrated by taking five of the largest Nationalist electoral divisions in Tyrone County and contrasting them with five of the same county's largest Tory electoral divisions. We will see the great number of Nationalist votes thus made ineffective, allowing the lesser Tory votes to carry other divisions.

The five largest Nationalist electoral divisions in the Omagh Rural Council area and the voting strengths of the two parties are:

	Voters	Nationalist	Tory	Ineffective Nationalist votes
Carrickmore	473	394	79	314
Creggan	623	617	6	610
Crockanboy	506	471	35	435
Fallagh	448	425	23	401
Loughmacrory	451	409	42	366
	2,501	2,316	185	2,126

In other words 85 per cent of the Nationalist vote was rendered ineffective.

In the following Tory areas a much smaller Tory vote is spread effectively over a large area. The five largest Tory electoral divisions in the Omagh Rural Council area are:

	Voters	Nationalist	Tory	Ineffective Tory votes
Benchran	429	188	241	52
Dunbreen	350	137	213	75
Gortin	350	136	214	77
Mountjoy Forest West	366	150	216	65
Kilskeery	349	92	257	164
	1,844	703	1,141	433

Only 37.9 per cent of the Tory vote was rendered ineffective.

It is obvious from these figures that what has happened is by design. The ineffective Nationalist vote is five times as large as the ineffective Tory vote. The Nationalist voters are asked to pay 2,316 votes for five seats, whereas five seats are secured by the Tories for only 1141 votes or less than half. By this means, applied all over the Omagh Rural Council area, a large Nationalist district was handed over to Tory management. A total of 8,459 Nationalist votes were unable to secure a majority on the Council, that majority being won by the 5,381 votes of the minority.

What happened in regard to Omagh Rural Council happened also in regard to every Rural Council in the County of Tyrone, the political distribution of whose membership is shown in the following table for before as well as after the gerrymander:

		Nats.	Tories	Nat. % of Population
Castlederg	Before	7	7	50.8%
	After	6	10	
Clogher	Before	7	9	50.8%
	After	5	11	
Cookstown	Before	8	6	52.9%
	After	7	9	
Dungannon	Before	9	8	52.0%
	After	6	13	
Omagh	Before	26	13	61.5%
	After	18	21	
Strabane	Before	10	9	54.2%
	After	8	20	
Tyrone Co. Cl.	Before	15	11	57.2% [1]
	After	12	15	

Thus in one county the minority, by a careful assignment of electoral divisions, took control of every Nationalist rural area and converted its own total of 63 seats before the gerrymander to 99. At the same time it reduced the seats held by the majority from 82 to 62, although the ratio of the two electorates had not in the meantime changed.

This manipulation of boundaries occurred not in one county only but wherever the Nationalists were not in such overwhelming majority that they could not be dislodged. Keady urban area in County Armagh with 81 per cent Nationalists escaped, so did Newry Town in Co. Down with 79 per cent and Strabane Urban

[1] These are from the Census used at the time, that of 1911; no other census was taken until 1926.

in County Tyrone with 75 per cent. But in areas where the Nationalists are as much as from sixty to sixty-five per cent, as well as where they are below sixty per cent, a rearrangement of electoral divisions dispossessed them of majority rights.

We have given instances from Rural areas. Urban districts provide similar examples.

Armagh City has a Nationalist majority of 57.2 per cent. The Tory 42.8 per cent control the City Council, getting 12 seats to the Nationalists' 8.

Enniskillen Borough Council has a Nationalist majority of 55.8 per cent. The Tory minority control the Council by 14 seats to 7.

Omagh Urban Council has a Nationalist majority of 62 per cent. The Nationalists get only 9 of the 21 seats, the Tory minority get the other 12 and control the Council.

Observe the new "democracy" at work: 55 per cent, 57 per cent, 62 per cent—it is all the same—the minority gets a substantial majority of the seats.

This method, whose effectiveness the figures demonstrate, is applied across the whole partitioned territory from Down in the East to Derry in the West. It is perfectly in keeping with Partition, which is itself a giant gerrymander. By that major boundary manipulation a minority in the whole of Ireland was given a veto on the majority's right to decide policy for the nation, just as today by boundary manipulation minorities in Nationalist areas inside the partitioned territory are allowed to veto the local majority.

While in the area taken as a whole the Tories predominate numerically, they have local majorities in less than half the area. In half of Armagh and half of Down, in all Tyrone and all Fermanagh, in Derry City and part of Derry County and in the northern tip of Antrim, those against Partition are in majority. Not one of the Six Counties is without its Nationalist areas. The capital town in five of the Six Counties is Nationalist.

If these areas were free to elect representatives of their choice, there would be Nationalist Councils in more than half the severed territory. That in the Tory view must be prevented at all cost.

The local electoral divisions were gerrymandered in 1923 and the divisions for the Belfast Parliament in 1929. As the concentration of Tory votes in Belfast and within a thirty mile radius of it provides the party with a majority of seats in the Par-

liament, [1] the manipulation of Parliamentary boundaries within
that radius was designed mainly to keep the number of Nationalist representatives as low as possible. (Nationalists are more
than a fourth of the City's population but they get only 2 of
Belfast's 16 seats, one for every 57,470 people; whereas the Tories
have a seat for every 23,480.) In Derry City and in Fermanagh
the gerrymandering of Parliamentary constituencies has been
just as ruthless as in any local-government area, again for purely
political reasons.

Derry City has a particular place in Tory mythology, though
it is a Nationalist stronghold. By a special arrangement of wards,
the majority is prevented from electing a representative City
Council, as we have seen earlier. They are also prevented, but
by a different method, from electing a Member of Parliament.
For Parliamentary purposes Derry City is an obvious unit, and
its population comprises as we have seen, 31,620 Nationalists and
18,479 Tories. However, political arithmetic is no obstacle to
the determined gerrymanderer. Part of the City was cut away
altogether and put into an already Nationalist constituency (the
Foyle Division). Then a carefully chosen series of rural areas,
some of them eight miles away, were grafted on to the now
truncated city. By that means a Tory majority was created for
what is still absurdly called the City Division.

Thus the Parliamentary as well as the municipal representation
of the second city of the partitioned area was secured for the
minority.

The Tories also considered it necessary to break up the Nationalist counties of Tyrone and Fermanagh, whose area is over
a third of the whole partitioned territory. They concentrated on
Fermanagh and created three Parliamentary constituencies in
which the population was thus divided:

	Nationalists	Tories
Enniskillen	8,900	10,600
Lisnaskea	8,300	9,200
South Fermanagh	12,200	3,700
Totals	29,400	23,500

Notice the same pattern as in Derry. Fermanagh has 29,460 Nationalists and 23,580 Tories. By drawing such an electoral
boundary as will make one overwhelmingly Nationalist constituency (South Fermanagh), the Tories provide themselves with
two constituencies in which they have a small but sufficient

[1] The area within 30 mile radius of Belfast elects 34 of the 52 members
of the Parliament, and 30 of these are Tories.

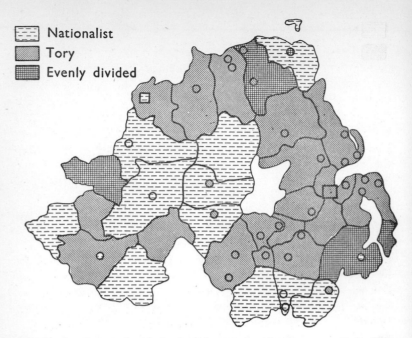

Nationalist
Tory
Evenly divided

Map showing the results of elections for rural and urban councils in 1920, before the Belfast government was established

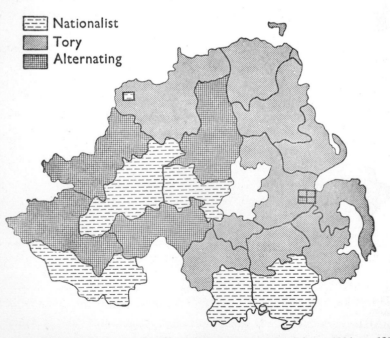

Nationalist
Tory
Alternating

Map illustrating the results of parliamentary elections from 1884 to 1918

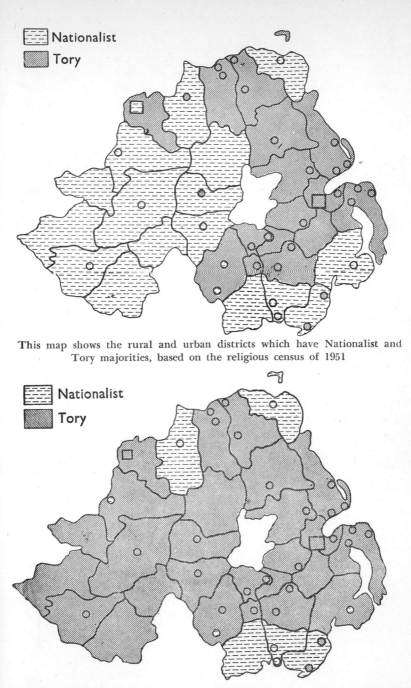

This map shows the rural and urban districts which have Nationalist and
Tory majorities, based on the religious census of 1951

The universality of the policy of gerrymandering since the Belfast government was established is seen in this map showing the results of the 1955
local elections. In most areas in which Nationalists are in majority they
are prevented from returning a majority of the councillors

majority. Thus, despite adult suffrage and the secret ballot, the minority gets twice the representation of the majority. And having done this the Tories can point to a two-to-one Parliamentary representation to support their contention that Fermanagh wants to remain partitioned from Ireland!

The attack on the electoral rights of the Nationalists comes from two directions. Not only are those who have the vote deprived of its value by gerrymandering, but as many as possible have been denied the franchise altogether under a new Act. An interesting parallel was provided in this matter. In 1945, both the British Parliament and the Belfast Parliament had before them legislation determining who should vote in local elections. The British Act extended the franchise, declaring that anybody aged twenty-one years or over was entitled to vote. (Free Ireland had given this right to its local electorate more than ten years earlier.) The British Act, however, contained a lengthy section excluding the local voters of the Six Counties from the benefit of adult suffrage, and the Act going through the Belfast Parliament actually restricted the franchise and took the vote from many who had it. The property qualification was made more onerous, and in addition a new form of plural voting was introduced, giving wealthy business firms up to seven votes each.

A member of the Administration openly admitted that the aim of the Act was to disfranchise the Nationalists where they formed a majority. It has notoriously succeeded in that aim. The Parliamentary electorate of 17,255 Nationalists in Derry City is reduced to 10,671. The Tory voters fare much better; their numbers are cut down by less than 2,400.

The constituency (Lisnaskea, Co. Fermanagh) which elects the Prime Minister of the Six County Government provides another example. There 12,037 people have the Parliamentary franchise. Those who can vote in local government elections have, however, been cut down to 7,523. But this reduction—achieved by the application of the residential and property qualifications— does not affect the two parties equally. The number of Nationalist voters is cut from 7,097 to 4,142, but the total of the Prime Minister's supporters only from 4,940 to 3,380. [1]

Even this, as the figures show, leaves the Nationalists in a majority. That majority is then made ineffective by gerrymandering. The electoral boundaries are so arranged that the Nationalists have large majorities in thirteen of the 31 electoral

[1] Figures cited from the Electoral Registers by Mr. Cahir Healy, M.P.

divisions, their ineffective votes allowing the Tories to win
control of the other eighteen with small majorities. This gives
them a majority on the Council. [1] The Tories are able to win
a seat for every 187 votes, the Nationalists having to poll 317
votes for every seat they get. The disproportion of seats with
regard to *population* is even more marked. The Tories get one
seat for every 435 persons: the Nationalists one for every 925
persons.

The universality of gerrymandering needs no other proof than
this disproportion. It can be cited for almost every local-government area in the whole Six Counties. From the most important
public body to the least the disparity exists.

Here is a list of examples giving one for each kind of public
body from the full analysis which was published elsewhere. [2]

	Seats per Party		Population per seat	
	Tory	Nationalists	Tory	Nationalist
Derry Corporation	12	8	1,541	3,665
Armagh County Council	23	5	1,638	7,098
Lurgan Borough Council	15	0	551	none for 5,499
Omagh Urban Council	12	9	180	397
Irvinestown Rural Council	14	8	424	851

It is obvious that only a carefully organised plan could have
produced this uniformity of discrimination.

The plan is indeed so carefully organised that it can be seen
in operation on any of the electoral maps. The All Party Anti-
Partition Conference published in 1950 a series of coloured
maps giving illustrations of the process. The maps embraced
electoral divisions in the areas of the Omagh Rural District
Council, the Enniskillen Rural District Council, the Lisnaskea
Rural District Council, the Armagh City Council and the
Derry Corporation. [3]

In the Omagh area the Nationalists had in 1920 a majority
in 8 of the 13 electoral divisions mapped. Then the gerrymander came into effect. Nationalist divisions were amalgamated
and the Tory divisions sub-divided, so that without any change
whatever occurring in the population the 13 electoral divisions
were reduced to 9 and of these only 2 were left with Nationalist
majorities.

[1] In 13 electoral districts the Nationalists have an average majority of 145,
but the average Tory majority in the remaining 18 is 62.
[2] *One Vote Equals Two.*
[3] Ibid., pp. 8, 9, 18.

HOW GERRYMANDER WORKS
LISNASKEA

Before Gerrymandering

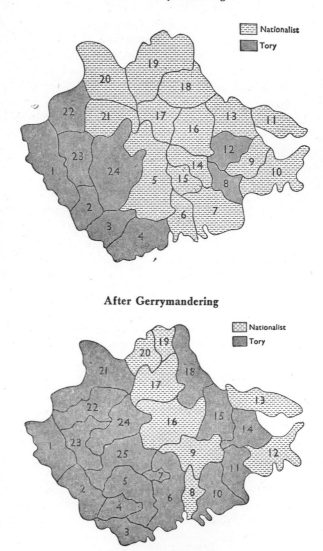

In the main part of the Lisnaskea Rural District before 1922 there were 24 Electoral Divisions, of which 15 had Nationalist majorities and 9 Tory majorities. The area was gerrymandered in 1922 and the boundaries so rearranged that majorities were created for the Tories in 17 of the now 25 Electoral Divisions, leaving only 8 Divisions in control of the Nationalists.

HOW GERRYMANDER WORKS
ENNISKILLEN

Before Gerrymandering

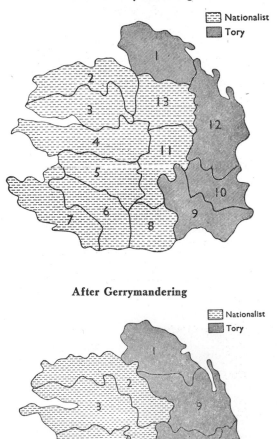

After Gerrymandering

In the western part of the Enniskillen Rural District before 1922 there were 13 Electoral Divisions of which 9 had Nationalist majorities and 4 Tory majorities. The area was gerrymandered in 1922. The Nationalist Electoral Divisions were greatly enlarged in order to reduce the nine held by the Nationalists to four. The boundaries of the Tory areas were then manipulated so as to give them five Divisions instead of four they had, thus turning a two to one Nationalist majority of seats into a minority.

THE ARMAGH GERRYMANDER

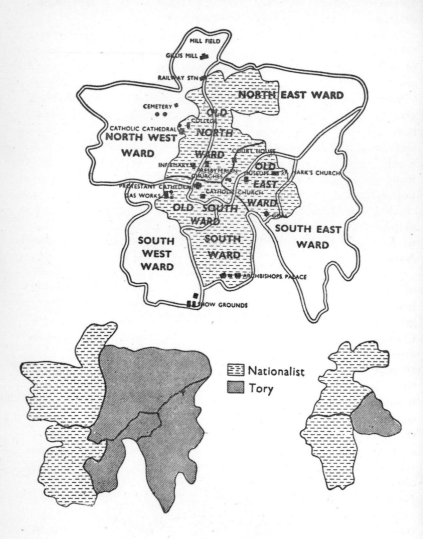

The diagram and maps show how Armagh with its Nationalist majority was made safe for the Tories. The City prior to 1946 is shown, shaded, in the centre. The South and North wards were Nationalist and the East ward Tory (as illustrated in the key below on the right). The City created by the 1946 gerrymander is shown in outline. With the rural additions, the wards were increased to five, of which three, the North-East, South-East and South were given to the Tories (as illustrated in the key on the left).
The Tories thereby controlled the City Council

The same process in the Enniskillen Rural District reduced 13 electoral divisions, 9 of which were Nationalist, to 9 electoral divisions, 4 only of which were Nationalist.

In Lisnaskea an area covering 24 electoral divisions was shown. Of these 15 were Nationalist and 9 Tory. But after the alteration of boundaries 25 new electoral divisions had been created in the same area and of these 17 were Tory and only 8 Nationalist. [1]

The cities—Armagh and Derry—were handled in a different way. In Armagh, as would be expected in a city with a population nearly 60 per cent Nationalist, the City Council was Nationalist. Prior to 1934 there were three electoral districts or wards. Though the population had *declined,* the city boundaries were enlarged so as to bring in much rural territory whose population was predominantly Tory. Five wards were now created. Three of the five were so arranged as to have a Tory majority, and as a result the City Council passed from Nationalist to Tory control, though the citizens remained still in majority Nationalist. [2]

Derry Corporation, is the example *par excellence* of the art of gerrymander. In a period of less than twenty years the wards had seen four major changes in an effort to prevent the rapidly growing Nationalist majority from electing a Nationalist City Council. Prior to 1919 there were five wards; in 1919 these were altered to four; in 1922 the number was again increased to five, though a different five; then in 1936 it was changed back to three, but a different three. In addition to altering the electoral boundaries other methods were used to nullify the numerical superiority of the Nationalist voters. The number of seats on the City Council was reduced from 40 to 20. The number of representatives allotted to each ward bore no relation to the number of persons in the ward. The voting qualifications were altered so that, as set out in the beginning of this chapter, more Nationalists than Tories were removed from the electoral registers. Even the siting of housing estates was governed by the central consideration that the Nationalists must not so gain in residential votes as to challenge the Tory minority's control of the city.

The result of this elaborate system is eminently satisfactory to the Tories in Derry. For every 933 votes they get a seat: the Nationalists get one seat for every 2,157 votes. The Tories have

1 Ibid., p. 18.
2 Ibid., p. 14.

a double reason for this strange electoral system: to provide themselves with an argument that Partition has a democratic basis, and at the same time to reduce to political impotence, even where they are in majority, those who oppose Partition.

The existence of public bodies controlled by the Nationalists would, in the Tory view, disclose the facts and demonstrate to the world the lack of homogeneity in the severed territory. To have a chain of Nationalist Councils running from East to West would blow the misconception of a solid "Ulster" sky high and would expose the geographical absurdity of the boundary. It would do something equally feared by the Tories. It would encourage the Nationalists to hope. It would keep them organised. It would give them authority and responsibility in these border communities.

On the other hand to take control of the Nationalist areas away from the Nationalists would help to dismay and disperse them. With the control of each public body goes the giving of employment, the building and allocation of houses, the spending of public moneys on health schemes, education, public libraries, public works, local amenities, etc.

All this implies considerable power over the life of the community. If Tory control of the Councils could be secured, therefore, the Nationalists could be excluded from public employment, be denied their proper share of housing and contracts for public works; they could be discriminated against educationally, and generally be treated as a subject section of the community. [1] Tory control would deny them hope and drive them to seek employment and residence elsewhere, until the Border areas could be made, like three-quarters of Belfast, the undisputed preserve of the Tory Party.

Some to whom the facts of gerrymandering are new may regard as exaggerated these statements as to its purpose. But the general attitude of the Tory leaders to the Nationalist majorities in the Border Counties has been frankly stated by themselves. Three prominent members whose importance to the Party has

[1] The *Voice of Ulster*, official organ of the Ulster Unionist Council, says in its issue of November 1949: "Vital as were the votes cast in Ulster's great Election last February, equally vital are Local Government votes. By the latter the Ulster people put into office those who can wield for weal or woe, the power transmitted by our Stormont Government. Nor is this power negligible when one considers the making of appointments, the letting of houses, and the provision of health, medical, education and other services."

been recognised by recent appointment to public posts have put their views on record.

The late T. L. Teevan was recently named a member of the Ulster Unionist Council and was selected as candidate for the Tory party in West Belfast in the General Election of October 1951.

It was Mr. Teevan who stated with brutal frankness that houses and employment must not be given to Nationalists or Catholics lest majorities in important electoral districts be lost. He himself was then chairman of the Limavady Rural Council, which had a majority of Tory representatives, although the majority in the area are Nationalists. On 15 January 1950, speaking at Enagh Lough in Derry, Mr. Teevan stated it in sectarian terms:

> What have we done? In the great strongholds of Unionism in Ulster they are still asleep, while we on the outskirts have to fight for our very lives. In Londonderry City and County, where we should have been on our guard, our majority has dropped from 12,000 to a perilously low figure. How did that came about? Through the ruinous and treacherous policy, pursued unwittingly perhaps, of handing over houses owned by Protestants to Roman Catholics. It is also caused by the great employers of labour in the North of Ireland employing Roman Catholic labour. [1]

The chairman at Mr. Teevan's meeting, Mr. J. C. Drennan, J.P., President of the North Derry Unionist Association, put it even more bluntly:

> They should return members to local authorities who would not be afraid to support the Unionist cause when houses became vacant. Then let them get down to the employers of labour. [2]

Another prominent Tory witness of the purpose behind gerrymandering is Mr. E. C. Ferguson, M.P., who in October 1949 resigned from Parliament to take up the post of Crown Solicitor for Co. Fermanagh, to which the Six County Government appointed him. Speaking at Enniskillen, capital of the county, on 9 April 1948, he said:

> The Nationalist majority in the county, notwithstanding a reduction of 336 in the year, stands at 3,684. We must ultimately reduce and liquidate that majority. This county, I think it can safely be said, is a Unionist (i.e., a Tory) county. The atmosphere is Unionist. The Boards and properties are nearly all controlled by Unionists. But there is still this millstone around our necks.

[1] *Londonderry Sentinel,* 19 Jan. 1950.
[2] Ibid.

In a word, everything except the people are Unionist! The millstone was the County's Nationalist majority, which had been insufficiently liquidated by refusing to employ or house them.

The third important witness is Major L. E. Curran, then Parliamentary Secretary to the Minister for Finance, later Attorney General, and recently appointed a member of the High Court. This "liquidation" of a Nationalist majority would according to him, be best achieved by the wholesale disfranchisement of Nationalists not in Fermanagh only but in other Border Counties also. He was in charge of the Bill already mentioned limiting the franchise in local elections; and on 10 January 1946 in the Belfast Parliament, he referred to the danger "of the Nationalists getting control of the three Border counties plus Derry City". Describing them as disloyal he was reported in a Tory paper as saying:

> The best way to prevent the overthrow of the Government by people who had no stake in the country and had not the welfare of the people of Ulster at heart was to disfranchise them.

That a Government should introduce a Bill for the sole purpose of disfranchising its opponents would have produced a political crisis in a democracy. No crisis was precipitated in the Six Counties. The majority in the Belfast Parliament accepted the reason given by Major Curran as an excellent one for passing the Bill into law. Though Major Curran wrote to the newspapers correcting another passage of the same speech he did not question the accuracy of the passage about disfranchisement.

One minor difficulty arose in this matter: it was soon surmounted! The official report of the speech does not contain the tell-tale passage. It can, however, still be seen in the Tory Press of the next day, 11 January 1946, where it was reported, and in the *Northern Whig* was emphasised by being put into specially large type.

This whole incident illustrates how little exaggeration there is in saying that in the partitioned area, electoral as well as other laws are designed to extinguish the rights of the Nationalists inside the border.

In the case of this particular Bill the Nationalists were directly robbed of their votes. In other cases disfranchisement is achieved indirectly. In the Chapter on Discrimination it is shown how houses built out of public funds are refused to families in dire need of proper shelter, if these families are Nationalist. The result is that Nationalists are compelled to leave the area or to seek lodgings with another family. In either case the right to vote is lost in that district in which the Tories wished to "liquidate" it.

This link between votes and houses has long been a feature of political life in the Six Counties. It partly explains why in the long period from 1922 to recent years the record for housing in the area has been deplorable. "I was 20 years on the Public Health Committee of Belfast Corporation", said the present Minister for Education, Mr. Harry Midgley, in the Belfast Parliament on 20 March 1946. "We got reports of insanitary dwellings and what did I find on pursuing the question further. I found that in between the war years there never was a scheme, not one single scheme, of slum clearance carried out in Northern Ireland." [1]

Another member of the Government, Mr. J. E. Warnock, K.C., Minister for Home Affairs, speaking of Fermanagh in the Belfast Parliament on 18 May 1944 said, "No cottages have been built in that county under the Labourers Acts since 1912" (i.e. for thirty-two years). The explanation for this widespread neglect is provided by another Tory group. On 6 June 1936 a meeting was held of the Tory members of the Omagh Rural District Council, on which, though the area is strongly Nationalist, the Tories have a strong majority. These Tory Councillors passed a resolution asking for a change in the law relating to the letting of labourers' cottages. The existing law was that if a particular family, being badly housed, applied for a cottage, and one were built, it should be given to that family. To avoid the Nationalists having the benefit of this law the Council built no cottages. In time their own followers became badly in need of new housing. Even then the Tory Councillors would not build. As a preliminary they asked that the law be changed permitting them to erect out of public funds cottages for their followers only.

> If this change were made (said their secretary, Mr. Robert A. Parke, in a letter to the Deputy Whip of the Government Party, Sir Wilson Hungerford, on 6 June 1936) it is believed it would enable the Unionist party to improve their position without risk from the other side.

A new house meant new votes. The danger was real as, due to the unusually bad conditions under which the Nationalists were compelled to live, they were certain to have first claim on new cottages.

[1] Northern Ireland Debates, 20 Mar. 1946, vol. xxx, col. 294.

In a resolution urging the change in law, which accompanied
Mr. Parke's letter to the Government Whip, the Councillors said:

> We would point out that in certain districts cottages are required
> by Unionist Workers but we hesitate to invite representations as
> we know there would be a flood of representations from the Na-
> tionalist side and our political opponents are only waiting the
> opportunity to use this means to outvote us in divisions where
> majorities are close. [1]

The change in law was not granted, and despite the fact that
over 40 per cent of the houses in Tyrone were totally unfit for
human habitation, no cottages at all were built.

These are not momentary acts, wrongs done in the heat
of party combat. They are part of a long-standing, carefully-
devised plan. The effect of these injustices does not fall on the
Nationalists only. The injustices have corrupted the whole
foundations of local government. Not only are the rural and
urban councils, the Borough Councils and the City Corporations
unrepresentative of the people, which, it is pretended, elects
them; but the constant tampering with electoral freedom has
killed in the electorate as a whole any desire to participate in
local government. To-day, and for many years, a contested local
election in the Six Counties, particularly in the rural areas, is
so rare as to be a notable event. It is no exaggeration to say, as
the figures below will show, that nowhere in the world where
democracy exists can there be found a parallel to the situation
in the partitioned area. There a majority of all seats on elective
Councils, a majority as high as almost 80 per cent, are filled
without a vote being cast, not once but in every election for
thirty years.

Before 1922, there were instances of unopposed returns in the
North-eastern area of Ireland. But they were nothing like what
has now become the custom. It was in 1923 that the local
electoral divisions were gerrymandered. The elections immediately
before that date showed how keen an interest in local politics
fair electoral conditions will stimulate. For practically every
urban seat there was a contest, and for the great majority of
rural seats.

> Out of 126 Borough and Urban Council areas (reported the *Irish
> Independent* in January 1920) there were contests in all but nine.
> One hundred and forty candidates are contesting the 60 seats in
> Belfast. [2]

[1] Northern Ireland Debates, 23 Mar. 1937, vol. xix, col. 731.
[2] *Irish Independent,* 17 Jan. 1920.

The system of election was P.R.; the divisional boundaries had generally not been tampered with, and men and women readily offered themselves for service on the public boards.

The change showed itself as soon as the alteration of electoral boundaries had taken place, and it continues to this date.

The *Belfast Newsletter* (Tory) of 16 January 1926 put the fruit of gerrymandering in one sentence which was not even intended to be cynical:

> No matter how the voting goes there will be a Unionist majority on the new Council.

For every election year from 1923 to 1952 one could find quotations such as this:

> Little interest was evinced in nominations for the urban councils and in the majority of cases there will be no contests. In some there were fewer candidates than seats to be filled and it is suggested that the retiring members in these cases may be deemed to have been elected.

This is from the *Belfast Newsletter* of 6 January 1923.

In 1927, the *Banbridge Chronicle* published this comment:

> Greater apathy in connection with local affairs could scarcely be imagined than that shown by the result of the nominations for urban and rural district Councillors this week.... Even the retiring members themselves, with a few exceptions did not appear deeply concerned or manifest any desire to retain office.... The same apathy prevailed as far as the County Council was concerned.

In more recent elections the *Irish News,* Belfast, referring to the Enniskillen Urban Council, said in 1949:

> For the first time for many years there will be a contest for one seat.

Referring to contests for the Castlereagh Rural Council the *Belfast Newsletter* of 21 May 1952 said:

> It will be the first challenge to the Unionists for at least 20 years.

It was not only that there were no contests. The apathy has been so profound that in every election year the candidates have been fewer than the seats!

This petrification of local democracy did not arise from lack of work which the Corporations, County Councils, Urban Councils, might have been doing. In each of the six partitioned counties the scope open to enthusiastic public bodies has been and is likely to remain very wide indeed. Both in urban and rural areas overcrowding and the occupancy of houses totally unfit for human habitation are grave problems, as the figures in the Official 1944 Housing Survey (the latest available) show.

In Belfast, for example, over 28,000 houses were then either overcrowded or unfit for human habitation, and the number is somewhat similar to-day. In other urban areas the total was 16,461. In rural areas 66,794 houses were overcrowded or unfit for human habitation, ranging from 30 per cent of all houses in Co. Down to 57.9 per cent in Co. Fermanagh. In the same rural areas there was an average of 31 per cent of all houses without water, 39 per cent of all houses without separate sanitation, and the houses without either gas or electricity were 83 per cent of the whole, being 70 per cent in Co. Down and over 90 per cent in both Tyrone and Fermanagh.

On 24 June 1952 a debate was held in the Six County Parliament on housing conditions in Belfast. Mrs. Irene Calvert, Member for Queen's University, Belfast, described conditions in Lonsdale Street of that city. Of one house which other speakers declared was not exceptional she said:

> The kitchen of the house is let at 11/- per week and in that kitchen there are nine of a family living, a father, mother and seven children. When I say "children" they are all over the age of 10 years and they are all past the age at which the sexes are normally segregated. In actual fact, nine members of a family are living, eating and sleeping in the kitchen.

Describing how other rooms in the house also contain families, one comprising a mother and six children, Mrs Calvert went on:

> The conditions in the house are frightful. There are about 50 or 60 people living in that house and there is one toilet for the whole house. I think that fact speaks for itself. The two attics are damp, many of the rooms are infested with bugs and clocks and other vermin are running all over the place ... I know it is not easy but if you take a house of this kind where there are eight families living and some of those families have seven or eight children what kind of families are those people going to bring up in the next generation? [1]

Other speakers in the debate were Dr. Rodgers, M.P., and Dr. Eileen Hickey, M.P. Dr Rodgers said: [2]

> I can tell the Hon. Member also that the case which she has quoted is not the only one of its kind. I know of a house where there are 30 people and there is only one wash basin available. This is a common question ...

[1] Northern Ireland Debates, 24 June 1952, vol. xxxvi, cols. 1208, 1210.
[2] Ibid., col. 1212.

Dr. Hickey said:

> Lavatory and washing conditions in the Lonsdale Street area are
> simply shocking and so are the lighting, cooking and heating arran-
> gements. I passed through the area this morning and tried un-
> successfully to count the number of broken windows. I should like
> to say that the people who are housed in such sub-human conditions
> end by being dehumanised themselves and they exploit each other. [1]

There was and is, therefore, an immensity of urgent work
for public bodies to do, yet even in a crowded industrial city
like Belfast there is no enthusiasm to do it. Over four out
of every ten seats on the Belfast Corporation have been filled
without contest in the period 1923 to 1955. The exact percentage
is 42.7. The average in other urban bodies is higher still. There
has been only one year in the last thirty when a majority of the
urban seats in the whole North-east of Ireland were contested,
i.e. 1946, when even in the Six Counties the urge for a new
postwar world was felt.

The figures for all the ten local elections in the urban areas
since Partition are as follows: [2]

YEAR	SEATS VACANT	SEATS UNCONTESTED	%
1923	479	381	79.6
1926	404	213	52.8
1929	379	198	52.3
1932	344	280	81.4
1936	340	252	74.2
1939	322	201	62.5
1946	446	131	29.4
1949	433	239	56.5
1952	496	275	57.4
1955	478	244	51.0

Average of uncontested seats 1923-55 59.6%

Where else in countries claiming to be democratic is there a
parallel to this — sixty per cent of all urban seats left uncontested? That it could occur in crowded areas where industrialism
and its effects have produced so many social difficulties reflects
a collapse of public faith in democracy. Usually the existence
of such difficulties attracts public-spirited men and women to
contest vigorously for membership of the electoral bodies. In
the Six Counties partisan interference with the electoral system
has killed this spirit of public service.

[1] Northern Ireland Debates, 24 June 1952, vol. xxxvi, cols. 1215-6.
[2] The totals of "Seats Vacant" differ as some bodies renewed only part
of their membership in these main electoral years.

But if the urban areas are apathetic even in face of pressing problems, what can be said of the rural districts? The following is an analysis of the local-government elections held in the rural areas of the Six Counties since these areas were gerrymandered in 1923.

YEAR	SEATS VACANT	SEATS UNCONTESTED	%
1924	742	709	95.6
1927	742	702	94.6
1930	742	706	95.2
1933	742	711	95.9
1936	742	717	96.7
1939	742	722	97.4
1946	742	684	92.2
1949	742	703	94.8
1952	742	688	92.7
1955	742	703	94.8

Average of uncontested seats 1924-1955: 94.9%

Despite the wide opportunities for constructive public work, 95 seats in every 100 on the local-government bodies in the rural areas have never been contested in almost a generation.

If we take all local-government bodies, Corporations, Borough and County Councils, Urban und Rural Districts Councils, the average of the seats which have been filled without contest is nearly 80 per cent over the whole period from 1923 to 1955. In not one of the ten elections for rural and urban bodies since 1923, have there been enough candidates for all the vacant seats!

For the Six Counties as a whole in those years there has been a total shortage of candidates of 932. In 7 out of the 10 election years Antrim was more than 10 per cent short in the number of candidates put forward. In 1955 it was 14 per cent short. For every year from 1923 to 1939 Armagh was short over 10 per cent. Derry was 17 per cent short in 1939, and for each election before that year there were more than 10 per cent of the seats without candidates. The shortage of candidates in Down ranged from 5 per cent in 1945 to 17.4 per cent in 1932. The percentage in 1955 was over 9 per cent. Tyrone, although there was no shortage of candidates in 1949, had an average shortage over the period 1923 to 1945 of above 8 per cent. Fermanagh has the distinction of being short of candidates in only five of the ten elections years! The appendix to this chapter gives examples, from each of the Six Counties, of important public bodies for which over the period 1924 to 1955 there have not only been practically no contests but for many seats no candidates.

Next to the Corporations of Belfast and Derry, the most important of the local bodies in the Six County area are the County Councils, which have very substantial powers. Nevertheless, an average of 94 per cent of all the County Council seats have been uncontested since 1924, as this table shows:

County Council Elections.
1924—1955

Year	Seats	Seats Contested	Unopposed Returns	% of Unopposed Returns
1924	129	11	118	91.5
1927	129	11	118	91.5
1930	129	7	122	94.5
1933	129	10	119	92.2
1936	129	4	125	96.8
1939	129	6	123	95.3
1946	129	11	118	91.5
1949	129	5	124	96.1
1952	129	3	126	97.6
1955	129	4	125	96.8

The number of electors on the County Council register was 368,315, but in 1955 in

Antrim	of the 100,368 electors,	3,663 voted
Armagh	of the 47,764 electors,	none voted
Derry	of the 40,298 electors,	2,479 voted
Down	of the 104,756 electors,	3,386 voted
Fermanagh	of the 21,322 electors,	965 voted
Tyrone	of the 53,807 electors,	none voted.

These important Councils were returned although less than 3 per cent of the County Council electors took part in the "election".

As this book is being prepared for the press the full results of the 1955 local government elections in the Six Counties have become available. The important figures have been inserted in the tables. In the few areas in which more than one candidate was nominated for a seat the novelty of a disputed election led the newspapers to such comments as "This is the first election for 50 years". [1] In some urban and many rural areas there were, as we have seen, fewer candidates than seats, a trifling matter easily set right under the special law which empowers the returning officer to deem the last holder of the seat re-elected!

The Nationalist representatives are still kept as few as possible, by requiring that for every seat they get a larger number of supporters vis-à-vis their opponents. Thus for the principal urban

[1] See *The Belfast Newsletter* of 3 June 1955.

bodies in the 1955 elections the Unionists got a seat for every 3,992 of their people. The Nationalists, however, got one only for every 9,163. In the County Council areas the Unionists have a seat for every 4,107, whereas the Nationalists have one for every 10,135. [1]

Along the Border from the West to the East the principal towns are Derry City, Strabane (Co. Tyrone), Enniskillen (Co. Fermanagh), Armagh City, and Newry (Co. Down). In these towns and their rural areas the Nationalists form 57.2 per cent of the population, but they can win only 38.6 per cent of the seats. The 42.8 per cent minority, on the other hand, secure 61.4 per cent of the representation. [2]

In contrast, local elections were held in the free part of Ireland within a month of the Six County 1955 elections. Of the 1,400 seats only 12 were not contested. Three thousand candidates, the nominees of six national organisations and many local groups competed for membership of Corporations, Borough Councils, County Councils, Urban Councils etc.

This short survey of the elections held in the Six Counties during the last thirty years makes one thing plain. Since Ireland was partitioned operative democracy has become non-existent in the separated part of Ireland. Half the Corporations, more than half the Urban Councils, and almost all the Rural Councils are returned without a single voter going to the booths.

Before Partition every seat in the Derry Co. Council was contested, in 1920. In 1924 there was only one seat contested, and in the 25 years since then there have never been less than 17 unopposed returns to the 19 seats, and the average is 18. There were 40 candidates for the 23 seats on the Antrim Co. Council in 1920. From 1924 to 1952 the average of unopposed returns was 22, and in 7 of the 9 elections not even enough candidates presented themselves. For the 15 seats on Lisburn Urban Council there were 30 candidates in 1920. Since 1924 the Council has been returned 6 times without a contest, and in 4 elections there were not enough candidates. In 1920, 20 candidates fought for the 9 seats of Tanderagee Urban Council. In 1923 there was no contest and in 6 of the 8 elections from then to to-day not a

[1] The figures are based on the *Census of Population of Northern Ireland,* 1951, published in 1954.

[2] See full analysis of the 1949 election results in *One Vote Equals Two,* published by the Mansion House All-Party Anti-Partition Conference. There has been no material change since 1949. If anything, the Nationalists position has worsened.

vote had to be cast: it was 9 candidates for 9 seats every time, except when there were not even 9.

Gerrymandering and electoral laws both directed at suppressing Nationalist representation have had their effect in every part of, and on every party in, the partitioned territory. Liberalism, Labour, Nationalism, Independent Tories, Independents all have gone down under undemocratic action and legislation. Their disappearance or diminishment has left the official Tories in the Six Counties grossly over-represented and all others grossly underepresented. Worse still, it has left democratic elections themselves a mere facade to deceive the uninstructed observer.

II. PARLIAMENTARY ELECTIONS

Before the Partition Act was passed two notable statements were made about the outcome of Parliamentary elections in the Six Counties. One was by the Six County Tory leader who was about to give up the leadership, Sir Edward Carson, the other by the leader who was to replace him, Sir James Craig.

Sir Edward Carson was looking into the immediate future: he saw how the English cities were tending to elect more and more Labour M. P. s. The same, he felt certain, would happen in Belfast. Speaking in the British House of Commons on 10 November 1920, Sir Edward Carson said:

> When they come to work the Parliament in these industrial districts the elections will turn probably on Labour questions probably on a Labour Government — and I am not at all sure that if there is to be a Labour Govrnment it may not be the first Labour Government there will be in this United Kingdom because they (the workers) have a great preponderance of voting power and it may be you will elect the Parliament entirely on Labour questions. [1]

Sir James Craig was also looking into the future. He was explaining to the House how dangerous it would be for his Party if the real Ulster, the province of nine counties, were the area to be cut off. That had been the claim of his Party at many crises in the 1912-14 days — the exclusion of all Ulster. This "clean cut" was put forward not to be achieved but so that the Home Rule Bill might be wrecked by it. But in 1920 there *was* to be Parti-

[1] Hansard, 10 Nov. 1920, vol. cxxxiv, col. 1225.

tion, and Britain was compelling the Tories of the North-east of Ireland to accept a Parliament they had not sought. The ardour in favour of the "clean cut" had weakened noticeably after 1913 when, by winning a by-election, the Nationalists held a majority of the Parliamentary seats in the province. The demand for the exclusion of all Ulster was abandoned, and Sir James explained why in a speech in the British House of Commons on 29 March 1920:

> If we had a nine counties Parliament with 64 members the Unionist majority would be about three or four but in a Six Counties Parliament with 52 members the Unionist majority would be about 10.[1]

Nor was this the view only of Sir James Craig. Ian Colvin in his *Life of Lord Carson* refers to Carson's visit to Belfast in March 1920 to discuss the extent of the partitioned area. He goes on:

> Meanwhile the Ulster delegates had been debating the horrid choice between six and nine ... on the six county basis the Northern Parliament would probably consist of 32 Unionists and 20 Nationalists and Independents, a majority of 12, although on a closer analysis allowing broader margins of safety, the reading gave 31 Unionists and 21 Nationalists, a majority of 10. On the nine county basis taking the constituencies as they were in the Bill the result worked out at the best at 33 Unionists and 31 Nationalists, a majority of 2, or, upon a less favourable estimate at 32 for either party.[2]

The significant points in these statements are the likelihood of Labour successes at the polls and the certainty that the Nationalists and Independents would win about 20 or 21 seats. Neither of these things happened. By a use of violence sustained throughout the whole campaign of 1921 the seats won by the Nationalists were kept down to 12, and as for Labour, it was destroyed the first moment it showed its head.

For this we have the witness of the newspapers of the time. In the daily Press during the months of March, April and May 1921 the arrest and imprisonment of Nationalist agents, organisers, candidates, polling clerks is recorded day by day. The homes of many of them were broken into and in several cases they were murdered and in most assaulted. Their literature was seized in the post, and by raids on local Committee rooms, and destroyed. Their posters were torn down by Special Constabulary. Their

[1] Hansard, 29 Mar. 1920, vol. cxxvii, col. 990.
[2] Colvin, *Life of Lord Carson*, vol. iii, p. 383.

voters were driven away from the booths and were then imper-
sonated. Even during actual polling their impersonation agents
were expelled from the polling booths and at the counting
of the votes others were arrested — four of them were taken into
custody at the Antrim count and held for three hours. Early
in March 1921 (Polling day was 24 May) the *Irish Independent's*
special correspondent wrote from Fermanagh:

> There are other preparations of a more sinister character proceeding
> apace in Fermanagh which have created very grave apprehension in
> the minds of the Nationalist population. The County is now al-
> most entirely policed by the new Ulster 'Specials'. All the members
> of this new force are ex-members of Carson's army. The political
> and religious prejudices of these custodians of the lives and pro-
> perty of the people cannot be concealed. They are frankly the
> enemies of the people and make very little effort to hide their
> prejudices. [1]

That was at the beginning of the election. At the end, the story
was the same.

Three days before polling, a Special Correspondent from the
Manchester Guardian toured the area. He wrote in his paper:

> They (the Special Constabulary) scoured the countryside for Sinn
> Fein workers and threw them into jail without charge. They
> destroyed election literature.... No sooner has it been discovered
> that a man was Sinn Fein election agent for a district than he has
> disappeared.... At Martial Hill, in Armagh, the Sinn Fein director
> of elections for the district was taken out of his house by Special
> Constables and made to go down on his knees.... and promise he
> would take no further part in the elections.... These are incidents
> in the election campaign. They will give an idea of the handicaps
> placed on any man or woman who wishes to vote against the
> Unionists next Tuesday. [2]

On Polling Day itself, the *Irish Bulletin* wrote of this universal
repression, giving scores of instances and adding:

> How well the Special Constables did their work of political persecu-
> tion is instanced by the fact that of the 19 Sinn Fein candidates, 8
> are in jail and 7 others are "on the run". [3]

In the Six County area as a whole, where they are more than
a third of the whole population, the Nationalists secured not
the 20 or 21 seats which Sir James Craig with his intimate knowledge of the area predicted, but 12. It was, and is, an important
difference, for if the Nationalists and allied groups could win 20

---

[1] *Irish Independent*, 3 Mar. 1921.
[2] *Manchester Guardian*, 21 May 1921.
[3] *Irish Bulletin*, 24 May 1921.

seats and all others thirty-two, they would have been strong enough to protect the rights of their people, especially with the uprise of the Labour Party predicted by Sir Edward Carson.

But there was no uprise of Labour either. The Tories saw to that. Two of the Labour candidates in Belfast spoke to the vote of thanks to the Returning Officer after the elections had been decided. They were Councillor James Baird and Mr. Harry Midgley. They described the conditions under which they were permitted to fight the elections. Mr. Midgley, speaking after the count, said, according to the *Belfast Newsletter* (Tory) : [1]

> As that was the first opportunity he had had of speaking in public since the elections started, he wanted to enter his unqualified protest against the way in which the defenders of civil and religious liberty had conducted themselves. He protested against the methods of coercion which had been resorted to. They of the Labour Movement did not believe that the partition of the working classes in Ireland would ever solve the problems of the country and for that reason they were going to work for that unity which would bring about political and economic emancipation.

Councillor James Baird also gave his testimony as to the extraordinary thoroughness with which the Labour campaign had been extinguished:

> During the election he had not been allowed to say a word. Since the day of his nomination he had been hunted and shadowed by Crown Forces and he was unable to conduct his campaign. Intimidation marked the polling and many seeking to vote were brutally assaulted. He had been threatened and a threat made to wreck his home. Your election (he added) has been carried out under the worst intimidation and marked by wholesale impersonation. [2]

The suppression here described by one of its victims was no chance affair. The three Labour Party candidates, Messrs. Baird, Hanna and Midgley, had engaged the Ulster Hall, Belfast's main auditorium, for 17 May 1921. The Hall was stormed and captured some hours before the meeting by Orange members among the shipyard workers, who then sent a telegram to Sir James Craig:

> Mass meeting of loyal shipyard workers who have captured Ulster Hall from the Bolsheviks, Baird, Midgley and Hanna, request that you address them for a few minutes to-night.

Sir James Craig replied not with any condemnation but with a telegram to "my shipyard friends in the Ulster Hall". The telegram regretted that as he had to speak at meetings already advertised he could not come but

---

[1] *Belfast Newsletter,* 26 May 1921.
[2] Ibid.

am with them in spirit. Know they will do their part. I will do
mine. Well done big and wee yards. [1]

There was no member of the Labour Party elected to the Parliament in the last election in 1953, just as there was none elected
in the first election in 1921, though Belfast, highly industrialised,
sent 16 members to the House. A Socialist Republican and two
Independent Labour candidates were returned unopposed, but
from Nationalist constituencies. The extinction of Labour by
violence has been but little eased by time.

Labour has made no progress whatever in the thirty years
which have seen several Labour Governments in Britain and
many in the British Dominions. This arises from the exploitation and the extension into politics of the religious divisions
in the partitioned area where there are 899,000 Protestants and
471,000 Catholics.

The Orange order thrive by spreading fear of persecution
among its members, a persecution which never comes. Describing
itself as an embattled Protestantism, it has created out of its
imagination a "Romanism" ready to hurtle itself around the
corner at any moment and extinguish all liberty in the Six
Counties. This keeping alive of sectarianism is regarded by the
Tory leaders as vital to the continuance of the party in office.
An incident illustrating it occurred at Clifton Street Orange
Hall, Belfast, on 8 October 1951. Mr. Nathaniel Minford, Tory
M.P., said at the end of a by-election speech on that date: "God
save the King and to Hell with the Pope". Protests came from
many Protestants, and Mr. Minford disclosed later that he had
visited party headquarters next day ready to apologise, but the
leaders deprecated the idea. The phrase might win them the seat.

Polling took place on 25 October, and the seat was lost by a
few votes. It was then suggested that the offensive phrase had
kept decent Tories from the polls, and the decision was taken
to appease them. On 10 November, a month after it was made,
the Tory Headquarters disowned the speech, and on 13 November
Mr. Minford publicly apologised for it.

There are many similar speeches which are not apologised
for, and a fear of persecution is inculcated, day in day out, by
newspaper, lecture, speech and pamphlet. It is designed to turn
the average Orangeman into a fanatic, and to deflect his attention from the ordinary political and economic interests on which
normal movements and normal party-politics are based. To make

[1] *Northern Whig*, 18 May 1921.

sure of his not voting on everyday issues the Six County Government has had one main slogan in every election since 1921: "The State is in danger". This note of panic has been sounded incessantly.

From the election Manifestos or Eve-of-the-Poll Messages issued by Sir James Craig (Lord Craigavon) or his successor, Sir Basil Brooke, now Lord Brookeborough, in the seven general elections since 1921, these phrases are taken:

> The fate af the Six Counties hangs in the balance. (1921)
> Defeat your enemies, save the Border. (1925)
> Scatter your enemies. The fate of the country lies in your hands. (1929)
> Defeat the designs of our enemies.... Ravenous eyes are concentrated on our province. (1933)
> Ulster's fate is in your hands.... Forces.... are at work to deprive us of our birthright. (1938)
> Ulster's Constitutional position.... is the supreme issue. It dominates every other question. (1945)
> Our country is in danger—Ulster's heritage is at stake.... Loyalists stand to your defences. (1949)
> Overshadowing all else is the Constitutional issue. (1953)

Faithfully, in answer to this cry for help against ravenous enemies, the Orangeman turns away from his trade unions, his economic hopes, his schemes for more democratic politics, and springs to the defence of what he has been told is in danger of being captured and destroyed by Rome.

It may seem absurd to outsiders, as it is absurd to the vast majority of Irishmen. It is, however, all very real to the average Orangeman. For several generations he has been filled by his leaders with a hatred of his fellow-countrymen of another faith. He thus is kept estranged from them, constantly being replenished with new mistrust and suspicions so that he remains easy to convince that what he holds dear is threatened by those whom he has since childhood been taught to dread.

One who is now the Tory Minister of Education in Belfast, and himself exploits sectarianism with the best of them, was in his Labour days more perceptive. Mr. Harry Midgley, speaking as Secretary of the Belfast Labour Party in the Ulster Hall, Belfast, on 12 October 1923, said:

> I notice the orthodox politicians in Northern Ireland are at present preparing their new bogey for the next elections—that is the Border question.... I believe that just as in the old days when they kept us at each other's throats over the Home Rule question they will

seek to perpetuate their old privileges by resurrecting a new bogey, and this time it will be the Boundary bogey. [1]

No sooner had the Six County Government settled into office than it set about depriving the Nationalist voters of as much of their electoral strength as could be shorn from them. The elaborate gerrymandering of the local electoral districts in 1922-3 already described was carried out. What was done with regard to local government was applied to Parliamentary government in 1929. The method of election was changed. The Boundaries were "revised" and the number of seats the Nationalists could win was reduced. The party which Sir James Craig himself thought on a population basis should win at least 20 parliamentary seats can now win but 10.

In Antrim a Nationalist population of 39,800 secured a seat in each of the elections of 1921 and 1925. The 1929 gerrymander suppressed all Nationalist representation and, although it gave a seat to every 25,730 Tories in Antrim, it leaves the Nationalists, who now number 51,038, without any. In Armagh of the four seats the Nationalists in 1921 and 1925 won two. The Constituency was so rearranged that since 1929 the Nationalists win only one while the Tories win three. To win Derry City for the 37 per cent minority, the grotesque "City Division" already described was formed. Fermanagh, a Nationalist County, was given three seats, but their boundaries were so drawn that the Tory minority got two seats while the Nationalist majority can get only one.

When the Bill making these changes was going through the Belfast Parliament in March and April 1929 [2] many M.P.s gave other examples of how unjust it was to the minority. William MacMullan (Labour) said P.R. was abolished to deprive Labour of seats in Belfast. T. Henderson, (Independent Unionist) said the Government had called for an Opposition and "when they got it they gerrymandered and abolished proportional representation to drive them out". S. Kyle, Leader of the Labour Party and J. Beattie (Labour) instanced the unfairness of the Bill to working-class candidates, who would no longer have even the meagre representation they had secured under P. R.; P. McAllister (Nationalist) predicted that the eventual effect of the Bill must be to bring the Nationalist representation which should be at least 17 down to 9. George Henderson, the only Liberal in the

1 See *Northern Whig* and *Belfast Newsletter*, 13 Oct. 1923.
2 Northern Ireland Debates, vol. x, col. 437 et seq.

House, pleaded with the Government not to pass the Bill. J. W. Gyle (Independent Unionist) protested against the Bill, which, he said, destroyed the only real safeguard for minorities.

The appeals of these representatives of all the groups, Labour, Liberal, Independent Unionists as well as Nationalists were all unavailing. The Second Reading was passed by 20 votes to 13, a majority of 7; and of the 20, 11 of the votes were from members of the Government, which thus perpetuated itself by this legislation. During the debate the Government vote fell as low as 17, i.e. less than a third of the House. In the elections held immediately after the Bill was passed the gerrymander it legalis-ed bore rich fruit for the Government. Kyle and McMullen (Labour) George Henderson (Liberal) and Gyle (Independent Unionist) lost their seats.

In this debate several speakers predicted that elections would now cease to be real and that there would be many unopposed returns. The constituencies, they said, had been so arranged that one party was made secure by the Bill and could not be disturbed.

That not only happened immediately after the Bill was passed but it has happened ever since. It is to-day a normal thing for nearly half the Parliamentary seats to be filled without a contest. In the first election under P.R. every seat had been fought for. In the first election under this gerrymandering Act there were 21 unopposed returns, or over 40 per cent.

For the six general elections held in the last thirty years under the 1929 Act, the average percentage of uncontested seats was 48.9 as is shown in the following Table (The four University seats filled from a small and separate electorate under the P. R. system have been omitted.)

Year	Total ordinary seats	Contested	Filled without contest		%
1929	48	27	22	or	45.8
1933	48	15	33	or	68.7
1938	48	26	21	or	43.7
1945	48	28	20	or	41.6
1949	48	28	20	or	41.6
1953	48	23	25	or	52.0
Averages 1929-53	48	24$^1/_2$	23$^1/_2$	or	48.9

Uncontested elections have become a tradition and there are eleven constituencies (more than a fifth of the total) which have either seen no Parliamentary election at all or only one in nearly thirty years.

The purpose of the measure indicated by Mr. T. Henderson (Independent Unionist) "to drive out the opposition" was completely filled. In 1953 one Socialist Republican and two Independent Labour M.P.s were returned for Nationalist constituencies. Eight Labour Party candidates stood. They were all defeated, and to-day in the most highly industrialised area in Ireland there is not one official Labour representative and outside the Nationalist areas not one Labour representative of any kind survived the polls.

APPENDIX to Chapter Fifteen

ANTRIM
Lisburn R. D. C. (15 seats)

Year	Seats Contested	Candidates Short
1924	3	—
1927	None	3
1930	1	6
1933	None	8
1936	None	7
1939	None	8
1946	None	2
1949	1	—
1952	1	5
1955	None	4

ARMAGH
Armagh R. D. C. (31 seats)

Year	Seats Contested	Candidates Short
1924	2	1
1927	None	15
1930	None	13
1933	4	13
1936	1	2
1939	None	—
1946	None	7
1949	None	11
1952	None	5
1955	None	2

DERRY
Coleraine R. D. C. (21 seats)

Year	Seats Contested	Candidates Short
1924	None	—
1927	None	3
1930	None	—
1933	None	3
1936	None	2
1939	None	7
1946	1	1
1949	None	1
1952	2	—
1955	2	3

DOWN
Banbridge R. D. C. (20 seats)

Year	Seats Contested	Candidates Short
1924	None	3
1927	None	5
1930	None	10
1933	None	11
1936	None	11
1939	None	14
1946	1	4
1949	None	6
1952	1	—
1955	None	4

FERMANAGH
Irvinestown R. D. C. (19 seats)

Year	Seats Contested	Candidates Short
1924	None	6
1927	None	4
1930	None	—
1933	None	—
1936	None	1
1939	None	1
1946	2	1
1949	2	—
1952	None	—
1955	None	—

TYRONE
Omagh R. D. C. (39 seats)

Year	Seats Contested	Candidates Short
1924	None	16
1927	1	5
1930	4	2
1933	None	9
1936	None	4
1939	None	4
1946	4	—
1949	None	1
1952	1	—
1955	None	3

CHAPTER XVI

THE IMPERIAL CONTRIBUTION

THE GOVERNMENT OF Ireland Act 1920, which erected the Six Counties into a separate area, imposed on the area a monetary tribute. Although described as an Imperial Contribution, the "Contribution" in actual fact was a deduction of a fixed sum out of the total proceeds of British taxation in the area. The sum so deducted was deemed to be the Six Counties' share of the costs of Empire Services for which the territory was to be responsible.

The sum was a contribution for the whole of Ireland (since Partition was intended to be a transitory arrangement only):

> Ireland shall each year make a contribution towards the Imperial liabilities and expenditure. (Clause 23, Section 1.)

That contribution for the whole country was fixed at £18,000,000 a year, of which the Twenty Six Counties would bear 56 per cent and the Six Counties 44 per cent or £7,920,000. The Act laid down that after two years a Joint Exchequer Board would re-determine the sum both parts of Ireland should pay. The Sixth Schedule set out the items in regard to which this Imperial Contribution was to be paid.

1. The National Debt Charges
2. Naval, Military and Air Force Expenditure
3. Civil Expenditure, i.e.
   (a) Civil List and Royal Family.
   (b) Expenditure in connection with the United Kingdom Parliament, the National Debt Commissioners, the Foreign Office, the Colonial Office, Trade Outside the United Kingdom and the Royal Mint.
   (c) Such other expenditure as the Joint Exchequer Board may determine to be Imperial.

The 1920 Act came into operation in May 1921. The Anglo-Irish Treaty was signed in December 1921. One of the understandings between the British Government and the Irish Signatories was that as an inducement towards the re-unification of Ireland, the Six Counties if they chose exclusion from a National Parliament must continue to bear the burden for the first two years of £7,920,000 per annum and then of whatever sum the Joint Exchequer Board decided.

This was an important qualification in both the eyes of the British and the eyes of the Irish signatories to the Treaty. The British Premier, Mr. Lloyd George, in a letter to Sir James Craig on 10 November 1921, stated if

> Northern Ireland remained a part of the United Kingdom . . . it is clear that the people of Northern Ireland would have to bear their proportionate share of all Imperial burthens such as the Army, Navy and other Imperial Services in common with the taxpayers of the United Kingdom.[1]

That this consequence of Partition would be an impulse towards unity was repeatedly stressed by the British before the Treaty was signed, and the Irish signatures were appended to that document in the belief that in this and other ways the British were determined to aid re-unification. Michael Collins, after the Treaty was signed, spoke of union being certain because not only would Clause XII enable Tyrone and Fermanagh to come back under a National Parliament but because

> the burdens and financial restrictions of the Partition Act will remain on North-east Ulster if she decides to stay out. No lightening of these burthens and restrictions can be effected by the English Parliament without the consent of Ireland.[2]

By the Act of 1920 no change could be made in the total of the Imperial Contribution for two years from May 1921. But in May 1922 the Six County Minister for Finance was able to announce that the British Government had agreed to reduce the Contribution, and it was reduced for the financial year ending 1922-3 by £1,200,000. It was not the amount of that reduction, big as it was, which was important. It was the fact that this substantial reduction was agreed to despite the undertaking over the Treaty and before the Boundary Clause came into operation. It constituted an assurance to the Orange leaders that the British Government would reward them if they refused to allow the unity of their homeland to be restored.

What followed merely confirmed this beginning. Instead of the Imperial burthens driving the Six Counties to seek relief by

---

[1] *Handbook of the Ulster Question*, (Stationery Office, Dublin, 1923) p. 32.
[2] Michael Collins, *The Path to Freedom*, (1922), pp. 94-95.

incorporation in a united Ireland, the gross Contribution was allowed to dwindle away from millions to hundreds of thousands, from hundreds of thousands to tens of thousands, until the net Contribution for the whole pre-war period 1922 to 1939 was little more than what the 1920 Act fixed for one year, and there was in fact no true Imperial Contribution at all.

The essential figures are shown in the folowing table. They include a column showing the receipt by the Belfast Government of the Land Annuities. These Annuities were, by the Act of 1920, made a gift from the British Government to the Six County Government as an inducement to accept and work the Partition Act. The same gift was offered to the Twenty-Six Counties if they too would accept. When they did not, Britain forced their collection as part of her own revenues.

Year Ended March 31st	Total Grants and Payments from Britain	Gross Imperial Contribution	Net Imperial Contribution	Land Annuities	True Imperial Contribution
1922	391,719	2,820,820	2,429,101	252,953	2,176,148
1923	3,699,665	6,685,645	2,985,980	645,528	2,340,452
1924	2,359,584	4,517,879	2,158,295	661,580	1,496,715
1925	2,310,130	3,175,000	864,870	663,601	201,269
1926	1,980,000	2,275,000	295,000	663,866	— 368,866
1927	1,059,273	1,350,000	290,727	667,774	— 377,047
1928	357,285	1,450,000	1,092,715	664,969	427,746
1929	726,393	1,175,000	448,607	665,410	— 216,803
1930	526,004	855,000	328,996	664,624	— 335,628
1931	740,654	545,000	—195,654	663,833	— 859,487
1932	458,352	298,000	—160,352	658,561	— 818,913
1933	109,250	75,000	— 34,250	655,465	— 689,715
1934	26,086	76,000	— 49,914	657,058	— 607,144
1935	137,499	24,000	—113,499	656,297	— 169,796
1936	904,904	365,000	—539,904	657,547	—1,197,451
1937	1,139,919	900,000	—239,919	654,494	— 894,413
1938	1,647,291	1,200,000	—447,291	657,000	—1,104,291
1939	1,788,790	1,300,000	—488,790	654,000	—1,142,790
1922-39	£20,362,789	29,087,344	8,724,546	11,464,560	—2,740,014

When Britain became involved in war with Germany the situation changed. The Six Counties found themselves automatically at war too. As the area had been turned into part of the United

Kingdom the British King declared war for North-east Ireland without the formality of prior consultation.

The war threatened to disorganise the Six County finances, but the British Government made immediate arrangements and the whole financial inter-relationship entered a new phase. The pre-war method of determining the amount of the Imperial Contribution was simple. It would be whatever sum remained of the total proceeds of taxation after the cost of Government in the area had been deducted.

Now it was decided that the local services were to be kept at the normal peace-time level, and if this minimum was exceeded it would be met by the British Government itself, as excess war-time transferred expenditure. This restraint on local spending meant that war taxation would be likely to provide a much greater residue. So it proved. In Britain existing taxes were steeply stepped up, new taxes were imposed. These became operative in North-east Ireland where 90 per cent of the total taxation is imposed by the London Parliament and goes straight into the British Exchequer. Part of it later is transferred to Belfast to meet the cost of administration and services. The rest, which never leaves the London Treasury, is as we know the Imperial Contribution.

An agitation arose in the Six Counties during the war in which members of the Tory Party called on the Belfast Government to retain some of what was being kept by Britain. On 23 May 1944 in his Budget speech of that year the Six County Minister for Finance described the impossibility of any such plan.

> I feel I cannot emphasise too strongly a fact which must be known to every Member of this House (he said) that this Reserved Revenue is paid into the Imperial Exchequer and not into our own. What we receive here is that part of it required to meet, together with our transferred revenues, the cost of local administration. The actual amount which we so receive, called the Residuary Share of Reserved Taxes is determined by the Joint Exchequer Board. It follows from this that the balance of our Reserved Revenue, which forms the Contribution, never leaves the Imperial Exchequer.

It is a contribution which is taken, not given!

The effect of the war taxes was to send the total revenues collected in the area sky-high, and, as expenditure on local services was pegged to a certain standard, each year there were large surpluses accruing to the British Treasury which were then credited to the Six Counties as "Imperial Contributions". But, as in the inter-war period, these papers credits were off set by British grants and payments, direct and indirect, and it was only in the medial years of the war period 1943-6 that there was any substantial Contribution, as the following table shows.

Year Ended 31 March	Gross Imperial Contribution	Direct Exchequer Grants and other British Expenditure	True Imperial Contribution
1940	3,000,000	4,084,623	— 1,084,623
1941	8,500,000	6,812,321	+ 1,687,679
1942	17,600,000	8,970,378	+ 8,629,622
1943	29,750,000	10,752,785	+18,997,215
1944	36,000,000	15,004,818	+20,995,182
1945	36,300,000	15,947,227	+20,352,773
1946	34,500,000	14,531,466	+19,968,534
1947	22,500,000	21,296,830	+ 1,203,170
1948	22,500,000	22,507,450	— 7,450
1949	22,500,000	26,617,636	— 4,117,636
1950	19,121,000	26,589,051	— 1,468,051

Years	Gross Imperial Contribution	True Imperial Contribution
1940-50	252,271,000	+79,156,415
1921-39	29,087,344	— 2,740,014
	281,358,344	76,416,401

(These figures are based on tables in Labhrás O'Nualláin's *Finances of Partition* revised in the light of information, regarding the years 1949 and 1950, contained in Six County financial accounts issued since the publication of Dr. O'Nualláin's work).

From this table it can be seen that on paper from June 1921 to 31 March 1950 £281,358,344 was credited to the Belfast Government by the British Treasury under the heading of Imperial Contribution. The fact was that for the entire thirty years period only £76,416,401 was actually held by London.

How far short this total falls of being any real contribution to Imperial expenses is shown by another table. This expresses the Imperial Contribution as a percentage of Britain's defence expenditure for the war decade:

Year ended 31 March	True Imperial Contribution £	British Expenditure on Defence	Proportion borne by Col. 1 to Col. 2
1940	− 1,084,623	626,400,000	−
1941	+ 1,687,679	3,220,000,000	0.05
1942	+ 8,629,622	4,085,000,000	0.21
1943	+18,997,215	4,840,000,000	0.39
1944	+20,995,182	4,950,000,000	0.42
1945	+20,352,773	5,125,000,000	0.39
1946	+19,968,534	4,410,000,000	0.45
1947	+ 1,203,170	1,653,400,000	0.07
1948	− 7,450	853,900,000	−
1949	− 4,117,636	753,200,000	−

This shows a contribution of less than a fifth of one per cent to defence expenditure during the decade in which an Imperial Contribution *was* made. There was therefore no real contribution whatever from the Six Counties to the other items set out in the Schedule to the Partition Act — National Debt Charges, the Royal Family, the Foreign Office, External Trade etc.

By the Partition Act the Six Counties were to bear their full share of all these expenses estimated in 1921 at £7,290,000. The area has never borne any such share. In seventeen of the thirty years there was no real contribution at all and the total sum contributed in those three decades — even in the low money values of the 1950's — worked out as an annual average much less than half the 1921 figure. Even when the yearly contribution from 1943 to 1946 averaged £20,000,000 it was not half of one per cent of the British defence costs alone, so it is evident what a real Imperial Contribution would have been like.

Dr Labhrás O'Nualláin's book, *Ireland — the Finances of Partition,* from which our tables have been taken, is the only authoritative work on this question. Dr. O'Nualláin, after an exhaustive analysis of Six County finances, says:

> The one incontestable conclusion that emerges from a study of the financial relations between the British and the Six County Governments is that ever since the establishment of the latter Government some thirty years ago it has for the most part been carried on the backs of the taxpayers in Britain. Despite the deceptive appearance of the large war-time *gross* Imperial Contribution the area is quite definitely not bearing a proportionate share of the Imperial liabilities and expenditure... Apparently they (the British Government) are indifferent as to whether the Six County area

does or does not make a proportionate Imperial Contribution so long as a Government is upheld in that area which is willing to hold fast to the *status quo* and resist all attempts to upset it. [1]

The financial clauses of the Partition Act, which Britain promised would be strictly enforced if the North-east did not rejoin the rest of Ireland, have in fact never been implemented. The difference between the vast sums the Six Counties would have been asked to pay if they had been implemented and the trivial amounts which the British treasury did in fact retain must be regarded as a bribe to ensure that Ireland's dismemberment was maintained. It was a bribe much more polite but no less discreditable than that by which the Union of Great Britain and Ireland was first achieved.

---

[1] *Ireland: Finances of Partition* by Labhrás O'Nualláin, pp. 186-7. Examination of the Six County financial accounts and the British Hansard reports for the period 1950 to 1955 reveals that the gross Imperial Contribution for that period, returned as £77,816,000, has been more than offset by British Exchequer grants and payments amounting to £91,755,301. Thus no true contribution has been made by the Six Counties towards the costs of Imperial services in respect of that period.

CHAPTER XVII

THE TWO AREAS

MANY SIMILARITIES

THE ECONOMIC AND social development and organisation of Ireland was the process of many centuries. It was as a unit that the
country lived its material as well as spiritual life, and partition
has not affected in any profound way the fundamental economic
or social structure of the nation. That structure is the same in
the two parts of Ireland, and reunification of the national territory would require no changes in this regard. Many aspects
of this basic similarity are to be observed:

1. AGRICULTURE

Both areas have agriculture as their greatest industry. In the
Six Counties, 165,404 are employed on the farms either as
working farmers or as labourers. That is 12 per cent of the population: in the 26 Counties 470,000 are employed on the farms,
which is 16 per cent of the population. There is a similarity
also in the size of agricultural holdings. Of the total number
of farms of more than one acre there is generally no great
divergence in the percentages of holdings grouped according to
acreage, as shown in the following table giving percentages of
the whole:

	Total No. of Holdings	Above 1 to 10 acres	Above 10 to 15 acres	Above 15 to 30 acres	Above 30 to 50 acres	Above 50 to 100 acres	Above 100 to 200 acres	Above 200 acres
Six Counties	87,542	28.8	10.0	22.9	17.0	14.6	4.5	2.2
Free Ireland	317,840	18.1	9.6	27.4	19.6	16.2	6.8	2.3

In both areas it will be seen that more than half the farms, 61.7
per cent in the case of the Six Counties and 55.1 per cent in the
case of free Ireland, are below 30 acres, and that in the farms
from 30 to 100 acres free Ireland has 35.8 per cent and the Six
Counties 31.6 per cent. Of the larger farms, over 200 acres,
there are slightly more in the Twenty Six Counties (2.3 per cent)
than in the North-east (2.2 per cent), but holdings of this size

are unusual in both areas. Of all the farms, those from 1 to 50 acres form 79.7 per cent of the whole Six County farming area and 78.6 per cent of that of the Twenty Six Counties.

Broadly speaking, therefore, the economic organisation of life as regards the rural areas is roughly the same in all parts of the country, and in the three Ulster Counties which escaped partition it is in fact almost identical with the partitioned area. In Cavan, Donegal and Monaghan, below the Border, the percentage of farms in the 1 to 15 acres group is 36.6 per cent against 39.8 per cent above the Border. The other major aspects of the agricultural economy of the partitioned area are similar to those of the rest of Ireland. "The heart of Ulster is its farmed country-side", says T. W. Freeman in his recent book *Ireland: Its Physical, Historical, Social and Economic Geography* [1] and he adds:

> All the three Counties, Antrim, Down and Armagh still have less than one third of their population in towns and are, in spite of numerous factories, almost as distinctly rural in their life as the rest of Ireland. [2]

This rural bias reflects itself also in the external trade of the area.

The sale of livestock to outside markets is, as in the rest of Ireland, the principal agricultural export and together with other agricultural products—bacon, eggs, milk, potatoes, poultry, grass seed, flax—forms the most valuable group in the Six Counties' external trade: in 1953 £72,500,000 as against £38,000,000 for linen exports and £38,200,000 for ships and air-craft. Of all the exports of the Six Counties 94 per cent go to Britain or through Britain to other countries, whereas 86.7 per cent of the export trade of the Twenty Six Counties is consigned to Britain and the Six Counties. Both parts of Ireland, therefore, have the same principal market, and this is particularly so as regards the exports of agricultural produce.

In the two areas the relevant agricultural statistics (1954) show the basic similarity in regard to livestock and cultivation. In both farming communities the main agricultural wealth is in livestock and livestock products. The cattle of the Six County area, [3] which is one fifth of the total area of Ireland, number

---

[1]   Page 495.
[2]   Page 495.
[3]   Figures from the Six Counties are from *Digest of Statistics*, No. 3, March 1955, issued by the Belfast Stationery Office.

957,000: in the Twenty-Six Counties there are [1] 4,504,000. Sheep in the North-east number 956,000 and in the rest of Ireland 3,112,842. The number of pigs fluctuates more considerably, and in the Six Counties it was 812,000 while in the Twenty Six it was 958,000. Poultry of all kinds were 11.6 million in the Six Counties and 16.0 million in the Twenty-Six Counties.

II. LAND USE

Land use in both areas is similar. Tillage forms a small proportion of organised farming. According to the 1954 statistics there is 20.5 per cent of the area of cultivable land under crops in the Six Counties and 15.6 per cent in the Twenty Six. Hay is grown in 18 per cent of the Six County land and 16 per cent of Twenty Six County land, and permanent pasture covers more than half the cultivable area in both parts of Ireland, 61 per cent in the North-east and 68 per cent in the west of Ireland. In both areas tillage expanded during World War II, but has since declined, despite all Government aids and exhortations to the farmers. The major agricultural problem from the point of view of the general community is similar both above and below the border: to step up considerably home production and to curtail imports of foodstuffs for both men and beasts.

Within these broad divisions in regard to livestock and tillage there are such dissimilarities as can be found if Munster is contrasted with Leinster or Connacht with both. In general, the Departments of Agriculture in Belfast and in Dublin have to deal with the same classes of farmers faced with the same difficulties, men who have to be encouraged and materially aided along the same lines in an effort to get them to achieve the same objectives.

III. FORESTRY

All Ireland with a forest area of less than 2 per cent is notably short of growing timber, and each Government devotes much attention to making good this lack. Of the Six Counties the area of woodlands was only just over one per cent at the time of partition, and action has been taken since 1922 to increase forested lands mainly by State planting, which has progressed at a rate in recent years of 1,700 acres annually. The latest figure

[1] Figures for the Twenty Six Counties are from the *Irish Trade Journal* of March 1955.

is a total of 36,385 acres planted up to 1954. [1] In the Twenty
Six Counties the rate of planting has been higher, and up to 1953,
168,200 acres had been put under forest, and since then approx-
imately another 12,000 to the end of 1954. [2] In both parts of
Ireland the work is going forward steadily despite the difficulty
shared in the two areas of securing land for forests with the
goodwill of the farmers.

IV. LAND DIVISION

Farmers will not readily part with even marginal land for
trees, for the first use of land is regarded as agricultural, whether
for tillage or for stock-raising. This desire for land is expressed
in the big steps made by the Governments of Dublin and Belfast
in the creation of new holdings or the enlargement of old ones
by the division of the larger estates or untenanted land. At the
establishment of self-Government there was less of this work to
be done in the Six Counties than in the Twenty Six, but a
contrast is useful. The first Land Act was passed for the Six
County area in 1925, and land division has since been practically
completed. A total of 805,000 acres were made into new farms
or the extension of existing farms. The number of those who
benefited was 38,500. In the Twenty Six Counties since the Land
Act passed in 1923, 79,727 allottees have had distributed amongst
them 1,244,000 acres. The division of land is also reaching its
final stages in the Twenty Six Counties.

V. TRADE

The trade of Ireland as a whole is far more evenly balanced
as between agricultural products and manufactured goods than
the separate returns from the two areas would suggest. The Six
Counties exports by value contain 70.6 per cent of manufactured
goods, whereas their agricultural exports are only 20.2 per cent.
The Twenty Six Counties has only 9.6 per cent of manufactured
exports and has 78.2 per cent of agricultural products. But if
the returns of the two areas are considered together the export
trade of all Ireland is found to be a balanced trade, manufactures
totalling 54.4 per cent and agricultural exports 35.6 per cent.

Another point of importance which arises from a study of the
trade of the whole country is that Ireland could provide substantial markets for each of the separated parts. Certain types of
Twenty Six County agricultural products would be available

[1] *Digest of Statistics*, No. 3, Mar. 1955, Table 67.
[2] *Statistical Abstract of Ireland*, 1954, Table. 87.

without restraint to North-east Ireland, and Six County manufactures would be at the disposal of the rest of the country. For instance in 1953 free Ireland imported £18.6 million pounds worth of machinery and electrical goods, of which only a tiny percentage came from the Six Counties, but the Six Counties exported in that year £18.1 millions under the heading of machinery, and it is obvious that in a united Ireland there could be a far larger market for machinery manufactured in Belfast.

In 1953, under the heading of textiles, which included cotton piece goods, linen yarn and piece goods, woollen yarns, artificial silk etc. the Twenty Six Counties imported goods to the value of £22.2 millions, and only a small percentage of this came from the Six Counties. In the same year the Six Counties exported £70.6 millions worth of textiles to the rest of the world. In an undivided Ireland a valuable home market would be at the door of the North-eastern manufacturers. In the eight years after World War II (to 1953, for which we have the latest statistics) the Twenty Six Counties spent an average of almost £4 millions yearly on apparel from outside, again only an insignificant percentage coming from the Six Counties. In that same period the Six County exports of apparel averaged £13.3 millions. The clothing industry in the North-east gives employment to about 30,000 people, but finds its principal markets in Britain and overseas. The Irish market which, in an undivided nation, would be available to Six County firms was in fact supplied largely by British manufacturers.

An example of how the process works the other way round is given in the footwear industry. There is a well-developed boot and shoe industry in free Ireland employing 9,300 people in 1951, and there is a market across the Border for imported footwear. Imports of footwear amounting in value to £5 millions were, in fact, purchased by the North-east in 1951. In an Ireland without a Border this is a case where the factories of the Twenty Six Counties could meet a considerable proportion of the North-eastern demand.

How the partition of the country affects natural economic development in Ireland is illustrated by the dependence of the North-east on flax from the European Continent. Flax can be grown in many parts of the Twenty Six Counties, and a nationally organised production of flax would make this great Northern industry much less dependent than it is now on outside sources of supply and free it also from the difficulties involved in fluctuating value and often the inaccessibility of foreign currency.

Other aspects of the External Trade figures emphasise the advantages which could be brought to both parts by united efforts properly directed. Free Ireland, despite the considerable hindrance to mutual trade which results from the Border, is the North-east's most valuable customer after Britain. In 1954 the Twenty Six Counties purchased eight times what all the British Dominions, Colonies and possessions put together bought direct from the North-east. [1] The Six County imports from the Twenty Six Counties were one and a half times as much as was sold to the rest of the world outside Britain. If there were no Border and trade was free between all parts of Ireland, the North-east would not be the loser in the exchange.

There is obviously little substance in the suggestion that union with the rest of Ireland would rob the North-east of its British market. The establishment of independence for the rest of Ireland had not that effect. The Twenty Six Counties' external trade was especially high in 1924 (the first year of separate returns) when, marked by an exceptional export of cattle, it reached a total of £119.9 millions. The next year it was £106.7 millions. The slump which hit world trade brought the figure to £68.8 m. in 1932 and, aggravated by the Economic War, to £54.5 m. in 1933. The same downward trend affected the external trade of the Six Counties which from £131.1 millions in 1924 and £120.2 millions in 1925 fell to £80.0 m. in 1932 and to £76.8 millions in 1933. The trade of both areas thereafter slowly climbed back towards normal. That of free Ireland was £70.3 millions in 1939 and of the Six Counties was £116.9 millions in the same year. Then came the Second World War, creating a new situation in which Twenty Six County trade shrank again while that of the Six Counties expanded. After the war the value of the trade of both areas advanced steeply. In 1953 it was £296.7 millions in free Ireland and £495.9 millions in the North-east, more than a four-fold increase on the pre-war figure in each case. Changes in money values explain much of this improvement but there was a considerable expansion in volume also. Free Ireland has not lost trade in the British market through independence.

VI. INDUSTRIES

In the industrial field the two areas have come in recent decades to have many similar needs and problems.

[1] *Trade Statistics of Ireland,* Dec. 1954 (Dublin Stationery Office, 1955).

The Six County area was widely industrialised when Ireland got self-Government in 1921. As in other nations—America, France, England are examples—industry flourished in the Northern part of the country. British policy was responsible also for this location of manufactories.

In the eighteenth and earlier centuries industrial development in the country as a whole was stringently subordinated to Britain's manufacturing and commercial needs. The Irish woollen industry, like other industries which threatened to become a competitor of Britain's, was suppressed. The linen industry of the North-east was not a danger to British interests and was encouraged, until it and the manufacture of textiles as a whole have become the first of the main non agricultural industries.

Shipbuilding was complementary to British needs, and its growth was stimulated, though it is interesting now to recall what were the beginnings of this great Northern industry. The first Belfast ship on record was the *Eagle's Wing,* built in 1636 to the order of Presbyterians from Antrim fleeing to America from persecution by the Episcopalians! Today shipbuilding is one of the three mainstays of employment in the North-east. The yards, which in 1853 occupied one acre of land on the Queens Island in Belfast Harbour and employed 100 workers, today occupy over 300 acres and employ 20,000. They now build not ships only, but aircraft, diesel and electric engines, and consumer goods, such as refrigerators, electrical equipment, etc. The industry was heavily hit by the first and second post-war slumps, mainly during the post-1920 period, in which unemployment went as high as one worker in every three, and in 1922 there were nearly 10,000 idle in the shipyards.

The engineering industry grew out of the demand of textile manufacturers for engines, boilers, water wheels, turbines, etc. It expanded from a few foundries at the turn of the nineteenth century to the great chain of engineering works today in which many thousands are engaged. Like the shipbuilding industry, engineering suffered in the interwar slump, but better times came with the rearmament programmes in 1938 and 1939, and in the July of the latter year 27,600 persons were working in the Engineering trades. The war brought a marked expansion to the industry as it did to shipbuilding. That growth has been maintained since the war ended.

The 1953 Census of Production [1] which groups, these trades—shipbuilding, engineering and metals—shows that 48,396 were employed in them, an increase of more than 150 per cent over the figure given for 1935.

But the greatest of the leading industries (after agriculture) is the Textile group. It includes the spinning and weaving of wool and worsted, the manufacture of thread, hosiery, cotton piece goods, sacks, ropes, felts, the finishing trades of bleaching, dying, printing. Linen is the most important of them all and provides work directly or indirectly for a fifth of the gainfully employed population. It depends largely on an export market, but wars and the consequences of wars have reduced that market drastically. The linen industry has had a varied career since it was established in the middle of the seventeenth century. Though the big majority of linen workers are concentrated in Belfast and its environs, the industry, unlike shipbuilding and engineering, has offshoots in Newry, Armagh and County Derry. The first world war disrupted a flourishing and valuable trade. Changing habits, the contracting market for luxury goods and the difficulties of securing flax from Russia and the Baltic countries administered a shock from which the linen industry has never recovered. In 1912 250.7 million square yards of piece linen were exported from Great Britain and Ireland and 90 per cent to 95 per cent of this came from the Six County area. This great trade had fallen to 89.9 million sq. yards in 1921, rose for some years to 110.8 million sq. yards and then began a downward movement again to 71.1 million sq. yards in 1935, and an average of 57.9 million square yards in the period 1936-38. This fall was mainly attributable to the fall in the exports to the United States market, which from an average of 138.9 million square yards in 1907-13 fell to 38.3 million square yards in 1919-28. After a period of moderate recovery it has again dwindled in recent years. In 1952 the total export to all overseas areas was 36.8 million sq. yards, and the export to the United States fell from 20.6 million sq. yards to 14.9 millions. [2]

This long decline has been reflected in the constantly falling employment the industry gave. In 1912 77,333 persons were engaged in the linen and hemp trades; this was 74,758 in 1924,

---

[1] *Report of the Census of Production of Northern Ireland*, 1953 (Belfast Stationery Office, 1955).
[2] *Belfast Newsletter*, 3 January 1953.

63,000 in 1939, and the Census of Production of 1953 [1] shows the number of linen and hemp workers that year to be 48,467. As the exports declined and the number of workers fell, the total of spindles and looms grew less and less. Only all-Ireland figures are available, but as there are only four linen mills in the Twenty Six Counties the statistics are sufficiently accurate to indicate the decline in Six County linen production. In 1921 there were 951,246 spindles and 37,600 looms in the linen industry in all Ireland. By 1939 there were 840,000 spindles and 25,500 looms, and in 1949 775,000 spindles and 22,000 looms.

Other major industries in the Six Counties are clothing and building and contracting, both of which have expanded in recent years: though they suffered greatly in the interwar slump, the unemployment in the clothing trades never falling below 24 per cent in the whole period 1930-9, and in building and contracting is was never less than 33 per cent for those ten years, and was actually 41.5 per cent in 1937.

Thus in the Six County area as a whole the interwar years disclosed a precarious industrial situation of stagnation and in many cases of decline. The all-over position was reflected in two of the industrial censuses taken before World War II. A fall in the general price level between the two censuses and also a change in the method of enumerating those in employment— all firms of less than ten employees being omitted—affect the comparison, but they do not account for the fall in both value and numbers which the 1935 Census disclosed. The Census of all industries in 1924 showed a total net output of Industry of £23,880,000 and an average number of industrial workers of 156,834, but the Census of 1935 showed a net output of only £20,005,000 and the number of workers at 140,176. Of these 140,176 there were almost as many women workers as men. The males employed were 53.5 per cent of the whole; the females were 46.5 per cent. This was nearly double the proportion of females employed in Twenty Six County industry, and the proportion of juvenile labour in the Six Counties was also well ahead of that below the border, 14.4 per cent of the whole against 10 per cent in free Ireland.

In the same period in which industry in the Six Counties was either stagnant or in decline, a very different situation existed

[1] *Report of Census of Production of Northern Ireland,* 1953 (Belfast Stationery Office, 1955).

in the Twenty Six Counties, where industry made substantial progress.

Between 1926 and 1936 the value of the output of industry increased by £10.7 millions or 32 per cent, and the number of workers by 51,373 or 39 per cent. The industries of free Ireland were not so susceptible to fluctuations of international trade, and there was much more diversification than in those of the North-east. Most of the leading industries, electricity, brewing, building and construction, bread, flour and confectionery, cement, sugar making and grain milling etc., had the advantage of drawing their raw materials from internal sources, and with the exception of brewing they cater primarily, if not wholly, for the home market.

There is a useful comparison too between the distribution of industry in the two areas. In the Six Counties Belfast has 57 per cent of all industrial workers and accounts for 60 per cent of the net industrial output. Industry is distributed better in the Twenty Six Counties, where only 43 per cent of the total numbers engaged and 50 per cent of the total net output is centred in Dublin and Dún Laoghaire, leaving 57 per cent of the total numbers and 50 per cent of the output to the other towns and provinces.

Since the war both areas have been re-planning their industrial production. The Government in Belfast has adopted many different methods, including loans, grants, the provision of sites and factory premises to attract industries from abroad. The Government in Dublin has granted tariffs and quotas as well as financial assistance to provide markets for those ready to establish new industries, and has itself in the beet sugar, turf and electricity undertakings taken direct part in the industrial revival. The effect of this policy pursued with vigour in free Ireland for over twenty years has been to build up industrial production to levels similar to those above the border.

The latest industrial censuses for both areas are those of 1952. They supply us with surprising figures. There were in that year in the Six Counties 201,015 persons engaged in industrial pro-duction in firms employing 10 workers or upwards, making with those in smaller firms 221,000 altogether. [1] In that same year

---

[1] *Report on the Census of Production of Northern Ireland,* 1953. The number of those employed by exempted firms (i.e. those employing 10 or less) was 14,000, according to this Report, bringing the total employment by all firms to 221,000.

the total employed in industrial production in the Twenty Six Counties was 221,295 on the slightly different computation of firms with less than 10 workers but not less than 3. [1] The value of the gross output of all industries in that year was £320 million in the Six Counties and £352 million in the Twenty Six Counties, and the Net Output "one of the most informative bases of comparison of industrial output" [2] was £92.2 millions above the Six County Border and £105.8 millions below it. These figures continued to expand during recent years, but the almost exact parallels have remained. As the population of free Ireland is over 2½ times that of the Six Counties it will be seen that the partitioned area is more highly industrialised, but how rapidly industry has increased in the Twenty Six Counties can be seen from a comparison with 1926 when the first industrial census was taken. Then the numbers employed in all industries was 102,515 [3]: it was 221,295 in 1952. The net output (though here the comparison is affected by the change in money values) was put at £23,078,000 in 1926. It was £105,800,000 in 1952.

The salaries and wages paid in industry in the Twenty Six Counties totalled just over £66.8 millions in 1952 (it was £13 millions in 1926 and £14 millions in 1938). In the Six Counties the figure for 1952 was £60.1 millions (£12,400,000 in 1935). One of the reasons for the lower wages total north of the Border is that the percentage of women workers in the Six Counties is much higher than in the Twenty Six Counties, and the lower wage-rates for women reflect themselves in the total. Out of 201,015 Six County workers recorded in the Census for Industrial Production for 1952, 73,684 were women. [4]

These totals for salaries and wages bear out an interesting point about the industrial wage levels in the two areas. It has been used as propaganda for many years that the wages in the Twenty Six Counties are much less than the wages in the Six Counties. In fact the industrial wages in Dublin and in other cities are in many cases higher per hour than in Belfast and the Six Counties generally. From a wage schedule compiled in 1951 covering many trades it was found that in the majority of cases the wages which skilled workers and unskilled labour can earn per hour in free Ireland were markedly higher than in Belfast

1 *The Statistical Abstract for Ireland*, 1954.
2 *Report on the Census of Production of Northern Ireland*, 1949 p.l.
3 *Statistical Abstract for Ireland*, 1954.
4 *Report on the Census of Production of Northern Ireland*, 1952.

and the North-east generally. The relative value of these wages is affected by the level of taxation on widely consumed goods and services in the two parts of the country. Tax and non-tax revenue for the current financial year (1955-6) in the Six County area is estimated at £78,820,000, or £58 5s per head of the population. In the Twenty Six Counties the tax and non-tax revenue is estimated at £110,623,000 or £37 0s per head of the population.

In the matter of manufactures both areas have had a similar problem in the post-war years. In the Twenty Six Counties industrial development had first been tackled in the late twenties, and then more actively in the period from 1933 to 1939. The post-war resumption of industrialisation benefited by the twenty years of interwar experience. In that twenty years largely by use of tariffs more than 100 new industries and more than 900 workshops and factories had been established in free Ireland, and the employment created in protected industries rose from 15,953 in 1926 to 21,198 in 1931; and in later years the total increased more rapidly until it was 94,336 in 1949 and 107,067 in 1954.

It was not until after the world economic collapse in the second interwar decade that the need for special encouragement to new industry was appreciated. In the Six Counties, which was already strongly industrialised, the first steps were taken in 1932 and the early efforts to encourage new establishments bore little fruit. From 1932 to August 1939 24 concerns received assistance, and of these 18 were in the Belfast region, 12 in the city itself and 6 within a thirty-mile radius of the city. After the war new Acts making more effective and attractive provision for the extension and establishment of industries were passed. This new legislation aided not only new concerns but extensions of existing undertakings benefited also with a view to expanded production and the creation of additional employment. Special steps were taken to encourage the establishment of industries outside the Belfast region. As far as can be gleaned from the sparse statistical material available 58 new or expanded undertakings were set up from July 1945 to the end of 1949 under these later Acts. In the whole period, 1932 to 1949, there were 95, of which 91 were still in production in 1950. Of these 28 were located in Belfast, a further 33 within the 30-mile radius and 30 others in the rest of the Six County area. Most of the undertakings were in the light industry class producing consumer goods of a type calling for considerable female labour.

Including the number of factories (52) established without Government aid, the factories built by the Government itself (22) to attract industrialists and the extensions to existing factories, the total new undertakings numbered 196 in the whole period from 1932 to February 1950. These were providing work on 30 September 1950, for 22,636 persons of whom 12,909 were men and 9,727 women and juveniles.

Among the post-war industries in the Six Counties as in the Twenty Six an important development has been in food-processing. Milk, formerly turned into either butter or cream, is now dried, condensed, or made into food products. Over 1,000 workers are already engaged in these milk processing operations. Canning and deep freezing of meat, meat products, fruit and vegetables has expanded greatly since the war. It is now an industry employing 2,400 (770 men and 1,640 women) whose output in 1952 was valued at nearly £3 million.

Since the war, in addition to the 900 factories and workshops that were set up in the Twenty Six Counties in the interwar years, there has been a considerable industrial expansion. In a relatively similar period, September 1945 to 30 July 1951, 331 new factories and workshops were established. These, which were mainly smaller units, employed 4,407 people. Something over half the industries (190 or 57.4 per cent) were set up in Dublin City and county and 141 in the rest of the country. As in the North-east there was a big development in the canning, processing and dead-meat trades, and the exports of these reached substantial proportions.

VII. HOUSING

When in 1921 and 1922 the British Government handed over their administration of Irish affairs for the greater part of Ireland to a legislature in Dublin and less fully to a Government in Belfast, they also handed over a legacy of desperately poor housing conditions. The British Acts under which housing could have been provided for workers and those with small incomes were never properly implemented, partly through insufficient grants from State funds and partly through inadequate use of their own powers by the local government authorities. As a result the ending of direct British rule left a legacy of slums in Irish cities and wretched rural housing conditions in both parts of the country which gained Ireland an unenviable reputation.

Both areas recognised that proper housing of the workers was one of the major social problems, and between 1921 and 1939 many statutes were passed to provide a solution. Subsidies were given to individuals, organisations or local authorities to enable them to build, and the powers of the various urban and rural councils to take advantage of Housing Acts were increased. In the Twenty Six Counties these powers were widely used. In the Six Counties, as stated in an official report, the increased powers had not up to 1947 "been used to any appreciable extent by any local authority in Northern Ireland". [1] Although five Acts were passed in the Six Counties between 1921 and 1939 to encourage the building of labourers' cottages, the number of these workers' homes erected during that period numbered only 3,556. The *Interim Report* commented:

> We believe that the rural district Councils have, speaking generally, not been enthusiastic about housing and have felt that they have discharged the liability cast upon them under the Housing Acts if they adopted the hand to mouth policy and built sufficient houses to satisfy the more pressing needs of the moment. This is not surprising for their allegiance is divided between their desire to keep down the rates and their duties to supply houses for the labourers under the Housing Acts. (Paragraph 60).

There was, as we have seen in an earlier chapter, another reason for the reluctance to build houses.

Taking all classes of houses erected with financial aid from State funds in the Six Counties the total from December 1921 to December 1939 was 38,583. Of these the local authorities built 2,644 in urban areas and 3,556 cottages in rural areas. The rest, 32,383, were built by private builders. In addition the Irish Sailors' and Soldiers' Land Trust built 1,251 houses for ex-servicemen. It is estimated that, in addition, over 9,000 houses were built without financial aid from State funds. So that there were about 49,000 houses erected in the Six County area in the eighteen years from 1921 to 1939.

Housing conditions in both the Twenty Six Counties and in the Six Counties called for not only the provision of new houses (to shelter the town populations which were constantly growing) but the removal of the wretched houses which had been inherited, or slum clearance as it is called. Legal powers to effect this removal of slums were contained in Acts operative in the Six County area. An official Report on Housing issued in 1944 [2]

[1] *Interim Report on Rural Housing in Ulster* (1947)
[2] *Housing in Northern Ireland*, cmd. 224, July 1944.

stated that those powers had not been used to any appreciable extent by any local authority throughout the area mainly because no grants had been made available by the Belfast Government to local authorities for this purpose.

In the Twenty Six Counties under the first Housing Acts 29,193 houses were built in the decade 1922-32, making an average of nearly 3,000 houses per annum. [1] In 1932 a comprehensive Act, the Housing (Financial and Miscellaneous Provisions) Act was passed. Under this Act housing in the Twenty Six Counties went ahead much more quickly, and from March 1932 to March 1939 56,263 houses were built and reconstructed by local authorities; 26,177 were built by Utility Societies and Private Individuals; 15,335 by the Irish Land Commission and in the Irish-speaking areas along the Western seaboard either entirely out of public funds or with the aid of State subsidies. Thus over 97,775 houses were built or reconstructed in seven years from March 1932 to March 1939, or 13,967 a year. Altogether from 1921 to 1939 126,968 new or reconstructed dwellings had been provided with financial aid from the State.

It is to be observed that whereas in the Six County area building by local authorities accounted for 6,000 out of 38,000 houses, or 15 per cent, in the Twenty Six Counties the local authorities and other public bodies built or reconstructed over 73 per cent of the 97,000 dwellings provided there from 1932 to 1939. The Twenty Six County authorities also used their slum clearance powers, and in the period of eight years from April 1932 10,874 houses in urban and rural areas were demolished as unfit and unhealthy.

At the outbreak of the Second World War the progress of housing in both areas slowed down. It came to a standstill in the North-east by 1941; and in the Twenty Six Counties, the annual rate of building (11,623 in 1939) decreased to 2,517 in 1943. Although over 16,000 houses were built in the war years, the industry did not begin to revive again until 1948. The war with its destruction of 3,000 houses in the Belfast area, had made a solution of the housing problem more imperative there and in the Six County area generally, and a Housing Survey taken in 1943 [2] disclosed an immediate need for 100,000 houses.

[1] 25,540 by Local Authorities. Utility Societies and Private Individuals, 3,595 by the Land Commission and 58 in the Gaeltacht.
[2] *Housing in Northern Ireland*, cmd. 224, July 1944.

In 1943 a survey of housing conditions was begun by the local authorities in the Twenty Six Counties also; and figures from it appeared in a White Paper, *Housing - A Review of Past Operation and Immediate Requirements,* which was published in 1948. It estimated that the immediate requirements then were for 100,000 houses, of which 60,000 were needed for the working classes. In each area the main housing needs were shown to be in the two chief cities, Dublin, which required 54.8 per cent of the total houses wanted for the whole Twenty Six Counties, and Belfast with 58.6 per cent of the needs of all the North-eastern area. In rural housing the need for better rural housing in the Six Counties is four times greater than in the rural areas of the Twenty Six Counties.

As soon as supplies became available after the Second World War building was resumed in both parts of Ireland. In the Six Counties an additional Ministry was added to those already established, the Ministry of Health and Local Government, which was given the special task of pressing forward with the erection of new homes for the people. At the same time several Acts of Parliament were passed providing substantial subsidies and other inducements to local authorities and private persons to build for themselves and others. A Housing Trust with powers to build in all parts of the Six Counties was set up. In 1948 legislation to aid the housing of farm workers and farmers was passed. By that year the housing drive had got under way in the North-east and altogether 51,381 houses have been built up to Dec. 1954 by all agencies north of the Border. Of these the local authorities built 20,216, the Housing Trust 13,174 and private builders and Government Departments 17,991. There were 6,737 other houses in various stages of construction. [1] In Belfast itself over 8,000 houses have been erected, but because slum clearance has not progressed at the same rate, the older houses are becoming still more delapidated and the number of applicants for new homes has remained steady since the war's end at over 20,000. The City Medical Officer of Health is reported in December 1952 in the Belfast Press as stating:

> In spite of the Corporation's progress in the erection of new houses in the city there are as yet few indications that the grave menace to health resulting from the unsatisfactory conditions in which many citizens are living is being overcome. [2]

1 *Digest of Statistics,* No. 3, Mar. 1955.
2 *Belfast Newsletter,* 27 Dec. 1952.

In the Twenty Six Counties revival of the building industry also dates from 1948. From April of that year the erection and reconstruction of houses has been as follows:

1948—49	4,168
1949—50	9,466
1950—51	14,922
1951—52	12,784
1952—53	16,191
1953—54	14,818
1954—55	15,100

making a total 87,449 of the 100,000 which the Survey of 1943-8 had found to be urgently needed. There were 6,077 other houses in construction and 2,974 in tender, all making a grand total of 96,500, so that 96.5 per cent of the Twenty Six Counties immediate needs were either met or being met. Before the end of 1954 the 270,000th new dwelling was erected since free Ireland secured self-government. In the North-east in the same period 91,110 have been built with State assistance.

This brief survey of the housing conditions in the two areas and the steps being taken to solve a problem fundamental to the well-being of all the Irish people emphasises how alike the difficulties and the needs are in the two parts of Ireland and how much better and more expeditiously the whole question could have been handled if Ireland had remained a unit and the Irish people were free to deal with the housing problem on national lines.

CHAPTER XVIII

UNEMPLOYMENT
FOLLOWS DISMEMBERMENT

BEFORE THE PARTITION of Ireland took place it was deeply feared by Irishmen generally that the separation of the industrial area from the country as a whole would have grave repercussions. The heaviest impact would, it was thought, be on the towns which were the marketing centres of areas now to be traversed by a border, particularly Derry and Enniskillen on the Six County side, and Clones and Castleblayney on the Twenty Six County side. Even more severely felt would be the detachment of large southern districts for which Belfast, Derry, Newry and Enniskillen were the distributing centres, and which would now be cut off, and similar northern districts separated from Sligo and Dundalk which were their distribution centres. The separation of these towns from what had come to be regarded as their natural economic hinterland was likely to mean loss of wealth and also loss of employment to many areas.

At the time the Boundary Commission was sitting, Mr. John S. Steele of the *Chicago Tribune* wrote in the London *Sunday Times* [1]:

> I have just returned from a journey along the boundary, during which I visited towns on both sides, and in all I found a burning desire for its elimination. No matter what their political affiliations, business men on both sides declared that it was proving ruinous, and many went so far as to say that they did not care what the eventual settlement was so long as the boundary was wiped out.

Mr. Steele from his observation was bearing out what had already been reported in the London *Times* in the previous September. There a special correspondent who had visited Ireland wrote: [2]

> There are also strong economic arguments in favour of union between North and South. The abolition of the present vexatious Customs frontier between the Six Counties and the Free State would unquestionably benefit Northern industry and commerce. Towns

[1] *Sunday Times*, 1 June 1924.
[2] London *Times*, 24 Sept. 1923.

like Londonderry which had an important commercial hinterland in what is now Free State territory would recover the trade which they have been steadily losing since Partition.

There had always been the fear that the area cut off would be too small for any State fashioned within it to be prosperous, and the intervening years have borne that out, certainly in the domain of unemployment. Belfast and its environs have for the last century been a place where humanity made more than ordinarily slow progress in the sphere of labour relations. Here, if anywhere, the political and economic were intermixed. The area was highly industrialised, and in the early years of the century the wages paid and the conditions of work were harsh even for that stark age. Yet, whenever the workers came in desperation to the point of revolt against either their inadequate pay or long hours or the wretchedness in which they were compelled to work and live, the ruling class, who were also the employers, had their old remedy close at hand. They turned the Protestant workers against the Catholic workers. It had never failed.

One who later was to become Prime Minister of England and was then leader of the British Labour Party referred in two speeches to this aspect of the Irish problem in the Home Rule debates in the British Commons in 1912.

The first was on 11 April of that year. Mr. Ramsay MacDonald then said: [1]

> In Belfast which has been held up to us this afternoon as a rich and prosperous and powerful city and as a great example of the beneficence of English rule in Ireland, you get labour conditions the like of which you get in no other town, no other city of equal commercial properity from John O'Groats to Land's End or from the Atlantic to the North Sea. It is maintained by an exceedingly simple device. When a slum landlord is cleared out he becomes religious. Whenever there is an attempt to root out sweating in Belfast the Orange big drum is beaten.... Whilst the poor working classes imagine that this is a religious trouble the people who pay the piper know perfectly well that it is an economic trouble....

In the second reference on 9 May 1912 to the same subject Mr. MacDonald said:

> We know Belfast. We know how much this religious strife has contributed to the power of those who have been constantly opposed to Labour in the whole history of Belfast. We know that there is

[1] Hansard, 11 April 1912, vol. xxvi, col. 1458.

> never a trade dispute, never a strike, never an attempt to combine
> labour in a trade union, never an effort to use that combination
> for the purpose of improving the condition of the working classes
> of Belfast but this old enmity between Catholic and Orangeman is
> sought to be stirred up by those whose interest is in the existing
> order of things.... [1]

This naturally led to insecurity among the workers and there
was from that and many other causes a large measure of unemployment in the North-east even before Ireland was divided.

Export industries had been the mainstay of that part of Ireland for many decades but in the aftermath of the First World
War these export industries suffered severely. There would
have been a better chance in the slump that was coming had
Ireland remained a unit, for Belfast then would have had as a
cushion against the fluctuations in world trade the home market
of all Ireland. The decline in the overseas trade might have been
offset by the increased demand of a free Ireland for manufactured
goods. This was made impossible by Partition; for the greater
part of Ireland, after its chief industrial area had been cut off,
was obliged to build up its own industries, and this could only
be done by a policy of Protection. And since the Belfast area had
been retained as part of the United Kingdom, the tariffs
against Britain became tariffs against Belfast. The border having
broken Ireland's economic unity, the consequential changes
became inevitable.

At the time Partition was passed, in December 1920, the
engineering and shipbuilding trades were passing through a
heavy recession, and the fear grew among the rank and file of
the Orange movement that their jobs were at stake. That fear
was exploited as Mr. Ramsey MacDonald had foreseen, and the
pogroms which disgraced the North-east for a period of two
years broke out just at this time. The unemployment of December
1920 mounted rapidly through the following Spring and early
Summer, and in June 1921 when the Belfast Parliament took
over the administration of the area the total was 103,000—of
whom more than half were in Belfast alone. This was almost
nine per cent of the entire population of the area, equal to nearly
four millions in Britain or nearly 250,000 in free Ireland.

Relief measures were put into operation, and by December

---

[1] Hansard, 9 May, 1912, vol. xxxviii, col. 633.
See also *Labour and Nationalism in Ireland* by J. Dunsmore Clackson, Dept
of History, College of the City of New York, pp. 361-372.

1921 the number had been brought down to 70,570. In 1922 unemployment was nearly a quarter of all insurable workers. In the three decades since Partition this widespread unemployment has remained chronic in the North-east, defying every measure taken to end it. It has fallen for periods and during World War II was brought down to a level comparable with that in other countries, but since the war the rate of unemployment has slowly risen, until in recent years it has again assumed considerable proportions. Taking the whole period, the average number of unemployed swung from 59,000 in 1922, to 34,070 in 1927, to 91,176 in 1938, to 48,000 in 1952 and to 39,550 in 1954. These figures for a population of 1,370,000 are altogether abnormal.

In the later half of the interwar years the situation was far worse than in the first half: the average number of unemployed from 1922 to 1930 was 50,369, but from 1931 to 1939 it was 73,160. That these totals were more than the reflection of a world slump is shown by a comparison with Britain. There the unemployed averaged 11.7 per cent of the insured workers in 1922-30, and 15.2 per cent in 1931-39: but in the Six Counties it was 19.3 per cent in the first period and 24.3 per cent in the second. A quarter of all the registered workers in North-east Ireland were unemployed nine years after Partition! Nor was it in shipbuilding and engineering only where the incidence was 33.6 per cent that the unemployment was heavy. It averaged 31.6 per cent in the building trade from 1924 to 1937 and was at an average 20 per cent in the clothing industry. In the linen industry the average was 21.2 per cent. In individual years the situation was often desperate. 57.1 per cent of the workers in shipbuilding and engineering were idle in 1934, 41.5 per cent in the building industry in 1937 and 34.8 per cent in the linen industry in 1938.

As far as can be judged, with world conditions as they were, much of this unemployment would have been endured, temporarily at least, if Ireland had remained wholly under British domination. Had she gained her freedom as an undivided country it would probably have been a different matter, for then the enthusiasm to create a new nation would have overcome many obstacles. Certainly the existing unemployment would have been mitigated in the North-east, if for no other reason than in the greater part of Ireland under British mal-administration industrial development had been retarded, and the community was determined to set up secondary industries and provide itself with much of what had until then been imported. That the level of unemployment in the Six Counties remained as high as it did, despite widespread relief work, was due to the injury direct and indirect done to the economy of the Six County unit as a whole, but most severely felt in the bigger towns. A natural market had been cut off, and nothing had been substituted. In Britain, as we have seen, the rates of unemployment were much less, and after a peak in 1932 they gradually declined. In the free part of Ireland it was also much less and has remained much below the Six County rate for practically the whole period of Partition.

Owing to different methods of compilation and the varying scope of laws relating to employment an exact parallel for the two areas over the whole period cannot be given. The data which can be compared are, however, significant. Taking the insured population in each area, the unemployment percentage for the 1923-31 period is as follows:

Average Insured Persons Unemployed in twenty six counties	% Unemployed	Average Insured Persons Unemployed in six counties	% Unemployed
20,484	7.8	51,778	19.8

During these years the insurable unemployed did not *rise* higher in the Twenty Six Counties than 13.2 per cent in its worst year, 1923, and it was 6 per cent or less for most of the period. But in the Six Counties it never *fell* lower than 13.2 per cent and was more than 23 per cent for four of the 9 years. In 1931 it was 27.8 per cent.

No close comparison is possible between the two areas again until after the passage of legislation in 1933 and 1934, when the registration of unemployed in the two parts of Ireland became not exactly the same but broadly similar. In each area the scope of the then existing social insurance schemes was widened. Rural workers were included and so were industrial workers who had been beyond the sphere of the insurable trades, and both were encouraged to come on the Live Register. From 1936, when these wider Acts became operative, to 1939, when the Second World War began, the position is shown in the following table:

TWENTY SIX COUNTIES

Year	Average no. of unemployed on Live Register (Unemployment Benefit and Assistance)	% of population aged 16 to 64 (1936 Census)
1936	94,595	5.08
1937	79,831	4.28
1938	83,612	4.46
1939	89,036	4.78

SIX COUNTIES

Year	Average no. of unemployed insured persons on Live Register (Unemployment Benefit only)	% of population aged 16 to 64 (1937 Census)
1936	66,458	8.13
1937	72,716	8.89
1938	91,177	11.15
1939	77,000	9.54

As this table indicates, unemployment among the working population in the Six Counties in the last four pre-war years was twice as heavy as in the Twenty Six Counties. In actual fact, it was much heavier, as persons in receipt of Unemployment Assistance are included in the Twenty Six County figures shown above but are *excluded* from the figures for the Six County area. Published statistics relating to the number of persons in receipt of Assistance in that part of Ireland do not differentiate between those persons receiving Assistance only and those getting both Unemployment Benefit and Assistance.

These figures, taken in conjunction with those among insured workers for the period 1923 to 1931, make it quite evident that for the whole period from the partitioning of Ireland to the outbreak of the great war, unemployment in the partitioned territory continued at a rate which put the Six Counties among the most depressed areas in either Great Britain or Ireland. The war modified that position but, as has since been seen, did not alter it.

The effect of the outbreak of hostilities on the economies of the two areas was widely different. To the Twenty Six Counties it meant a cutting-off from industry of fuel, of raw materials, machinery replacements and supplies generally. There was a slowing down of transport, short time in the factories and much redundancy in commercial life. Many palliatives were applied under the encouragement of the Twenty Six County Government. It was made possible for both commerce and industry to retain more workers than normally would be required. Nevertheless, the unemployment figures, especially in insurable occupations, in the first years of the war remained high, but by the response of workers to the call of national defence, by industry adapting itself to the harsh conditions and through workers emigrating to British war factories, the totals for the Twenty-Six Counties declined as the following yearly figures show:

Year ended 31 December	Average no. of claimants to Insurance and applicants for assistance.
1940	79,110
1941	69,331
1942	70,834
1943	62,186
1944	55,814
1945	56,122

In the Six Counties, which by Britain's participation in the war became itself a war-area, the improvement of the position came much earlier and was much more complete. Large war contracts were placed in the factories of the North-east, contingents of the British and overseas forces were stationed there, and the general expansion of Governmental agencies, incidental to war, all provided new employment; and the Six County figures fell spectacularly after 1940. The totals for the subsequent years, affected also by enlistment and emigration are shown in the following figures:

1940	73,359
1941	44,280
1942	21,432
1943	17,856
1944	16,016
1945	20,520

Expressed as percentage of insured workers in employment, those out of work fell from 20.9 per cent in 1940 to 5.7 in 1945 (similar percentages in Britain were 5 per cent in 1940 and 0.7 per cent in 1945).

The economic effect of the ending of the war took a considerable time to show itself statistically in the Six Counties, owing to the uncertainty of the peace and also because new work came with the immediate post-war boom: the number of workless remained low as compared with the pre-war years. There was however, as normal conditions began to return, a significant upward tend in 1946, and unemployment had by the end of 1951 reached the 40,000 figure and again became a problem of much gravity. The average figures for the years are: [1]

1946	31,200
1947	30,400
1948	28,000
1949	30,000
1950	26,900
1951	28,500
1952	48,300
1953	38,000
1954	32,900
1955 (first six months)	35,400

Only in 1948 was the rate of unemployment higher in the Twenty Six Counties than in the Six, though unemployment has been a grave problem below the border as well as above it. In every other year the rate for the North-east was not only higher but over the whole period considerably higher. It was sometimes twice and sometimes three times the rate prevailing in the free part of Ireland.

Even more marked is the Six County position when compared to that in Britain. It is asserted that those partitioned counties have the advantage of belonging to the United Kingdom. If unemployment is a reflection, as it should be, of the economic instability of a community, the Six Counties have suffered worse than Britain in every year since the incorporation of this Irish territory into the British system.

A comparison allowing for some differences is shown in a table attached to this Chapter. The relative position of the two areas is strikingly dissimilar and has been from the first year of partition to today. In the period from 1922 to 1955, the rate of Six County unemployment was never less than 30 per cent above Britain and was often 50 to 100 per cent above it. In the last pre-war years there were proportionately three times as many

[1] See *Monthly Digest of Statistics* No. 116. August 1955.

workless in the separated area as in Great Britain, and since the war that disparity has become greater. The Six Counties for the last seven years has often had five times as much unemployment as her cross-channel partner.

From one point of view these facts are more significant than any given previously. They emphasise the failure that has resulted from trying to make part of Ireland part of England. Had the Six Counties remained administratively what they are territorially, i.e. Irish soil, the incidence of unemployment would certainly not have been so markedly disproportionate. The effort to fit this area into a system whose economic structure is so fundamentally different from its own has led to the suffering, loss and frustration that widespread unemployment means to every community afflicted by it.

It has also meant a grievous loss to the rest of Ireland. Facing the future with its most industrialised areas separated from its territory the Irish community has had to build up separate methods of employment for its town populations. As we have seen, it has been well done, but a core of heavy unemployment remains, a problem for both Governments likely to be resolved only by the substitution of one National Government.

TABLE
Percentage of Unemployed:

Year	Britain	Six Counties
1922	14.1	23.4
1923	11.6	18.2
1924	10.2	16.6
1925	11.0	23.9
1926	12.3	23.2
1927	9.6	13.2
1928	10.7	17.0
1929	10.3	14.8
1930	15.8	23.8
1931	21.1	27.8
1932	21.9	27.2
1933	19.8	26.5
1934	16.6	23.4
1935	15.8	24.8
1936	12.4	20.2
1937	10.1	21.2
1938	11.8	26.2
1939	8.1	22.0
1940	5.0	20.9
1941	1.4	12.3
1942	0.6	5.7
1943	0.4	4.8
1944	0.3	4.4
1945	0.7	5.7
1946	2.4	8.4
1947	3.0	7.9
1948	1.5	7.2
1949	1.5	6.4
1950	1.5	5.9
1951	1.4	6.3
1952	2.0	10.3
1953	1.5	8.1
1954	1.2	7.0

EPILOGUE

PARTITION WAS UNNECESSARY.

THE STORY HAS been told of how Ireland came to be dismembered against all common sense and against the interests of both parts of Ireland and of Britain. The idea was from the beginning not Irish, but British. When first proposed it was scouted by every section of the Irish people, the minority no less than the majority, and though it has since had encrusted around it manifold vested interests, it is still being apologised for by leading members of that minority. [1]

The Partition idea was developed solely as the method by which any grant of any kind of self-Government to Ireland might be defeated. When Britain eventually decided to apply it every step was accompanied by deceit, and the pretence that it would lead to unity: it was finally imposed as a purely transitory arrangement, to disappear in a few years. It has produced a flourishing crop not only of economic evils but of injustices.

The crowning tragedy of this makeshift "settlement" is that it was unnecessary. Ireland was partitioned wantonly. The aim which was professed for it was easily attainable and is as easily attainable today without dismembering this ancient European nation.

The avowed purpose of partition was to satisfy the claim of a minority. That minority had, through the Conservative party in England, represented to the British public that its interests would not be safe under a Government elected by the whole of Ireland. Had these representations been examined they would have been found to be baseless. But at a time when the fears of

---

[1] "We never asked for Partition and we never wanted it," said Lord Glentoran, Belfast Tory leader, on 10 October 1946.
"The people of Ulster never wanted this Parliament.... The present Parliament of Northern Ireland was forced on the people of Northern Ireland against their will in 1920," said Sir Hugh O'Neill, M.P., leader of the Six County Tories in the British Parliament, speaking on 13 June 1947.
"We never wanted a Parliament," said Mr. William Grant, Six County Minister for Health, speaking on 5 June 1949, in Belfast.

the minority were being used by the British Conservatives as an electoral weapon against the British Liberals, no examination was likely, and so the suggestion that the minority would be persecuted came to be believed.

There had, in fact, never been persecution of the minority in those districts in Ireland where they formed only an insignificant part of the population and were, therefore, must vulnerable. The minority has always received more than their numerical share of public appointments. Their position in the industry, trade and commerce of the country was, and is, far in excess of their percentage among the people. They are twice or three times as numerically strong in most of the professions and in practically all the more lucrative grades of employment, as their numbers would warrant. They have their own schools, their own associations, their own newspapers.

The suggestion that the tolerant majority under which all this came about and continues would overnight become persecuting bigots could only have been believed in abnormal times when sensible thinking was blurred by political passion. But the creation of these fears did create a political problem, and the Irish national leaders, while able to demonstrate the complete unlikelihood of discrimination, expressed themselves as quite ready to accept safeguards that would reassure the minority. They went to extraordinary lengths in this. But every offer was rejected and perhaps nothing could have demonstrated more clearly the false basis of the claim for "protection" than this rejection.

From the beginning of the Home Rule controversy the majority leaders made many generous concessions to set the mind of the minority at rest. Speaking in the Home Rule debates in the British House of Commons on 16 April 1912, Mr. T. P. O'Connor, Nationalist leader, referred to the safeguards contained in the Home Rule Bill:

> I will first say a word about the safeguards... What are they? They enable any man in Ireland who regarded a Bill (in the Irish Parliament) as prejudicial to his liberties — religious or secular — or to his property, to go to the Privy Council... That is only the beginning of the safeguards. There is the safeguard of (the supremacy of) the Imperial Parliament. There are two bigger safeguards than all. There is the safeguard of the Protestantism of England which would not tolerate for one hour an attack upon their fellow-religionists in Ireland. There is another and even greater safeguard than that, and that is the character and history

of Irish Nationalists in regard to this question of religious tolerance. There is no charge against the Irish Nationalist more inaccurate, more cruel or more ungrateful than the charge of a desire to persecute and to use intolerance towards his Protestant fellow-countryman. [1]

On the second reading of the Home Rule Bill, Mr. Asquith, British Prime Minister, said in the House of Commons on 9 May 1912:

> We have sought to allay whatever legitimate fears and apprehensions they (the minority) may entertain by the safeguards we have introduced, and we have asked them repeatedly over and over again to say what further safeguards they want. [2]

Mr. Asquith spoke again on this subject in Dublin on 19 July 1912 and is reported as follows in the *Irish Times:*

> We have here inserted in this Bill the most complete safeguards against the possibility—we don't believe there is a possibility—but against the possibility of persecution civil, political or religious. We have offered in the plainest and most distinct terms—and I repeat the offer tonight—that if these safeguards can be shown to be insufficient in any respect we will consider sympathetically and carefully any practical suggestion for adding either to their number or their strength. That is the offer which, as my colleagues here know, more than once in the House of Commons has been met with a flat, blank and persistent refusal. [3]

The Nationalist leaders, all through the Home Rule discussions, in expressing their grief at the suggested division of their native land, emphasised their readiness to provide the fullest protection for the minority. Joseph Devlin in a memorandum to John Redmond wrote:

> We have over and over again asked for one instance of Catholic persecution of Protestants as such in Ireland and none has been forthcoming. But if this idea of the fear of persecution or unfair treatment has got a lodgment in the minds of Irish or British Protestants the inclusion of 'Ulster' with the right of going out after a trial period affords the best means of practically testing its (an All-Ireland Parliament's) reliability. As a second concession we would be in favour of giving 'Ulster' extra representation in the Irish Parliament. And as a third concession we would be prepared to accept such an arrangement of the Senate as would afford them an additional safeguard against unfair treatment. [4]

[1] Hansard, 16 April 1912, vol. 37, cols. 214-7.
[2] Hansard, 9 May 1912, vol. 38, col. 694.
[3] *Irish Times*, 20 July 1912.
[4] Denis Gwynn, *Life of John Redmond*, p. 259.

Redmond, himself, said at Newcastle on 14 Nov. 1912:

> There is no demand that we are not ready to consider carefully
> so long as it is consistent with the principle of settlement based
> upon the national self-government of Ireland. [1]

On the day Asquith announced the Cabinet's acceptance of
the idea of Partition, Redmond, speaking of the refusal to
establish an All-Ireland Parliament, said:

> For the sake of peace the Irish Nationalist representatives were
> willing to make great sacrifices.... of many of their most cherished
> ideals. I say we would have been able to make an exhibition of
> moderate and tolerant government which would completely disarm
> the fears and suspicions of all classes of our fellow countrymen and
> speedily lead to the complete unity of our people under Home
> Rule. [2]

The first proposals to partition Ireland were interrupted by
the First World War. They were resumed in 1916 and they came
under detailed discussion in the Irish Convention in 1917-18.
There the Nationalist majority again showed by practical
offers to the minority that every concession necessary to reassure
the Tories would be made. In the Report of the Irish Convention
is included a statement by Nationalist leaders. It contains the
following passage:

> The Ulster Unionists, who were in close touch with their supporters
> in the North, to our great regret did not see their way to give
> much co-operation in constructive work along the lines which the
> Convention was following.... Every one of the Dominions contain-
> ed a minority of citizens accustomed to identify themselves with
> Imperial interests who predicted a calamity for their country and
> the whole Empire if self government were fully conceded.... in
> order to make it easy for our esteemed fellow-countrymen to join
> on fair terms in one Parliament for the whole country, we went
> so far as to concede them a large measure of additional elected
> representatives in the Irish House of Commons. They would be a
> powerful and effective element in an Irish Parliament. [3]

The Report itself set out the actual concessions to which the
Nationalists had agreed.

1. 40% of the entire membership of the Irish House of Commons
   to be Unionist. (Their electoral strength would give them between 20% to 25% of the seats).
2. Of the 64 members of the Senate 31 would be either nominated

---

[1] Earl of Oxford and Asquith, *Fifty Years of Parliament*, vol. ii, p. 143.
[2] Hansard, 9 Mar. 1914, vol. 59, cols. 926-8.
[3] *Irish Convention Report*, p. 37.

by the British viceroy, elected by Irish residents holding British peerages, or chosen directly to represent Unionist views. In addition 15 others were to be chosen from leaders of Commerce and Industry of which the Unionists would get at least half— so that they could actually have a majority in the upper House.

3. In measures affecting the minority area on which agreement had not previously been reached the issues would be decided by both Houses sitting together—which would have the effect in all disputes of substantially increasing the 40% special representation the minority were given in the Commons. [1]

Lloyd George, in a letter to the Convention Chairman, on 25 February 1918 notes other offers to the minority and records the opinion—of some weight coming from the author of Partition— that they met all the objections of the minority. The British Premier wrote:

Turning to the other essential element to a settlement—the securing of an agreement to establish a single legislature for a united Ireland —the Government believe the Convention has given much thought to the method of overcoming objection on the part of Unionists, North and South, to this proposal. They understand that one scheme provides for additional representation by means of nomination or election. They understand further that it has also been suggested that a safeguard of Ulster interests might be secured by the provision of an Ulster Committee within the Irish Parliament with powers to modify and, if necessary, to exclude the application to Ulster of certain measures either of legislation or administration which are not consonant with the interests of Ulster. This appears to be a workable expedient whereby special consideration of Ulster conditions can be secured and the objections to a single Legislature for Ireland overcome.

Despite this readiness of the majority to satisfy every reasonable demand from the minority, the leaders of that minority would not consent to any scheme of self-government for Ireland. The reason was that which in the subsequent years continued to bring all efforts at a national and just solution to nought: namely, that the question was decided by men who thought not of Ulster and its well-being or of Ireland and its well-being, but of the necessities of British Conservative policy and British Imperial needs.

The division of Ireland's territory was certain to injure deeply the North-east as well as the rest of the country. It is obvious that if the industrial North of Britain was cut off from the South, both parts would suffer, or if the industrial North of France was separated from the agricultural areas, or the manufacturing North of America was partitionel from the Southern States, such

[1] Ibid. p. 26-27.

an injury to these lands would strike a vital, if not a mortal, blow at both the dismembered parts.

On every occasion in which Anglo-Irish relations have been under review, Irish leaders have made it clear to Britain and to the Orange minority that a re-unification of the island would not injure their true interests. The special needs and problems of the area in which the minority predominates would be left to the minority itself to deal with and solve.

In October-December 1921 when the Treaty was being discussed in London the Irish delegates expressed their readiness to give to those areas full local autonomy under a National Parliament in Dublin. Indeed earlier, Mr. de Valera, as President of the Irish Republic, said in an interview with the *Neue Zeitung* of Zurich of 3 May 1921:

> I feel certain the Republic would be ready to give to the Six Counties.... far more substantial powers than those they are to possess under the British Partition Act which was designed less to give local autonomy to Ulster than to foster political and religious rancour amongst us. [1]

That has ever since been the policy of the Irish majority. The head of the first Government after the signing of the Treaty was Mr. William T. Cosgrave, who remained in office from 1922 to 1932. In a statement published in the London *Times* on the first day of 1923, Mr. Cosgrave declared that in a united Ireland the North-eastern leaders

> would have retained their parliament of the Six Counties and their separate Judiciary and their Governor according to their pleasure. The whole six counties would be theirs to rule and control from Belfast to exactly the same extent as they do so at present under the 1920 Act. Apart from that, the Six Counties would have had.... a representation of fifty-one members in the Free State Parliament instead of thirteen members who now represent them at Westminster.

Mr. de Valera resumed office in 1932, and he too made public declarations on the same subject. An example is his statement in an interview with Mr. Hessell Tiltman, Special Correspondent of the London *Evening Standard,* on 17 October 1938:

> I believe Partition can be ended by peaceful negotiation and with due regard to the sentiments and susceptibilities of all sections. I'd say to the rulers of Northern Ireland: Keep your local Par-

[1] Dorothy Macardle, *The Irish Republic,* p. 967.

liament with its local powers if you wish. The Government ask only two things of you. There must be adequate safeguards that the ordinary rights of the Nationalist minority in your area be not denied them, as at present, and that the powers reserved to the English Parliament shall be transferred to the All-Ireland Parliament.

Statements in the same sense were made by the leaders of the Inter-Party Government which succeeded Mr. de Valera's régime. In the period of their term of office, 1948 to 1951, Mr. Costello, head of the Government, and Mr. MacBride, Minister for External Affairs, again and again emphasised their consent to the re-unification of Ireland on the basis of a local legislature for the minority areas and as well their full representation in the National Parliament. On his return to office Mr. de Valera restated this as the national policy.

The partitioning of Ireland has therefore been wantonly carried through by Britain. The purpose they gave to justify it, that it would protect minority rights, was already assured. The Irish minority have the fullest guarantee from those best able to give and fulfil it, of the protection of their civil and religious rights, their interests and their economy. Inside a united Ireland they know they would be a respected and cherished section of the Irish people.

In face of these facts to say Partition was necessary is absurd; to maintain it is in every degree unjust, and to oppose the Irish majority in their effort to bring it to an end is to oppose the very principles upon which stable Government must rest all over the world, if democracy is to endure.

BIBLIOGRAPHY

Adair, A. Shafto: *The Winter of 1846-7 in Antrim* (1847)
American Council of Learned Societies: *Report.... on population.... in the United States.* (1932)
Bagwell, Richard: *Ireland Under the Tudors.* (1885)
Birkenhead, (F. W. Smith) 2nd. Earl of: *Frederick Erwin, Earl of Birkenhead.* (1933-4)
Blake, Robert: *The Unknown Prime Minister: The Life and Times of Andrew Bonar Law.* (1955)
Biggs-Davidson, John: *George Wyndham, A Study in Toryism.* (1951)
Calendar of Ancient Records of Dublin
Calendar of Carew Papers: 1603-25.
Calendar of State Papers, Ireland: 1608-10.
Callwell, Major-General, Sir C. E.: *Field Marshal Sir Henry Wilson: His Life and Diaries.* (1927)
Chaillot, Louis: *Pope Adrian IV: A Friend of Ireland.* (1906)
Chamberlain, Sir Austen: *Politics from Inside.* (1936)
Chamberlain, Joseph: *Home Rule and the Irish Question.* (1887)
Chetham Society Publications. Vol. I (1844)
Churchill, Sir Winston Spencer: *Lord Randolph Churchill.* (1906)
Church of Ireland and the Present Crisis. (1886)
Clancy, J. J.: *Mr. Chamberlain in Ulster.* (1888)
Clarkson, J. Dunsmore, Ph. D.: *Labour and Nationalism in Ireland.* (1925)
Collins, General Michael: *The Path to Freedom.* (1922)
Colvin, Ian: *Life of Lord Carson.* (1934-6)
Concise View of the Irish Society. (1832)
Curtis, Edmund: *History of Ireland.* (1937)
Curtis, Edmund and R. B. McDowell: *Irish Historical Documents* 1172-1922 (1943)
Digby, Margaret: *Horace Plunkett, An Anglo-American Irishman* (1949)
Duffy, Sir Charles Gavan: *League of the North and South* (1886)
Dugdale, Blanche E. C.: *Arthur James Balfour.* (1936)
Dunraven, Earl of: *The Outlook in Ireland.* (1907)
Ensor, R. C. K.: *England, 1870-1914* (Oxford History of England) (1936)
Epitome of the Case of Irish Corporations. (1839)
Freeman, T. W.: *Ireland: Its Physical, Historical, Social and Economic Geography.* (1950)
Froude, J. A.: *The English in Ireland in the XVIII Century.* (1872-4)
Gerard, James W.: *My Four Years in Germany.* (1917)
Ginnell, Laurence, B. L.: *The Doubtful Grant of Ireland.* (1899)
Green, Alice Stopford: *Ourselves Alone in Ulster.* (1918)
Gwynn, Denis: *Daniel O'Connell.* (1929)
Gwynn, Denis: *History of Partition.* (1950)
Gwynn, Denis: *Life of John Redmond.* (1932)
Gwynn, Denis: *O'Connell, Davis and the Colleges Bill.* (1948)
Gwynn, Stephen: *The Letters and Friendships of Cecil Spring-Rice.* (1929)

Hamilton, Mary Agnes: *Arthur Henderson.* (1938)
Hammond, J. L.: *Gladstone and the Irish Nation.* (1938)
Handbook of the Ulster Question. (Dublin Stationery Office, 1923)
Hardinge, Sir Arthur: *The Fourth Earl of Carnarvon.* (1925)
Harrison, Henry: *Ireland and the British Empire.* (1937)
Harrison, Henry: *The Neutrality of Ireland.* (1942)
Hill, George: *Plantation in Ulster.* (1920)
Historical Collections relative to the Town of Belfast. (1817)
Historical Manuscripts Commission: *Stopford Sackville MSS.* Vol. I (1904)
[Horgan, J. J.]: *The Complete Grammar of Anarchy.* (1918)
Hyde, H. Montgomery: *Carson: A Biography.* (1953)
Interim Report on Rural Housing in Ulster. (1947)
Kenna, G. B.: *The Facts and Figures of the Belfast Pogrom* 1920-1922 (1922)
Kiernan, Thomas J.: *Study of Catholic, Ecclesiastical and Religious Statistics.* (1950)
Latimer, William Thomas: *History of Irish Presbyterians.* (1893)
Latimer, William Thomas: *Ulster Biographies.* (1897)
Lecky, W. E. H.: *History of Ireland in the XVIII Century.* (1906)
Macardle, Dorothy: *The Irish Republic.* (1937)
McNeill, Ronald: *Ulster's Stand for Union.* (1922)
Morley, John: *Life of William Ewart Gladstone.* Vol. III. (1903)
Murphy, Denis: *Cromwell in Ireland.* (1883)
Nicholson, Harold: *King George V: His Life and Reign.* (1952)
O'Brien, Richard Barry: *Thomas Drummond.* (1889)
O'Brien, William, M. P.: *The Irish Revolution.* (1923)
O'Nualláin, Labhrás: *Ireland. Finances of Partition.* (1952)
Oliver, F. S.: *The Anvil of War.* (1936)
Oxford and Asquith, Earl of: *Memories and Reflections.* (1928)
Oxford and Asquith, Earl of: *Fifty Years of Parliament.* (1926)
Pacata Hibernia. (1633)
Pakenham, Frank: *Peace by Ordeal.* (1935)
Petrie, Sir Charles: *Life and Letters of Rt. Hon. Austen Chamberlain* (1940)
Plunkett, Sir Horace: *Report of the Irish Convention.* (1918)
Popular Guide to the House of Commons. (1886)
Records of the General Synod of Ulster. (1890-8)
Report of the Census of Production of Northern Ireland, 1951. (1954)
Report of the Labour Commission to Ireland. (1921)
Report of the Select Committee on Orange Lodges. (1835)
Riddell, George, 1st Baron: *Lord Riddell's Intimate Diary of the Peace Conference and After.* (1933)
Ronaldshay, The Earl of: *Life of Lord Curzon.* (1928)
Spender and Cyril Asquith: *Life of the Earl of Oxford and Asquith.* (1932)
Shakespeare, Geoffrey: *Let Candles be Brought In.* (1949)
Shearman, Hugh: *Not an Inch: a Study of Northern Ireland and Lord Craigavon.* (1942)
Sibbett, R. M.: *Orangism in Ireland.* (2nd Edition, 1943)
Stevenson, J.: *Two Centuries of Life in Down.* 1600-1800. (1920)
Strauss, E.: *Irish Nationalism and British Democracy.* (1951)
Tone, William T.: *Life of Theobald Wolfe Tone.* (1831)
Toynbee, Arnold J.: *A Study of History.* (1939)
Woodburn, James P.: *The Ulster Scot.* (1914)
Ulster Unionist Council: *The Voice of Ulster.* (Nov. 1949)

INDEX